Houses

Far from

Home

British Colonial Space in the New Hebrides

MARGARET CRITCHLOW RODMAN

University of Hawai'i Press
Honolulu

Library of Congress Cataloging-in-Publication Data

Rodman, Margaret.
   Houses far from home : British colonial space in the New Herbrides /
Margaret Critchlow Rodman.
      p. cm.
Includes bibliographical references and index.
   ISBN 0–8248–2307–9 (cloth : alk. paper)—ISBN 0–8248–2394–X (pbk. :
alk. paper)
   1. British—Dwellings—Vanuatu. 2. Dwellings—Social aspects—Vanuatu.
3. Colonial administrators—Housing—Vanuatu. 4. Vanuatu I. Title

GT384.V35 R63 2001
392.3'6'0892109595—dc21
                                                         00–060759

Designed by inari
Printed by The Maple-Vail Book Manufacturing Group

In Memory of William E. Stober (1940–1997)

Contents

Illustrations

Acknowledgments

T he Social Sciences and Humanities Research Council of Canada (SSHRCC), York University, and the Wenner Gren Foundation for Anthropological Research generously provided funding for this research, beginning in 1993. With two exceptions, this book consists of material not previously published: the part of chapter two on the court buildings appeared in *History and Anthropology* 11, 4 (1999): 479–514. An earlier version of chapter 4 appeared in the *Journal of Pacific History* 33, 1 (1998): 29–49. I am especially grateful to Reece Discombe, Joseph Macchiusi, the late Will Stober, and Keith Woodward for their extensive assistance with this research. For permission to use the New Hebrides British Service and Western Pacific High Commission Archives, I thank the Records Branch of the Foreign and Commonwealth Office in Hanslope Park, United Kingdom, and the government of the Republic of Vanuatu, especially Ralph Regenvanu, director of the Vanuatu Cultural Centre. For their assistance in Vanuatu, I wish to express my particular appreciation to Regine Battick, Peter Bouchard, Yvonne deSomerville, Peter Fidelio, Ken Hutton, Reece Discombe, Gaby Stuart, and David Wanamay. Violet Bowhay, Shelley Butler, Matthew Cooper, Susan Frohlich, William Rodman, Clara Sacchetti-Dufresne, and especially Keith Woodward provided comments on various portions of the manuscript for which I am grateful. My thanks go to Jane Philibert for French transcription, and to her and Jean-Marc Philibert for discussions of the Condominium over good meals together. To Martine Bonnemaison and the late, and greatly missed, Joël Bonnemaison, I am thankful for hospitality and insights into the French side of things, especially in 1994 in Gascony. I wish to express appreciation to the following York University graduate students for English transcription and other research assistance from 1993 to 1999: Terri Aihoshi, Sean Brotherton, Virginia Caputo, David Cavers, Tim Epp, Susan Frohlick, Jacquelyne Luce, Joseph Macchiusi, Ana Ning, Annabelle Sabloff, and

Shiho Satsuka. Some people who participated in the study may be disappointed, or relieved, that they are not in the book; my heartfelt thanks to you all, for you helped to shape this book, whether or not you appear in it by name. Finally, my thanks go to Channing Thieme for inspiring me in Vanuatu in 1995 and to Channing Rodman for encouraging me during the writing process and for preparing the index.

HOUSE OF BAMBOO

The houses far from home in this book are dwelling places of memory entangled with a shifting present. They are in the New Hebrides, a chain of islands between Fiji and Australia in the southwest Pacific. France and Britain jointly administered this archipelago as the Condominium of the New Hebrides from 1906 until 1980, when the islands became the Republic of Vanuatu.* Some were homes away from home to British colonial servants. They were decorated with "one's things," an accumulation of possessions that might range from Aynsley china to zebra skins, carried between overseas posts. One's things made each house a home, linking remembered places as a family followed the course of a man's British Colonial Service career, for it was never a woman's in the New Hebrides. Most colonial servants retired to live at Home, as England was always known, even in official correspondence. For them, the dwellings in their photo albums from the New Hebrides are mnemonic of those houses far from home that now blur together in memory: Was that photo in the New Hebrides? Oh, no, that was Montserrat.

---

* The terms "Vanuatu" and "New Hebrides" appear to be, but are not quite, interchangeable in this book. Both refer to the same place but not the same time. Vanuatu is used with reference to the postindependence period. Melanesian citizens of Vanuatu are called "ni-Vanuatu" (both singular and plural); they were called New Hebrideans in colonial times.

Other houses became home to people, again mostly men, who came from somewhere else, never to live there again. They were self-made people for whom "home" was a product of experience. Often, it was something they built for themselves.[1] Many came from other out-of-the-way islands such as Réunion, Pitcairn, Corsica, Norfolk, New Guinea, or New Caledonia, but others also came from Australia, France, or the better-known islands of England and Ireland. Those who stayed made homes in the islands; many had no other place to call home. After as many as four or five generations there, settlers are now caught up in conflicts over citizenship, race, and the relationship of land to identity in postcolonial Vanuatu. For many settler families who left the New Hebrides, the places where they now live in Australia, France, or elsewhere are just houses far from home; and home, both bitter and sweet in memory, is still in the islands.

This book explores connections among such ideas as distance, exile, travel, and rootedness through the notion of houses far from home. Rather than disdaining such metaphors as "home" and "away," I intend here to unravel their edges and the threads that bind one idea to another. The notion of houses far from home can link many places in a life, on the one hand, and many lives to a place, on the other.[2] The book metaphorically considers housing as if it were both a verb and a noun. Housing as a verb is "to house" or housing as a process. As a noun a house is an object of study. The Establishments Office of the British government in the New Hebrides made grammatical sentences out of housing, so to speak. It was concerned with housing as a verb and a noun, with both the process of housing British personnel and with the housing stock in which they were accommodated. I examine such "sentences" and pose questions: How did people who were positioned differently in a particular colonial history at once create, see, and respond to the New Hebrides? How did they recreate, regard, and respond to Home? How can home, homes away from home, and houses far from home be understood within a framework that expands "home" from the domestic to the public sphere, a framework that is one of the "hallmarks of Euro-American feminist practice"?[3]

Nostalgia, a longing for a place as much as a time, figures in all that follows here, as do some people's desires to distance themselves from painful pasts in the islands. But the charged space between romantic nostalgia for life in the South Seas and recollection of the same place with a shudder is what sparks my interest. Imperialist nostalgia, the yearning for what one has helped (intentionally or otherwise) to destroy, seems an apt term to describe what I heard from some participants in this project.[4] But simply tearing down the house of colonialism is another kind of imperialism, a conquest that makes it harder to find among the rubble the meanings that were colonialism's posts, beams, shingles, and trim,

much less its occupants. Here I prefer to scrutinize the colonial house as an arti-fact while also puzzling over its literal and metaphorical architecture.

Houses, their complex meanings as homes and as colonial products and pro-cesses, provide the framework for this endeavor. They relate, in various ways, to other colonial lived spaces as well as to plans, designs, and discussions of other places that were never built. The houses in this book are a way of understanding the social history of particular colonial spaces. I use the term "colonial space" to include spatial practice (the process, the verb), form (the buildings, the noun), and meaning (the sentences).[5] At the broadest level, I take "colonial space" to mean the built forms of official and unofficial expatriate settlement and their usage. Colonial space is also a way of looking at the world, a mind-set that the built forms and discourses about them represent and reinforce, making it com-mon sense for participants to see the world in colonial terms.[6] The core colonial spaces in this study are official ones. The British Residency and the British Pad-dock are key, but officers' housing, district agencies, boats, and prisons are equally revealing. All suggest the variations and tensions, as well as the unifor-mity, of the British colonial project in the New Hebrides over time and from the perspectives of people (men, women, and children) situated differently with re-gard to that project.

Memories of houses speak of tensions between promise and poignancy. Like all memories, these allow people to enrich and shape their present lives and to un-derstand past experiences.[7] Recounted memories convey the sense of possibility as well as the sense of loss that comes with movement between and within places. Ar-chival materials carry the past into the present differently than oral remembrances do with both material immediacy and the distance of time past. They connect to the present through reading, not through listening. On delicate paper tied with faded red tape, handwritten jottings in minutes and on margins of typescript con-struct and comment on the exclusive and inclusive spaces of colonialism.

The book tacks between oral memories and archival documents, between different islands and actors, and sails across time to link spaces in an analytical framework that critically accepts the power of romantic ideas as well as political realities to shape people and what they do to places. James Clifford, in develop-ing an idea of traveling theory has prioritized a research agenda that would in-clude such questions as "How do different populations, classes, and genders travel? What kinds of knowledges, stories, and theories do they produce?"[8] I ask these questions not in general but in the particulars of multiple locations and multiple voices in the New Hebrides.

This is what George Marcus would call a "multi-sited ethnography," an approach to which I have contributed in earlier research.[9] Such an approach

should "try to represent multiple, blindly interdependent locales, each explored ethnographically and mutually linked by the intended and unintended consequences of activities within them."[10] This study also considers some locales that are not "blindly" but quite explicitly interdependent, such as the Colonial Office in London and Port Vila in the New Hebrides. Another anthropologist, Mary Des Chene, has suggested that the multi-sited form of ethnography might be "well suited to research whose central focus is a historically linked group of people or an institution that has, over time, caused many people, from diverse locales, to traverse similar circuits."[11] It is hard to imagine a more suitable case for multi-sited treatment than British colonial servants in the New Hebrides.

In doing the multi-sited research for this book, I visited many people in their homes in the United Kingdom and in Australia, as well as a few in France. Although their current houses told me a lot about these people, the houses and other buildings that are the subject of this book are all in the New Hebrides, albeit widely scattered. I use these buildings as windows through which to glimpse and puzzle over some of the variety of the colonial project that was the New Hebrides, which itself was one small room in the house of empire. Each chapter has at its heart a building the reader enters, exploring from there particular dimensions of race, space, gender, and power in terms of the social history of the New Hebrides.

Woven Worlds

The house at the heart of this opening chapter is my own. My own home away from home in the New Hebrides, and the feelings it evokes in memory, led me into this project. My mind's eye kept returning to this small bamboo house on the edge of a South Pacific village where I lived in 1978–1979, 1982, and 1985.[12] As I tried to find the doorway for starting this book I kept remembering how the house glowed at night. It glowed like a loosely woven basket sheltering a candle, for indeed the house was made like a basket, with walls woven out of split and softened bamboo. Even the floor was woven. When I stepped outside at night, pale golden light from kerosene lanterns inside the house twinkled through the warp and weft of the woven walls. The glowing house was mesmerizing, beautiful and tame compared to the dazzling sky full of stars a thousand miles from the interference of city light. I wanted to "write space" so that the houses in this book would glow like that, shedding light on political spaces through domestic ones.

I remember that bamboo house with nostalgia for a place where my family lived simply and peacefully, for a time when my son and daughter were children. (Sean went on all field trips from 1978 on. My daughter, Channing, came on each

field trip beginning in 1982 when she was two.) I speak of that house as comfortable despite the stench of mildew everywhere and the discomfort of always sitting on floors, benches, stones, or mats, never able to lean back against anything except the occasional tree. Sleeping was much more comfortable; with hot, humid afternoons and cool nights, we did a lot of it. In 1978, six-year-old Sean slept on a mat on the springy bamboo floor, as did our black-and-white puppy, Riki. Captain Cat slept draped over a rafter. My husband, Bill, and I shared a simple and comfortable bed—a raised wooden platform with a foam mattress. From the window we could glimpse the sea far down the slopes of coconut palms; pictures of horses from a Minolta calendar decorated the bamboo bedroom walls.

Our house was, and is, on the edge of Waileni Village in the Longana district of Ambae Island, although it is no longer the same house in quite the same place. In 1978, the house was new. It was about twenty-five feet square, with a front room and two small sleeping areas at the back. We enjoyed the fact that the house did not stand out, except for having more windows than was usual in village houses. The windows marked it as more than a sleeping place; it looked a bit like an office. It was, in fact, both of these. We were proud that we did not have to occupy housing intended for visitors to the village, as we had on our first field trip to the New Hebrides in 1970. Then, we had lived in the back of a cement meeting house in another village on the coast. It was hot and buggy, and although the building materials were permanent, living there made us feel transient. We struggled to overcome the villagers' categorization of us anthropologists as just another kind of expatriate who passed through from time to time, such as the British or French district agent, the cooperatives officer, or the head of the Boy Scouts. We struggled, too, with the terms of the colonial equation of which, although we did not like it, we were a part. We tried with limited success to make a home out of the meeting house and with somewhat more success to make a place for ourselves in the area.

The house where we lived in 1978 was a great improvement in terms of comfort, the image of our place in the community, and our own construction of identity. We designed it, paid for the materials and labor, arranged for a local carpenter to build it, and, later, donated it to the community as a rest house when we left. As the piles of bamboo stacked on the building site became a house, a refrain echoed in my mind: "Bamboo roof, bamboo walls, it's even got a bamboo floor, house of bambooooo." Actually, our house of bamboo had a corrugated galvanized iron roof and guttering to catch enough rainwater to fill a two-hundred-gallon steel tank. This was our only source of water. An unprecedented drought was under way when we moved in, and the tank took a month to fill. We learned that two adults and a child could get by on two five-gallon buckets of

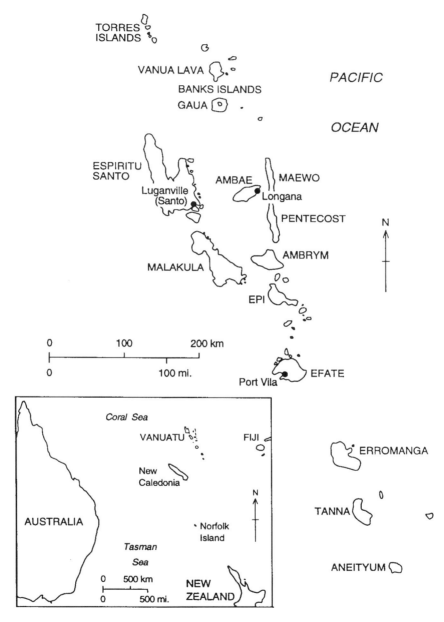

Figure 1. Map of Vanuatu. Annotated original. Carol Randall, Cartographic Office, Department of Geography, York University.

water a day, for washing, cooking, drinking, and bathing. This was only enough water to flush the average toilet twice, but we had no toilet. Instead, we had an outhouse with two footprints to indicate where one squatted over the hole in the cement slab and a couple of huge, yellow-backed, harmless spiders that bounced entertainingly when their webs were tweaked.

The kitchen was a separate building with a coral floor and thatched roof. Separate kitchens were common in villages and mission stations and on plantations because of concerns about fire and because rats prefer kitchens with food to houses in which there are only sleeping people. We created a bathing area in a back corner of the kitchen, curtained with a blue-and-white calico of hibiscus flowers suitable for a Hawaiian shirt. Most houses did not have a washing area in the kitchen as we did, but all had a private area outside the house that adults used for personal cleanliness under cover of darkness. All the children went to "swim" at twilight, none in the sea. The squalls of soapy toddlers being rinsed with cold water was a familiar evening sound. For us, including our children, bucket baths in a big aluminum washtub, with water heated on the propane burner, were as soothing as the best hot bath in Canada.

While easily romanticized, my memories of living in the islands, like those of most of the people with whom I spoke for this book, are mixed. The place evokes poignant contrasts between the opportunities my children enjoy in Canada and the limited futures of their island playmates in terms of travel, education, and income. These contrasts emphasize global inequalities in very personal ways that cannot be overcome by the occasional check for a child's school fees, the rare meeting of an islander in Canada, and increasingly frequent email in the lingua franca, Bislama.

For anthropologists, "the field" is both a methodological ideal and a concrete place: "The field is a home away from home, a place of dwelling."[13] Anthropologists have typically located themselves ethnographically through descriptions such as the one I have just given of our glowing house. Except for stories of the anthropologist's arrival, "the field" has tended to be constructed as spatially static and timeless. It is a place that rarely includes nonresident outsiders other than themselves. Anthropologists, myself included, have seldom paid much attention in their writing to the comings and goings of other outsiders such as missionaries, traders, or government officials. Yet these people were passing through another way of life as much as we were, albeit with different goals and strategies. They were also dwelling "in the field" in ways similar to ours. As James Clifford argues, "Why not focus on any culture's farthest range of travel while *also* looking at its centers, its villages, its intensive field sites? . . . How is one group's core another's periphery?"[14] This view requires new representational strategies, one of which I develop here. The culture in question is British; its farthest range, the New Hebrides; its

centers, villages, and intensive field sites, the British Residency, British Paddock, and British and French District Agencies. Here I examine the culture of British colonialism, a project that evokes salvage ethnography documenting a dying breed. I take up Clifford's call to investigate the intercultural figure of the traveler. I do so through a concern with transitory and permanent practices of dwelling, exploring both movement and rootedness through houses far from home.

Colonial Assistance

Writing about memory, home, loss, and possibility is made more poignant by the death of the complicated, at times infuriating, yet always helpful scholar who made much of it possible. Will Stober, an ex–colonial officer who lived in Birmingham after leaving the New Hebrides, arranged interviews for me with about fifty people who had worked in the New Hebrides.[15] In July 1994, and again in the spring of 1995, he drove me at a breakneck pace all over England in his aging red Citroen. We went from Northumberland to the south coast, from Norfolk to Herefordshire, and even to Fishguard in Wales. He found people willing to talk to me whose experiences in the islands ranged from assignments for Volunteers in Service Overseas to resident commissioners who held the highest British office. Some whom we were unable to interview contacted me at Will's prompting, making written submissions that included detailed drawings of their "houses far from home." One of the most artistic, submitted by the senior geologist with the British Residency in Vila from 1967 to 1974, is reproduced here (figure 2).

Will Stober threaded our way through the Foreign and Commonwealth Office bureaucracy which, along with the Government of Vanuatu, finally granted us permission to work in archives that no researcher on Vanuatu had seen for more than fifteen years. I enjoyed working in the archives with Will not only because of the wealth of information we uncovered there but also because he so clearly thrived on this kind of sleuthing and his enthusiasm for it was contagious. Anything Will did not remember about the colonial period in the New Hebrides he could usually find in his large collection of books and papers, piled neatly in stacks that nearly covered the floor of the study in his small flat.

His handwritten letters to me often filled ten pages, with twenty or more numbered enclosures that might include current film reviews or a photo from the early colonial period. My letters to Will were usually a laundry list of detailed historical queries, posed with the confidence that he knew, or could find, the answers. His obsession with the time and place of the colonial New Hebrides was useful for me, but it probably hindered his ability to live in the present and

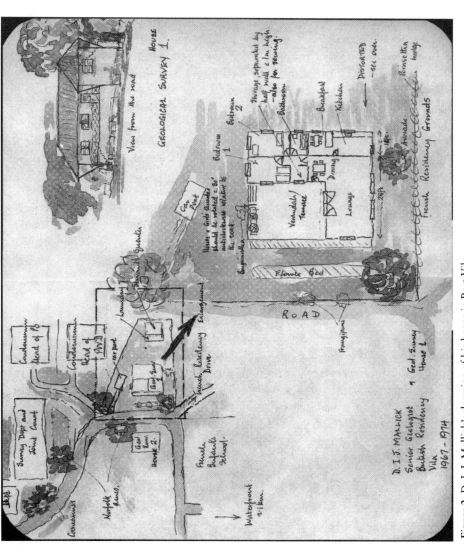

Figure 2. D. I. J. Mallick's drawing of his house in Port Vila.

deal with his life in England in the 1990s. He died tragically as the New Year began in 1997. I have felt Will's absence in more than the unanswered questions piling up on my desk. His presence is evident in almost every British interview and archival document. His loss is one that all researchers on the history of Vanuatu share, and one that those of us who worked closely with him feel most keenly. This is certainly not the book Will would have written. His would have been much longer, more detailed, and would have had even more endnotes. But I hope it is one that he would respect and, insofar as he could, enjoy.

Will Stober and I amiably argued some of the finer points of the colonial history of the New Hebrides, between ourselves and in discussions with other contributors to the project. This book is dialogic in this and other ways. One ex-colonial officer whom I interviewed had prepared a long list of questions to pose to me in response to questions I had circulated to potential participants. For example, I had asked if their housing was designed or modified in any way to respond to indigenous housing styles. He let me know that this question made him laugh. There were no considerations other than budgetary ones, he claimed, and the predominant style was "southwest Pacific corrugated Edwardian." Keith Woodward, who served in Port Vila from 1953 until 1978, was a major contributor to this project. Encumbered with a serious visual impairment even while in the islands, he had honed his memory, remarkable for remembering the sequence and detail not only of events in the New Hebrides but of the British contribution to and interpretation of those events. He was willing to give up considerable time to my project. He listened to and commented on a taped reading of the first draft of this book and related publications. In Australia, Violet Bowhay, daughter of a third-generation settler in the New Hebrides, commented on chapter 7. The cross-talk, critique, and commentary that all of these exchanges generated made me continually check my facts and be willing to question every one of them. One person's situated knowledge bounced off against the others', and I have enjoyed letting the contradictions as well as the confirmations play out in this book.

My personal experiences having lived in Vanuatu gave me something in common with the people I interviewed. Among the British, I had credibility as one who had served my time and knew the basics, although many felt the need to set me straight about the rest. I knew the social significance of whether one belonged to the yacht club or the BESA (pronounced "beeza").[16] I knew enough to ask the wives of former British colonial officers how they felt about employing a house girl. Did their children swim at Pango Point? I could picture the scene. With former district agents I could compare experiences of living through droughts and hurricanes in outer islands.[17] We could all exchange views on Jimmy Stephens, the leader of the Santo Rebellion at the time of independence in

1980. I found myself comparing notes on the French with the English, on the English with the French, and on politics with everybody.

With all the participants in the project, I was a white insider but always an outsider too. I could never join any of their tribes—colonial officer, wife, or child. I was always on the border, part and not part of experiences that I could identify with but not share. Most anthropologists would not be surprised to read this. Anthropologists work on the edge. I constructed and lived on some boundaries that I had the privilege of choosing, including borders between home and away. I walked some lines and watched the people I worked with walk others, teetering at times between belonging and renunciation, desire and loss, or even life and death. I crossed borders that could be peaceful or tense—between administrators, settlers, or islanders, for example. I write about these border crossings in this book and intend to write more in research I am beginning, in an effort to improve communication among groups of people who have not understood each other very well.

The research for this project was conducted over a series of summers, tucked in between my obligations as a teacher and as director of our graduate program in social anthropology at York University in Toronto. The research began with an exploratory trip back to Vanuatu in 1993 funded by the Wenner Gren Foundation for Anthropological Research. I had been away for eight years while the country had been closed to researchers. I received three years of funding for the project, beginning in April 1994, from the Social Sciences and Humanities Research Council of Canada. The summer of 1994 was spent conducting interviews in Britain and France and in archival research at the Foreign and Commonwealth Office in the Midlands. In April and May 1995, I conducted more British interviews and more research in the archives with Will Stober.

Initially, I had intended to do an equivalent amount of research on the French side of the colonial equation, but I have had to save that for another occasion. I had no idea when I began how many people in Britain were keen to talk about the New Hebrides. Nor did I know that the archives would prove to be such a treasure trove. I ran out of time and money to do research on the French administration of the New Hebrides.

In June 1995, I went back to Vanuatu, where my family joined me a month later. There I conducted about twenty-five interviews with settlers and islanders, visited six islands, and listed 117 historic sites for the Vanuatu Cultural and Historic Sites Survey. This last project was my contribution to the country in exchange for being given a research visa.[18] The summers of 1996 and 1997 were spent trying to organize the archival and other textual material, transcribe tapes in Bislama (the creolized pidgin of Vanuatu), label some five hundred slides, and index everything else: seven hundred minutes of videotape, a few French inter-

Figure 3. Will Stober and John Leaney (left to right) drawing houses far from home. Author's photo.

views transcribed by my friend Jane Philibert, and the large number of interviews in English that student assistants had transcribed.[19]

Houses on the Move

To return to 1978 and our bamboo house in Vanuatu: We had asked the local carpenter, Joel Mera, who built the house, to put in lots of windows. We did not want windows with glass panes or louvers, just large openings in the walls. He thought we were compromising our privacy: he worried that people could look in. In more conventional bamboo homes it is perfectly possible, as he knew, to peer out through the gaps in the woven bamboo and observe the passing scene without being observed; but we wanted a breeze as well as a broader view. Joel Mera warned that we were inviting storm damage, but he cut the window openings anyway—two large ones and three smaller ones. When we first moved in, we propped the shutters open with three-foot poles in the daytime. As Joel had predicted, children clung to the window ledges and peered through the two open doors. Adults chatted with us through the windows if they were uneasy about actually coming inside. They did not cross the boundaries into each other's houses, much less enter houses of visiting North Americans, unless they were close kin or very close friends. Most socializing took place in the domestic space

outside houses, shady packed-earth clearings that filled many of the purposes of Western living rooms.

When it finally rained and the shutters were closed, to everyone's relief the windows did not leak. There were no screens. We burned mosquito coils when the bugs were bad, but at night there were no mosquitoes this high in the hills. There *was* malaria, although drug-resistant malaria was not the major problem in 1978 that it later became for islanders, and for me. Resistant malaria nearly killed me in 1985. I was sick again in 1996, more than a year after leaving Vanuatu, with ordinary *Vivax* malaria.

Like the British colonial families I interviewed, we were pleased by the view from our bamboo house. We could and did set aside our anthropological awareness of the power of such gazes and of the primacy of the visual in our own tradition of constructing landscape. On one side, the windows of our bamboo house overlooked the distant sea, a fifteen-minute walk through coconut plantations and food gardens below us. From the front, we looked out at a Tahitian chestnut tree. Its gnarled roots provided benches for Chief Mathias Tariudu, our mentor and Bill's adoptive father, who visited daily. His stories and explanations filled our notebooks and raised new questions for me about customary land tenure, the subject of my dissertation research. Some of these questions could be answered only by walking along trails to plantations and gardens, which I did with Mathias and others.

From all the windows of our house we could see other houses more or less like ours. They had fewer openings in the walls because the houses were used mainly as containers for possessions and sleeping people. Most had dirt floors, a few were concrete, but none of the other floors in this village were bamboo, which was considered pleasant under foot but high maintenance. In 1978, there were seventy-two people in the village, all ni-Vanuatu. I mapped the village, and on subsequent visits in 1982, 1985, 1993, and 1995, I could trace the patterns that "moving houses" made. I found that some houses had moved slightly between my visits, while others had moved quite a lot. Very few had stayed exactly where they were according to the earlier map. These movements reflected, among other things, passage through the life cycle, feuds, friendships, migration, storm damage, and changing fortunes.[20]

Houses of bamboo do not last long in the best of circumstances, often no more than ten years. The necessity of periodic repair and reconstruction provides frequent opportunities for change. Domestic cycles place demands on housing in Vanuatu, as anywhere. But bamboo houses, more than houses made of masonry or wood, can change easily in response to changing household needs. Instead of moving house when family size changes, or building an addition, as people do in North

Figure 4. Mathias Tariudu and Channing Rodman under the Tahitian chestnut tree, 1982. Author's photo.

America and Europe, ni-Vanuatu can construct an additional house—for example, for teenage boys—using natural materials that are freely available or inexpensive. Frequent hurricanes speed the process of destruction, and rebuilding after a storm is an all-too-frequent chore. In 1985, for example, 90 percent of the housing on Ambae was destroyed in a single storm. Thatched roofs and bamboo walls are constructed in prefabricated panels; in most cases, some panels from walls and roofs that had blown off could be salvaged. Often they did not end up on the original house, which might be rebuilt in situ, moved slightly, moved a lot, or rebuilt as a smaller dwelling, or a kitchen. Social relationships in the village could be read out of the built form by noting such things as whose walls ended up on whose house, which way the houses faced, and who lived in them at various times.

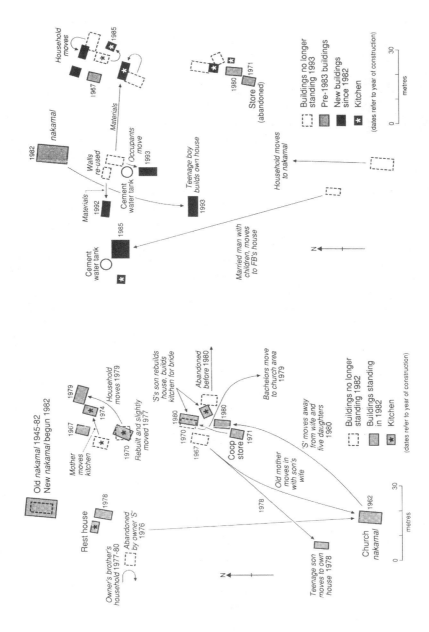

Figure 5. Waileni Village. From M. Rodman 1995. With permission from Cambridge University Press.

In the end, our house moved, too. When we visited in 1985, the floor and walls had been repaired, but the house posts were weak. The house was remarkably well built, and it lasted, with further repairs, until 1992. When we received word that our house had finally fallen down in a hurricane, we sent money to have it rebuilt. We knew that a widow and her daughters had been living in the house and that they would make room for us if we returned. When we arrived in August 1993, we found that part of the old walls had made their way down to Mathias' son's place while other bits were used to build a dwelling to our west, where the widow and daughters were sleeping. To local people, our house was still our house, complete with our Canadian flag (but no longer the Minolta calendar photos). As I began the research for this book on houses, it was disorienting to find that our own house in Vanuatu, while familiar, was in some ways not the same at all. The house was not even where we left it. It had moved about ten meters, its orientation had changed from north to east, and the layout had changed completely.[21]

Some expatriates who lived in Vanuatu also had moving houses. One missionary's house started life on Norfolk Island. It was a teacher's house, a modest structure, but its movement traces the history of the Anglican missionary enterprise in the New Hebrides. Mavis Salt told me about it when Bill, Channing, and I had tea at her British flat in August 1994. After nearly twenty years in the islands, from 1955 to 1976, she had retired to a modest flat near Cheltenham. We had known her as the headmistress of a girls' school near Lolowai, an iridescent harbor formed from a volcanic crater that had long ago opened to the sea. Lolowai, at the eastern tip of Ambae, was the headquarters of the Melanesian mission of the Anglican church. Bill and I remembered Mavis Salt's talent for making wine from tropical fruits. We had greatly enjoyed visits to her home at the school in the 1970s. Mavis Salt told me that her elderly bishop in the islands referred to the teacher's house in letters home to England as

> a "work-box of a house," you know, the old-fashioned needlework boxes with the different compartments? That was the house he was talking about, that we finally lived in. And the story is that in the earlier days, as you know, the missionaries wouldn't live in the islands. There weren't antimalarial tablets or anything, and they didn't know how to cope with malaria, so they lived on Norfolk Island, which was a bit cooler. They went up to the New Hebrides in the cool season and lived amongst the people in the cool months, then brought them back to school when it was hottest in the islands. There was quite a big settlement on Norfolk Island. Well, they finally [had antimalarial tablets] and realized they could live all the year round in islands without dying; I mean some of them did at first, but they were safe in the end.

Figure 6. Teacher's house moved from Norfolk Island to the Banks, to Ambae. From Mavis Salt collection, with permission.

Then the house was transported bit by bit. I imagine it was on stilts in Norfolk Island, but it was eventually on stilts [in the New Hebrides] anyhow. But they took it to the Banks Islands where the work flourished best in the early days. You know, Mota was the cradle really of the Christian, Anglican missionaries. They had a school for boys and a school for girls, and it was there for quite some years, and then one of the bishops got tired of waiting down at Lolowai in the hurricane seasons and having to hang about and not being able to get up and visit the schools. He sort of said in exasperation, "We'll move the whole school down here." So boys and girls, in fact, the two separate institutions were moved down, and this particular house came to be the head teacher's house for the girls' school.

Mavis Salt's story shows how fears of malaria in the New Hebrides encouraged missionaries to maintain a colonial nomadic cycle. They made seasonal forays out from Norfolk Island, which seemed more hospitable because it was more temperate and familiar. Early missionized colonial spaces were tentative and temporary, without permanent or "proper" housing. Progress in medicine, success in converting and educating New Hebrideans, and the seemingly wasted time involved in continuing to follow the seasonal migration to Norfolk Island led to better-appointed mission stations. Precut timber houses, ordered from Australian companies such as Burns, Philp, facilitated the kind of mobility that

Mavis Salt describes. Not only villagers' dwellings, anthropologists' houses, and missionaries' buildings moved. Houses were traded among, and sometimes physically moved between, the Condominium, French, and British governments, as well as private citizens.

Framing the View

The house Mavis Salt described, like all the houses far from home in this book, frame colonial views.[22] The view was explicitly important to expatriates whose cultural background included a landscape tradition. Islanders had no such tradition, no formal framing of "nature" with a foreground and middle distance and a backdrop of trees, hills, or the sea.[23] The category of "colonial landscape" is produced, it has been argued, to map "desire" or the goals of colonialism.[24] Desire in this case included dimensions of domination and surveillance but also education, salvation, and medicine. It involved visual enjoyment of the sight of the sea and the land, wild or ordered by colonialism, and of the land's seemingly "disappearing" people.

The importance of the view, and of siting houses to command a view, recalls Michel de Certeau's theory that any subject with will and power soon tries to create its own place, differentiated from the more general environment.[25] As subjects, he has in mind businesses, armies, or scientific institutions, but the British effort to establish an official presence in the New Hebrides fits his description perfectly. Theirs was certainly "an effort to delimit one's own place in a world bewitched by the invisible powers of the Other."[26] The Other for British colonial officers included seemingly uncivilized settlers as well as islanders. (For settlers and islanders, of course, the British officials were equally "Other.")

For example, a lack of what the British called "suitable" housing, and what de Certeau would call a "proper" place, was a continuing problem in the New Hebrides for various reasons. As we shall see in the next chapter, high-ranking officials were concerned that improper accommodation would send a message of weakness. Colonial statements of power made through buildings were clearest at the top. Both the French and British resident commissioners' homes were perched on hills overlooking Port Vila harbor, and each other. The British even situated their Residency on the highest point of an islet in the harbor.

Views were consciously important to the participants in this research, but many were less aware of the cultural lenses through which they looked out the window. They gave me abundant examples of gendered and racialized spaces, while rarely identifying them as such. Much was taken for granted, perhaps, be-

cause all the British colonial officers in the New Hebrides were male, and, until the final years of empire, all were white. "Hmm, I just don't remember where the kitchen was in that house," mused one retired colonial officer. His wife, however, had clear memories not only of where the kitchen was but of lying on the floor to fix the temperamental kerosene refrigerator.

Colonial families had no monopoly on gendered spaces. Indigenous spaces also were strongly gendered. No women were allowed in a traditionally male space of the *na gamal,* which in the north is a building and in the south of the archipelago is a clearing. Menstruating women spent their periods in a "small house" built for that purpose. While nowadays these practices are not so strictly observed everywhere in the islands, spatial boundaries between men and women are still evident in daily life.[27] For example, women sit with women and men with men at church and other social gatherings.

Racial boundaries are also evident in ni-Vanuatu spaces. Chairs brought out in a village clearing for white visitors to sit on could be both a sign of respect and a statement about the transience of visitors and their physical weakness. By far the strongest racial boundaries, however, demarcated colonial spaces. These boundaries, while constantly changing, characterize the entire colonial and postcolonial period. A regulation made in 1907 restricted the movement of natives at night in town. Over a period of many years, archival files described particular houses as suitable for Melanesian (especially New Hebridean) "natives," other "races" (such as Fijian or Chinese), or "whites." New Hebrideans always had their place and were expected to know it. Even in the 1990s, I saw a white woman berate a ni-Vanuatu gardener for stepping across the threshold into the main house to call for her. House girls, of course, were expected to be in the house, and it was accepted that they knew many intimate details about the lives of the people for whom they worked. Perhaps this is one reason why participants in the research so often spoke of their house girls as "really almost members of the family." I have never heard a house girl say the same about an employer.

There were other boundaries that no servant should cross: bureau drawers were off limits, although petty theft and trying on the mistress' clothes were common transgressions that many colonial wives told me about. Masters could and did cross intimate boundaries. Occasionally, a colonial officer's affair with a house girl became general knowledge, but this was probably the tip of a rather large iceberg. Ironically, employers rarely if ever entered their servants' homes, even if there were domestics' quarters adjacent to the main house. In this sense, house girls had more private space, albeit with a much lower standard of living, than their masters and mistresses.

Dialogue about Houses and Homes

With few exceptions, the people I interviewed were candid about their housing and their domestic lives. The exceptions did not surprise me. People who had had bad experiences with the press or with other researchers and one or two who were writing their own books on the islands were understandably reticent.

Most participants found the project uncontroversial. My questions, they said, seemed innocuous. If I had done a study of politics leading up to independence, I have no doubt that retired colonial officers would have been more guarded in their dealings with me. Most of the wives would have said little or nothing. Yet discussions of housing and lifestyle revealed many aspects of colonial politics and culture. Some were bemused by my interest in their New Hebridean houses. Why not study colonial homes in Kenya, which had some style and grace? It is true that there was nothing architecturally remarkable about colonial housing in the New Hebrides. It lacked the charm conveyed in such books as *The Romance of British Colonial Style*.[28] Mostly prefabricated or owner-built, housing in the New Hebrides, for colonial officers, missionaries, and settlers alike, was relatively inexpensive and primarily functional. Two notable exceptions were some of the French housing throughout the colonial period, which expressed a preference for a southern French villa style, and the buildings constructed in the earliest days of the Anglo-French Condominium, which figure in chapters 2 and 3. Even these were not grand in comparison to colonial edifices in India, Fiji, or almost anywhere else in the British empire.

My fascination with absolutely unremarkable, ordinary houses of ordinary people living in seemingly insignificant islands baffled people I interviewed. "Mais ce n'est pas très interessant!" a ninety-year-old French woman exclaimed as she let me photograph the museumlike interior of her old wooden home in Santo. My landlady, an indomitable character from a settler family who told her life story to my tape recorder in the fastest French I have ever heard, corrected her friend. She knew what I was about. "Si! C'est très interessant—pour *elle*." I write in the conviction, or at least the hope, that what follows is interesting for more than me. The subject is an anthropological history of British administration through its colonial spaces in a unique world at the geographical and temporal end of empire. It is a critical exploration of how such spaces and places both expressed and shaped a colonial process. These buildings are doorways that ask the reader to enter into a new understanding of ways that the people experienced, remembered, and wrote about their houses far from home.

THE CONDOMINIUM

Fom 1906 to 1980, a French Tricolore and a British Union Jack flew at equal height in the capital, Port Vila. Or so both sides claimed. Now there is a single flag, available to much of the world on computer software that will also play a music-box version of the rousing national anthem, "Yumi, Yumi, Yumi." This is not pronounced "yummy, yummy, yummy," as Australian tourists may be told; it is no paean to cannibalism. Rather it is "you-me," an inclusive "we" that has proved elusive in Vanuatu, where colonial divisions exacerbated indigenous ones. Three languages are common in town—English, French, and the pidgin called Bislama. English and French are the languages of education. The national anthem is sung in Bislama. For ni-Vanuatu as well as many other residents, Bislama is the most common language. More than a hundred languages, all Austronesian, are spoken throughout the eighty islands.

When I show slides of Vanuatu, they tend to go something like this: a map of the Pacific, a map of Vanuatu, then a series of slides on the capital, Port Vila. I explain that Port Vila had a population in 1995 of about twenty-five thousand. It has Chinese general stores and a fresh produce market. French wines and fine cheeses are beyond the reach of most ni-Vanuatu, enjoyed only by some expatriates and the ni-Vanuatu elite. The climate is pleasant by many North Americans' standards, although very humid, with an average high of 29° C and a low of 19° C.[1]

My slides include a view of the town from the sea, showing a line of two-story office buildings and a new park on reclaimed waterfront land; the covered market where ni-Vanuatu women sell fresh vegetables, fruits, live chickens, and shell necklaces; flamboyant trees in bloom; residential homes for business and government people; and the increasingly numerous homes made of bits of iron sheeting and other odds and ends that house islanders who have come to town and found little or no employment.

I never gave much thought to the tendency to start the show with Port Vila. Visitors generally arrive in Port Vila, so I thought it was logical to start there. Not so for John Salong, a ni-Vanuatu from Ambrym who earned his university degree in Canada. He borrowed our slides for some lectures he was giving. Sure enough, he began with the two maps, but then he went straight to the rural islands. He showed photos of gardens and villages, the "real Vanuatu" as he called it, sure that this was more authentically his country than Port Vila. I question the notion of authenticity—I don't think there is a "real" Vanuatu—but it would be hard to argue with John's conclusion that Port Vila is not like the rest of Vanuatu. Nor has it ever been.

Port Vila is a popular destination for middle-class tourists, mostly Australians, and for budget travelers from around the world looking for a little adventure, but not too much. Port Vila's soft life—wine, hot showers, croissants, nightclubs—makes development workers and anthropologists queasy. They prefer the characters, dust, and pickup trucks of Luganville (population about five thousand) on the northern island of Santo, which is the only other municipality in the country. Predictably, I've always found Santo more congenial, although the prospect of a meal in one of Port Vila's restaurants has sustained me for months on Ambae.

To me, Port Vila smells of burning green leaves from manicured gardens and wood smoke from "bush" kitchens, of gasoline and diesel because Port Vila is where the cars and trucks are, of sweet frangipani blossoms, steamy rain on asphalt roads, dark-roasted coffee from a French café, fresh *pain au chocolat* at dawn from a Chinese bakery. Visually, Port Vila harbor offers infinite variations on the blue and green that Melanesian languages treat as one color. The faux-native bungalows of Iririki Island Resort look back at the town from the islet in the harbor that was the site of the British Residency and Presbyterian hospital. Sailing yachts moor in the channel between Iririki and the main island. Cruise ships dock regularly at the main wharf, clearly visible from town but fifteen minutes' drive around the bay. The town itself is built on four tiers of coral limestone that form natural terraces, rising to a height of approximately a hundred meters.[2] It looks a bit like the fictional African capital, Celesteville, in the children's story of Babar the Elephant.[3] As in many colonial and company towns, the most prestigious buildings are higher up; but even the lower buildings facing the harbor

have a view. The whole idea of "the view" was very important to colonial sensibilities, as I suggested in the introduction. It remains an important aspect of real estate values. Stairs rise from the seafront market to the government offices in Independence Park (once the British Paddock), then another steep hill leads to the Supreme Court, which used to be the Joint Court of the New Hebrides. I often walked into town for the start of the business day at 7:30 A.M. from the Kaiviti, a homey budget hotel on the south side of town. To reach Independence Park from downtown, I climbed a long cement staircase, walking very slowly, hoping to avoid that moment when despite my best efforts the perspiration would start to drip down my face. To reach the Supreme Court was worse.

By 1995, when I last visited Vanuatu, the Supreme Court was the only historic government building that had been recognized as important for preservation. Originally built as the home of the president of the Joint Court, it was used as American Island Command Headquarters in World War II; it later became the Joint Court of the Condominium, replacing the dilapidated original Joint Court. The Supreme Court, a two-story frame building with huge Norfolk pines flanking the entrance, was all that remained of the half dozen relatively grand buildings constructed in the early days of the Condominium between 1907 and 1912. Today, Vanuatu offers remarkably little in the way of colonial architecture compared, for example, to Fiji or Kenya or Montserrat. Perhaps it was a perverse curiosity, then, that drove me to study historic architecture where there seemed to be almost none. It was a curiosity well rewarded in the archives, and even in the streets once I learned to look.

As we shall see, Port Vila was constructed out of seemingly empty space, which in turn was the creation of Britain and France. It was all wishful thinking.[4] The two powers were intent on the impossible task of building an impressive capital in a colony that wasn't a colony, where almost no one might be impressed, in a place whose volcanic islands were far more imposing than its towns would ever be.[5] These were not the first houses far from home in the New Hebrides—those belonged to missionaries, settlers, and, thousands of years earlier, to the first islanders—but they were among the most unusual.

Romilly's Dilemma

Colonization is easier if the space to be administered and settled is empty. Since almost nowhere really is empty, the illusion can be created that the land is wilderness, vacant or poorly used. The illusion of empty space clears the field for constructing colonial places that are linked in a system of administration and

Figure 7. Supreme Court, Vanuatu. Photo by William Rodman, with permission.

shaped by local versions of imperial cultures.[6] For colonial officials in the New Hebrides, the illusion of empty space was so complete that to the earliest administrators there seemed to be no place at all to live. The symbolic dimensions of housing as a metaphor for social status, and even as a metaphor of the self, are clear in the situation that faced Hugh Hastings Romilly. He was appointed Her British Majesty's first consul for the New Hebrides in June 1888, but he didn't receive his commission until five months later. Then, at the end of December 1889, when the seals and stamps finally arrived that would allow him to collect fees and otherwise do his work, his position was suddenly abolished. Romilly found all of this frustrating, but especially his housing, or lack thereof: "[i]n the New Hebrides themselves there was no house available in which he could have lived in accordance with the traditions of civilized life."[7]

Romilly's dilemma—how to find suitable housing—was remarkably hard to solve. Three dimensions of the problem need further discussion here. First, administratively speaking, there was only empty space. Second, for Romilly's purposes, the New Hebrides, while empty of suitable housing, was filled with inappropriate lodgings. Bamboo houses and other native accommodation were everywhere, but they simply would not do. Third, he tried to avoid staying in the houses of settlers because he suspected them of engaging in precisely the illegal activities he was supposed to police.

The first part of Romilly's problem was that there was no designated administrative space in the New Hebrides. While there were numerous settlers and mis-

sionaries in the group by the 1880s, the only land-based governmental activity, except for punitive expeditions, had been the occupation of Port Sandwich, Malakula, and Havannah Harbour, Efate, by French troops in 1886. One reason given for sending in the troops was as a response to the deaths of more than twenty settlers in the islands between 1882 and 1886. Australian opposition to French annexation of the New Hebrides was also a factor in the decision to raise France's military profile in the islands. The occupation intensified the diplomatic crisis: up to this point Britain and France had resisted pressure from Australia and New Caledonia, respectively, to annex the New Hebrides. Instead they had adopted a "hands off" policy. But in 1887 Britain and France began cooperating in a policy of joint minimum intervention. They formed a joint naval commission:

> The British and French naval commanders were to preside over the Commission in alternate months: two British and two French naval officers were to be members besides the President. In the event of any disturbance or danger, the Commission was to meet and take action; independent action was not to be taken except in emergency, nor was military force to be used unless the Commission considered it indispensable.

Added to this unworkable chain of command was the fact that ships of the naval commission did not sail during the six-month hurricane season.[8]

The second part of Romilly's dilemma was that living in a New Hebridean bamboo or "grass" house was out of the question. These were not even considered houses but rather huts or hovels. Simple dwellings made of natural materials symbolically partook of nature themselves as did those who lived in them, who seemed to the colonizers to be untamed, wild, naive, and sometimes savage. While not literally "empty," indigenous houses might as well have been. Throughout the archival material, grass houses are always presented as appropriate for New Hebrideans but inappropriate for Europeans. For those who were neither "native" nor "white," evaluating the suitability of particular housing types was a way of debating racial categories. For example, there was much discussion of whether it was acceptable to house a Fijian in what had been the public prosecutor's residence. In any case, a grass house was not part of Romilly's universe of possible accommodation.[9]

The third aspect of this dilemma was the greatest irritant for the consul. The settlers whom Britain and France were supposed to protect and control not only lived in accommodations that were generally unsuitable for receiving visits from the consul; their lifestyles were also a problem. It was unseemly, Romilly was sure, to live with traders who were suspected of dealing in various sorts of illicit

activities, notably illegal sale of liquor to the natives.[10] Romilly wrote his mother in May 1889: "I am feeling somewhat depressed at my utter inability to do my work properly, and the indifference shown by the Home Government. I am seriously thinking of buying a *tent* and pitching it somewhere in the group. It will be a most undignified proceeding, but I don't see what else is to be done."[11]

The "indifference shown by the Home Government" was an enduring problem. In the end, Romilly did take up lodging with a trader, Donald MacLeod, out of a lack of alternatives. Romilly reported, "The dirt and filth of this place are wonderful. . . . I never go into the store or liquor-bar below, as I do not wish to see my host's barman selling grog to the natives." Poor Romilly, unlike most other British civil servants in my study, never could find one of those "houses far from home." Even as British consul for the New Hebrides, he had to base himself in (French) New Caledonia, to the dismay of both French and British.[12]

A Unique Form of Government

Not suprisingly, French and British settlers were no happier with this situation than the consul. Although the British at least fell within the jurisdiction of the Western Pacific High Commission, French settlers had no legal system available to them. They could not even legally marry without going to New Caledonia to do so. Frustrated French settlers in the New Hebrides took the law into their own hands in 1889 and created the municipality of Franceville. "This was an ambitious attempt at local government" that had strong local support.[13] Internationally, however, it was frowned on. Britain and France, in a rare moment of agreement with regard to the islands, brought a rapid end to the upstart municipality. A few years later, the predominantly French planters at Mele made another attempt, establishing the municipality of Faureville in 1895. "This attracted less attention; at least one marriage was solemnised before its locally-elected officials . . . and others may have followed until, in 1901, the Governor of New Caledonia was at last given jurisdiction over his fellow citizens in the New Hebrides, with a deputy resident at Vila. The British made a similar appointment."[14]

Internationally, the Joint Anglo-French Convention that formalized a policy of minimum intervention in the New Hebrides in 1887 was closely tied to the 1888 convention regarding British and French interests in the Suez Canal. In 1904, the Entente Cordiale affirmed Britain's and France's support for each other's colonial policies, in opposition to Germany. A year later, the deputy commissioner, Captain Ernest Rason, telegraphed that a combined Anglo-French force had avenged the murders of French seamen on Malakula: "Party attacked

Figure 8. Port Vila harbor from town showing Iririki Island, circa 1965. Photo by John Yaxley, with permission.

by natives: district occupied, houses demolished. . . . *Entente cordiale* perfect. South-west Malikula quiet."[15] On this occasion the Entente Cordiale may have been perfect, but such punitive actions were hit or miss. The same official had complained only a few months earlier about "the want of government in the islands who can punish native murderers of white men." Repatriated laborers from Queensland were allegedly increasing the incidence of such crimes. Captain Rason had warned his high commissioner:

> It is at present openly spoken of that if the Mixed Commission do not succeed in bringing to justice and executing the murderers . . . when the men-of-war have left the group during the hurricane months, a band of settlers will proceed to take justice on the murderers themselves. . . . In these circumstances I am of the opinion that they will be acting with exactly the same justice and the same right as those settlers of the Middle States of America acted before the Government of the United States sent troops to punish the Indians.[16]

Locally, complaints about lack of government, land disputes, and threatened French annexation came from a variety of sources. English-speaking missionaries repeatedly lobbied for extensions of governmental control.[17] Settlers also complained to the British government: "I BEG to protest against Frenchmen interfering

with my property," wrote a settler on Epi in 1905 (emphasis in the original). He continued, "They have stolen corn and the British flag, struck my labourers, . . . and now they want to take my land. Ought not these affairs to be settled by the authorities?"[18] On the French side, efforts to attract settlers were also hampered by a lack of government: "A country where crime could not be punished or payment of debts enforced, where no marriage could be contracted that was valid in French law, could hardly hope to attract a good type of settler."[19]

The Condominium, which went into effect in December 1907, was predicated on the further mutual surrender of independent action by Britain and France; it was to be a land based rather than a naval administration. A British resident commissioner and his French counterpart would reside in Port Vila and make all decisions jointly. The perception of seemingly vast but bridgeable cultural differences between the two "races" is evident in the way the British judge, Thomas E. Roseby, spoke about the French in 1910: "In this Group we have the contact of those two European races which have perhaps most profoundly influenced the modern world; but differing as they do in language, in temperament, in their outlook on life, each has something to learn from the other."[20]

The fact that they were "resident" commissioners meant that they had to be housed appropriately, and not in New Caledonia. In fact, privileged spaces were not "found"; they were created, redeemed as building sites from the fictional wasteland of early colonial space. Iririki Island, for example, was deemed suitably empty despite the persistent, and eventually successful, land claims of nearby Ifira islanders. The Presbyterians were already using half the island for a hospital and were willing to lease the other half to the British government on the condition that the French never be allowed to gain exclusive control of the New Hebrides. In a re-creation of European geography in Port Vila harbor, a site on the mainland was selected for the French resident commissioner's home, while the British settled on Iririki, separated from the French by a narrow channel.

Dealing with the divergent British and French legal systems was not so easy: "This juristic experiment is by no means a simple one, the more particularly as it is without definite precedent, even in the Mixed Courts of Egypt or the Hague Tribunal."[21] Codified French law, like that of most of Europe, contrasted with English law based largely on precedent, yet the two systems had to be administered side by side in the New Hebrides. Judge Roseby's publicly expressed hopes for the Condominium anticipated today's European Union; the Condominium, he felt, could provide experience useful to international unification of European law. British and French law, he predicted, would prove to be much less different than commonly supposed: the Condominium "will remain, I think, as one of the interesting juristic experiments of history. In my opinion it will go on to exem-

plify that the essential ideals which inspire the administration of justice in these two great nations differ much less than their outward form."[22]

The Condominium lived up to only one of these high expectations: it was interesting. As an experiment it was a failure largely because the "scientists," to extend Roseby's metaphor, could seldom agree about how to proceed, and what they could agree on made the laboratory procedure cumbersome at best. In 1914, a protocol (not ratified until 1922) increased the resident commissioners' powers and those of the legal structure. Yet no matter how it was amended, the Condominium began as inefficient and remained ineffective. "It is a sad thing for the morale of a country," a resident lawyer commented in 1914, "when *all* of its inhabitants are agreed as to the inefficiency of its administration."[23] From 1906 until independence in 1980, the Condominium was a source of frustration: "It satisfied no one."[24]

The Structure of the Condominium

Under the Condominium, British law applied to British nationals and *ressortissants*. Citizens of other countries residing in the New Hebrides were expected to opt officially for either British or French jurisdiction. Melanesians would be covered by a Native Code. The Joint Court capped the judicial structure. The court was intended primarily to resolve large numbers of thorny land disputes and to provide a mechanism for the official registration of title to land by nonindigenous individuals and entities. It also decided other cases between British and French, as well as between Europeans and islanders. British and French courts handled cases involving their own nationals. Native courts (after 1914) heard disputes between islanders.

A neutral president, initially appointed by the king of Spain, was central to the judicial structure. The first president of the Joint Court "was truly neutral, having understood little French, less English, and no Melanesian; but this was no additional handicap, because he was also deaf."[25] Because of the unique structure of administration, the number of officials in the Condominium was unusually large for a place the size of the New Hebrides. In particular, the number of high officials was much greater than the four usually found in a Crown Colony.[26] These included a British and a French resident commissioner, a French judge, a British judge, a public prosecutor, a Native advocate, and a registrar. The large number of high officials led "to jealousies, intrigues, grievances and slights" that, even if imaginary, became all too important "in a country entirely cut off from the outer world save by a monthly steamer."[27]

The Condominium was commonly referred to as the Pandemonium in popular

literature on the islands. The Joint Court became "the Joy Court" in a satirical play in three languages about "this Tower-of-Babel tribunal, which played at law in pretentious and portentous splendour" by the lawyer Edward Jacomb.[28] Later commentators also regarded the New Hebrides as a "high musical comedy of one of the strangest political situations in the modern world" in which "an uneasy symbiosis" of three governments prevailed: English, French, and Condominium.[29] One colonial officer, Reid Cowell, even wrote a musical in the style of Gilbert and Sullivan, *Pandemonia, or a Franco-British Fantasy*. The play expressed Cowell's views on the administration of the New Hebrides in the mid-1950s better than any memoir.[30] A verse from the musical captures the silliness of fictional British resident commissioner H. H. Ian Maby-Abell's need to consider even the smallest issue jointly with his French counterpart, a need that was all too real in the Condominium:

> In my house on my island I think when I sit,
> Think jointly, conjointly, conjointly.
> And say to myself I am making a hit,
> Thinking jointly, conjointly, conjointly.
> It is co-operation alone I must seek,
> If I can't get it now I will get it next week
> If I firmly resolve to think ere I speak,
> Think conjointly, conjointly, conjointly.[31]

While often described as a dual system of government, the Condominium was in fact considerably more complex. Some services, particularly social services such as health, education, and cooperatives, were provided in duplicate, by the British and the French. There were three systems of government housing: British, French, and Condominium. For many public services, however, the Condominium was the only provider. These included postal service, telegraphs and telephones, customs and agricultural advising and development, survey, lands registration, mining, development of rural water supplies, and meteorology. Like the Christian Trinity, the Condominium was at once threefold and unitary. But it was best known as dual.

Port Vila: Vision and Reality

Port Vila, the largest town in the country, has always been rather small. Surprisingly, about 1910, half a dozen official residences and two public buildings were constructed on a comparatively grand scale. The rich archival material on the

New Hebrides reveals the complementary, overlapping, contested, and competitive roles of both individuals and nations that were expressed in the processes of designing, building, and using colonial dwellings and offices.[32] The life course of these buildings illustrates many of the hopes and many of the problems of the Condominium as an experimental form of administration.

The Condominium was an explicitly juristic experiment, as the quotes from Judge Roseby earlier in this chapter indicate.[33] As the New Hebrides was neither Britain's nor France's laboratory, the experiment had to be one in joint administration. There were limited funds for the experiment, especially on the English side. "Both Britain and France were reluctant to invest in an area not fully under their own control."[34]

The buildings to house the Condominium were an opportunity to make, and to contest, a series of assertions in built form about the nature of a unique form of law and order. Both the promise and the problems of the Anglo-French Condominium are evident in the construction of these buildings in Port Vila circa 1910 and in their subsequent decline. What notions of the New Hebrides as a juristic experiment were asserted and explored through these buildings? What does the failure to adequately maintain the buildings, or to build others on this scale, reveal about various views of the New Hebrides as a colonial enterprise? If the buildings were far too grand for the community they served, why were they built at all?

The new buildings expressed the Condominium's promise to develop legal structures for solving a big problem: land disputes between Europeans, and with islanders, that were inhibiting investment and development in the New Hebrides. Other major issues concerned the illegal sale of liquor to islanders and the related issue of regulating labor recruiting, both of which provoked conflicts along national lines. In addition to legal innovation, the other major promise of the Condominium was to improve transportation and communication in the islands. Appropriately, the post office, with facilities for telecommunication, was the other major building constructed at the same time as the court.

Why did the new government express these promises in built form? The buildings were, I suggest, a clear statement that the government had landed and taken root. Before 1906, alternating French and British naval patrols were the only visible evidence of government, and these, as we have seen, did not sail during the lengthy hurricane season. Government presence was largely punitive and always transitory. Medical service and education were almost entirely in the hands of the missions.[35] As the experience of Romilly, the homeless consul, suggests, there was nowhere for permanent government officials to stay. Creating a land-based physical presence focused on constructing the primary government buildings necessary to operationalize the Condominium, not just the British Residency on Iririki and

the French Residency on the main island. Building the Condominium almost incidentally created Port Vila as a small capital town in the process.

The history of Port Vila is a variant on a well known phenomenon: colonial ideas often were expressed in architecture, urban design, and, more generally, in built form. Certain colonial towns were "laboratories" for urban planning and design.[36] Especially in Morocco, Indochina, and Madagascar, aesthetic images "focused overwhelmingly on colonial 'space'—groups of new monuments, streets of new housing, magnificent ruins from the past, as well as quaint scenes of 'native' bazaars," and the like.[37] The elaborate public buildings and official residences in Port Vila, coupled with the very fact that the government presence established its land base at this location in the New Hebrides after 1907, made strong statements about colonial space. Yet the town was not a laboratory for urban planning. In fact, the town itself was a low priority for the Condominium.

There was no history of an urban native population or indeed of any urban population at all. The indigenous people were horticulturalists who lived in scattered settlements seldom larger than a hundred residents. In contrast to the places Wright describes, there were no " 'native' bazaars" to be found in the New Hebrides, much less in Port Vila, and thus no "quaint scenes" of them to be created. Creating images to attract visitors, which was part of French urbanism in other colonies, would have been ludicrous in the New Hebrides; the only places for visitors to stay were in private homes and, by World War II, a few modest hotels with minimal amenities, such as pit latrines.

The development of a colony requires a gaze that constantly negates what is actually perceived "in favor of what it might become."[38] Port Vila's urban form in the early 1900s provides a good example of this wishful thinking. Although Presbyterian missionaries writing for *The New Hebrides Magazine* repeatedly touted the town as a civilized, domesticated place for families to settle, few other observers expressed such a rosy view. Planters themselves cautioned newcomers that "it is not possible for them to successfully establish themselves by planting alone."[39]

By the mid-1890s, there were 119 people of European origin living on thirty-four plantations in the Vila area. Fourteen of these plantations were clustered in what is now a peri-urban settlement called Mele, about eight kilometers to the northwest. The rest were scattered. Port Vila itself was just a small commercial and planting center, by no means as important a site of European settlement as Mele; but it offered both "vacant" and plantation land, a harbor, and the possibility of some independence from the larger settler community at Mele.

By the late 1880s, two steamers called monthly at Port Vila. One was French, sailing from Noumea, the other English, sailing from Sydney. "[T]here was certainly nothing approaching a 'town' as such," but some of the distinctive signs of what would become the Condominium were already apparent in that the

few buildings clustered on the waterfront made up a "half-French, half-English settlement; each English building has its French counterpart, and the notices on the doors of the shops are in both languages."[40]

When Port Vila was designated in the 1906 convention to be the seat of government and of the Joint Court, the town was officially a municipality with a mayor, Monsieur LePelletier, and a five-member elected governing council. The expatriate population numbered "about 25 Britishers and less than a hundred French."[41] No figures are available regarding the native population or imported Tonkinese laborers, but only those connected with plantations would have lived in town at that time. The Presbyterian missionary publication *The New Hebrides Magazine*, always a booster of (Christian) settlement in the islands, observed that Port Vila was becoming quite civilized. Bridges and roads were much improved, and "fine teams," "dog carts," and cyclists had become common sights. Another positive sign that "settlers have come, not merely to make a 'pile,' but to stay" was reportedly evident in built form—"comfortable homes"—and social structure—"family life."[42] "Vila still flourishes,"observed the same magazine in January 1907. "It now boasts of a butcher, a baker, a plumber, a barber, and an aerated water manufactory."[43] Writing from a secular background and for a different audience (his mother), the young lawyer Edward Jacomb arrived in Port Vila to find that there was no hotel, one restaurant, and only a single, "primitive" boarding house with one room for guests. Yet the Veuve Cliquot flowed like water at a wedding soon after Jacomb's arrival; and the resident commissioners, awaiting the boats and buildings necessary to carry out their duties, "could do little except amuse themselves, and so life for them becomes one long round of dinner and other parties from year's end to year's end." Evening dress, even in Presbyterian households, was "*de rigeur* at local dinner parties."[44]

By 1909, however, the municipal government was moribund. Application was made in 1910 to reestablish the municipality of Port Vila, but the proposal was overruled by the high commissioners because the time was "not yet ripe for the experiment."[45] While taking on the additional responsibilities of municipal governance, the Condominium administration had little effect in town and still less anywhere else in the islands.[46] The two resident commissioners, "unable to cope with the Group [of islands] as a Group" started by trying to organize the capital. For fourteen years their activities were practically confined to Efate Island.[47]

White Space

In 1910, British Resident Commissioner Merton King, far less sanguine than the missionaries about the level of civilization in town, felt that the court officials

soon to be sent out to the New Hebrides should be warned "of the terrors that await them here. That they cannot purchase anything, or scarcely anything, that a civilised being wants, and that servants are unprocurable. . . . A degraded type of Mongolian from Annan and Tonkin [i.e., Vietnam] can be procured as servants in Noumea, but they are mostly worthless as I know to my cost."[48]

Except for the presence of the maligned Melanesian and Indochinese servants, the Condominium created white space as part of the juristic experiment. Not only did the Condominium hold out the promise that land disputes with islanders would be resolved in favor of whites, but the "natives" themselves would recede from view. This assumption applied to both the outlying and urban areas. In general, native people were believed to be disappearing as a result of diseases introduced by Europeans; these diseases killed as much as 95 percent of the population in some areas. The rural areas were largely beyond the administrative reach of the Condominium, especially in the early days when there were few if any district agents. The Condominium itself administered to white interests, not those of indigenous people. While one might question Oliver's assertion that the missionaries were politically impotent, it is true that "the Condominium . . . had its tragic side. France looked after Frenchmen and British after British, but only the politically impotent missionaries looked after the forty thousand natives. . . . In fact, the missions appear to have been the only effective champions of native welfare in the New Hebrides."[49]

Port Vila had not been a site of native settlement, although residents of Little Ifira (or Fila) Island in the harbor claimed the land and used its resources.[50] Islanders were discouraged from moving to town by a variety of factors, including distance from their home gardens and their hunting and fishing territories, lack of work in town, and lack of accommodation. Archival documents discuss the need to provide housing for "natives" coming to court and the allocation of £20 to construct "a suitable native building."[51] In the end, it is unclear whether such a house actually was built with Condominium funds, or where it would have been situated. The only provisions that seem certain to have been made for islanders and others visiting the court were spittoons placed on the verandah: "The natives spit a good deal. Whether they would always hit the spitoon is another question."[52]

A Condominium regulation further demarcated Port Vila as white space. In 1907, the British and French resident commissioners acted jointly to restrict the movement of natives in town between 9:00 P.M. and 5:00 A.M. Sale of alcoholic beverages to islanders already was illegal, but the law was rarely enforceable because the government lacked presence. White traders did brisk, illegal business, largely in rural areas in connection with labor recruits, but also in town. British Resident Commissioner King opined, "Such a measure is, I am of the opinion, very necessary in view of [drunken] and disorderly scenes that result on

certain nights of the week; and its adoption and enforcement cannot, I think, but materially aid in the suppression of the illegal sale of alcohol to, and its consumption by, the natives of Port Vila."[53] Natives employed by nonnatives were exempt from this restriction only if they carried written permission from their employer.[54] In Port Vila drunken and disorderly behavior (not just on the part of natives one might add) could be an irritant to government officials living there. These and other regulations concerning, for example, sanitation were juristic ways of trying to ensure a certain quality of life for expatriate officials, as well as invoking the benefits that would flow from such regulations more generally to the white, native, and Asian residents.

Grand Buildings

With the creation of the Condominium, "the first necessity was the provision of accommodation and offices." In 1908, "there were not more than forty houses in the whole of Vila, and apart from private hospitality it was well nigh impossible for a stranger . . . to secure lodging."[55] By 1911, five large houses, called in accordance with the customs of the time "cottages" in English and "hôtels" in French, had been built for each of the following: (a) the Spanish president of the Joint Court, (b) the British judge, (c) the French judge, (d) the public prosecutor, and (e) the registrar of the court. The Joint Court building itself (f) was still under construction. The new post office (g) was completed and opened for business by early 1910. A house for the commandant of the French *milice* (h) was planned (see figure 9).

The numerous new homes and offices constructed around 1910 were precut timber buildings sent to the New Hebrides on ships. Walls, roof, and floor were generally Oregon redwood. Doors were sugar pine. Kauri wood was used for shelving, and tallow wood for sills.[56] The houses, although precut, required as much as sixteen months to construct because the competent carpenters needed to assemble them were scarce. A few carpenters, such as Raveton, were recruited from New Caledonia; others were English or Australian, and one, who made himself indispensable for twenty years, was a Scots Presbyterian named Kenneth McKenzie. He was seconded to the British Residency by the Presbyterian mission and served as director of works from 1908 until 1928.[57]

The town, such as it was, developed along the seafront where Burns, Philp and other firms had small stores and wharves. Port Vila was a port before it was a town, although an unimpressed visitor as late as the 1930s supported the view that it was neither: "On a dit de Port-Vila qu'il n'y avait ni port, ni ville."[58] MacClancy, writing in 1981, agrees: "Born out of necessity not for elegance, Vila was a town for pioneers and beachcombers. Convicts who had served their time in prison at Noumea

	Building	Architect	Land purchased from	Builder	Source of materials	Completion date	Building cost
a	President of Joint Court's house	Joseland & Vernon	Société Française des Nouvelles Hébrides	M. Julienne	Sydney	1910	£ 8,505/2*
b	British judge's house	Joseland & Vernon	Société Française des Nouvelles Hébrides	M. Raveton	Sydney	March 1910	£ 4,048
c	French judge's house	unknown	Société Française des Nouvelles Hébrides	M. Binot	Noumea	1910	£ 2,275
d	Public prosecutor's house	Joseland & Vernon	Société Française des Nouvelles Hébrides	M. Julienne	Sydney	Aug. 1910	£ 8,505/2*
e	Registrar of the Joint Court's house	none	Annie Petersen	Kenneth McKenzie?	Sydney (renovation of existing cottage)	1910	unknown
f	Joint Court building	unknown	French government	M. Julienne		Sept. 1912	£ 10,000
g	Post office and Treasury	Joseland & Vernon	Annie Petersen	M. Raveton	Sydney	March 1910	£ 3,000
h	Commandant of French police's house	unknown	M & S Rossi	unknown	unknown	unknown	unknown

Sources: WPHC 447/1920 and NHBS 227/1908; for (f) and (g), Jacomb 1914.59.
[a] Labor and materials cost combined for these two buildings.

Figure 9. Condominium buildings discussed by BRC King, January 1911.

'haunted the beach' . . . and earned a living selling grog to [natives]." [59] The buildings along the narrow, muddy main street, rue Higginson, contrasted with the grandeur of the planned Condominium buildings. The new post office was to be in the commercial heart of town on the coastal strip. The Joint Court, and residences for the French judge, British judge, and Spanish president, would overlook the port from

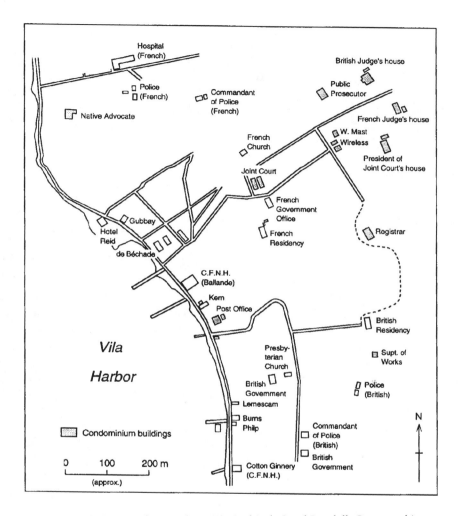

Figure 10. Sketch map of Port Vila, 1926. Archival. Carol Randall, Cartographic Office, Department of Geography, York University.

sites on the naturally terraced, raised coral limestone slope above the harbor.[60] From these hillside sites it was possible to make clear statements in built form about commanding the view and about superiority.

Not only were the new Condominium buildings situated up the hill, they were scattered. The sketch map from 1926 shows the location of the new Condominium buildings relative to the main commercial landmarks in Port Vila.[61] That the sites were scattered, rather than in a compound, was partly a

consequence of problems obtaining land and of the hilly topography above the narrow coastal shelf. But these factors did not prevent the British from later organizing their offices and most residences in a rectangular space known as the British Paddock on one of the limestone terraces. The scattered sites of the judicial buildings suggest, probably unintentionally, the cultural differences and independent attitudes that characterized the British and French, in this first, supposedly joint, building project.

Post Office

The postal service assumed particular importance because the Condominium post office would replace Burns, Philp's mail service. The commercial firm of Burns, Philp and Company received a subsidy from the Australian government to provide monthly steamer service to Port Vila and about a hundred other sites of European settlement in the region. The service had been "the salvation of British interests in the New Hebrides."[62] In March 1910, the post office was the first of the new public buildings to open, symbolically transferring colonial control over communication from a powerful commercial firm to the Condominium administration. The post office and treasury were the only new structures to be situated near the seafront rather than on the hill above the town, a popular statement in built form, for it was "deemed to be importantly necessary" for the post office (but not the other Condominium buildings) to be "near the principal places of business, and easily accessible to mail steamers."[63]

Like several other new buildings and in the spirit of the Condominium, the post office was built by a French-speaking Noumea carpenter, Georges Raveton, according to plans by English-speaking Sydney architects, Joseland and Vernon, who designed many of the early British and Condominium buildings. The British and French resident commissioners quibbled over the cost, the moiety of the difference which they were to share equally; the penciled recalculations of the British resident commissioner, Merton King, cover the back of an invoice in the archived files.[64]

The new postal service together with customs duties would provide one of the very few sources of revenue for the Condominium. Such revenues, it was hoped, would help to pay for construction of the principal buildings and offset some of the Condominium's operating costs. There seems never to have been a realistic expectation that this would amount to much; the joint powers had agreed each to pay a "moiety of the difference" between such revenues and actual costs. The post office was administered by the Condominium postal agent; he was charged with issuing stamps in both francs and pence and with mail delivery in and around the

town.[65] The stamps, which became collectors' items, were one of the very few sources of revenue for the Condominium.[66]

Officers of the French Residency always wrote letters in French; those of the British Residency corresponded only in English; but Condominium officials could use either official language to try to get what they wanted. Clearly, the postmaster's life was not easy, even in the new building. Postal Agent Deschamps, in a struggle to obtain blinds for the verandah, resorted to English (sort of) when he wrote in 1917, "The reverberation of the sun on the sea is simply insupportable!"[67]

Mail delivery was also a problem. French planters at Mele continued to feel isolated not only from the French government but even from Port Vila. The international postal incident described in figure 12 points to the kinds of communication difficulties that frequently arose, and still arise, in the islands. It also gives the flavor of the Condominium, suggesting some dimensions of the seemingly trivial problems that required the attention of officials at the highest levels, including the British and French resident commissioners, the Western Pacific high commissioner, and the secretary of state for the colonies. The incident conveys some of the tensions, as well as shared understandings, between the French and English. It suggests the logistical problems, among many other kinds of difficulties, that beset the Condominium. Above all, it illustrates the degree to which some events in this backwater of two empires were scrutinized by the metropolitan powers and how

Figure 11. Post office, undated. From Reece Discombe collection, with permission.

AN ATTEMPT TO IMPROVE the postal service precipitated an international incident. In August 1931, rumors reached the British Colonial Office in Downing Street that the French had taken the law into their own hands. The British secretary of state for the colonies, Cunliffe-Lister, wrote to the Western Pacific high commissioner to express his concern. Was it true that "an entirely French Postal Agency has been set up . . . which is independent of and in any respect competes with the Condominium Postal Service?" The secretary of state wanted to have detailed information so that he could consider lodging a protest with the French government.

There was indeed a breakaway postal service in the making. French Resident Commissioner Antoine Carlotti had decided to set up rural mail delivery to Mele, paid for out of French funds. Carlotti, in acting on his own initiative to solve a problem for rural French *colons*, had violated the Condominium practice of always consulting the other resident commissioner before doing anything.

The British resident commissioner had no objection to improving postal service to Mele and making a French policeman available to carry letters, but insisted that this must not be *advertised* as a French service, because to do so would be in violation of the Protocol. A joint letter was sent from both resident commissioners to the Condominium postal agent, M. de Gaillande, to find out why there were problems with the existing mail service to Mele. The postal agent responded acerbically, in French on an English typewriter without accents, that the "existing" service had never functioned regularly. If he had managed to deliver mail at all to Mele it was only through his own initiative and the use of telephone linemen who came to Port Vila from Mele to work. He would need to hire another postman or else have a saddle horse at his disposal. The horse would be better suited to the muddy roads than a man on foot.

In pencil beside this paragraph of the postal agent's letter is written the single word "Captain." This "excellent" horse provided weekly postal delivery service on behalf of the Condominium from Port Vila to Mele and back for more than a year. Captain was replaced by a bicycle in July 1932. (Presumably the roads had improved.) A joint letter from both resident commissioners informed the Condominium treasurer that the horse should be sold. M. de Gaillande offered to pay two pounds for Captain, but this was rejected as less than the animal was worth. In the end, the French Residency bought the horse for four pounds, a purchase price with which the British Residency officially concurred.

Figure 12. For Want of a Horse . . . An International Postal Incident.

easily a seemingly simple unilateral initiative for improving the quality of local settlers' lives could become an international incident.

Judges' Houses and the Joint Court

The judicial system, with its prospect of resolving land disputes, was even more important to the Condominium's hopes than the postal service. The importance attached to the judicial system is evident in the size and grandeur of the houses built for officials of the court and in the court building itself. These were by far the largest and fanciest buildings in Port Vila.

The British judge's house provides an example of one of the smaller cottages.

The house of the British Judge was a large two-storied wooden house on the highest point of the slope behind the Joint Court. . . . On the ground-floor were a huge dining-room, a billiard room, library, and hall with pantry and kitchen attached. On the top story were a roomy landing, a bedroom the size of a billiard room, three other bedrooms, and two bathrooms. Ten-foot verandahs surrounded the house on both stories, and seventeen or eighteen double doors on each story led to the verandahs."[68]

The first British judge himself was less impressive than his house, at least to Edward Jacomb, who was assistant to the resident commissioner at the time. The judge was Thomas E. Roseby, who made the comments on the New Hebrides as a juristic experiment. He arrived in Port Vila on the SS *Tambo*, 9 November 1908. Edward Jacomb's diary conveys both the details of colonial etiquette and the contrast between the fancy house and the slovenly judge. Jacomb seems uncharitably to make no allowance for the likely effect of a long journey by ship on the judge's appearance:

I had, for some reason, to go off to the ship myself and the boat in which he was being conveyed . . . passed me on the way. He stared very hard at me but was clearly determined to make me salute him first, which of course I did. He then made a too effusive reply. Later, when I was introduced to him at the Residency I was even less impressed—he was over-stout for his age and gave the impression of greasiness, unwashedness and being unsufficiently shaved; his finger nails were bitten down to the quick, and his clothes looked as if he had been sleeping in them and anyway off the peg [not made to measure].[69]

Even the British judge's house, which cost nearly £5,000, was not so elaborate as that of the president of the court, which was "so vast that most of the rooms were shut up and unoccupied."[70] The house had seven bedrooms, two bathrooms, a reception room, a morning room, a dining room, a smoking room, a library, a pantry, a vestibule, a porch, a kitchen, two storerooms, a servant's bedroom and bath, and twelve water tanks.[71]

The building that housed the Joint Court was the grandest structure of all. Sited on a promontory above the center of town, where the National Reserve Bank now stands, the Joint Court would have been visible from the harbor and from many parts of town. A war memorial constructed in front of and slightly lower than the court became the focus for ceremonial activity. Offices flanked the central auditorium, or courtroom: "It looks like the inside of an enormous square bandbox with little oblong windows (which will not open) let in round the tops of the

walls. . . . Both floor and benches are coated with a sticky varnish which militates against walking and encourages sitting." The symbolic expression of power through space must have been obvious. A barrier with a little door divided the public viewing area from the judges' stadium, counsel's table, and bench for the accused. The judges' stadium was a raised structure with four steps. The public sat on benches, the judges in chairs without arms; the president of the court sat between them in a chair with arms. Jacomb in his comic play *The Joy Court* describes the styles worn despite the court's location in a hot, humid town about as far from London, Paris, or Madrid as one could get:

> The President wears a black gown with plush collar, white lace cuffs and a black sexagonal hat with a nob on the top. The French Judge also has a sexagonal hat and a black gown with a tail of rabbit skin thrown over his shoulders. The British Judge wears a wig and gown, the Public Prosecutor (a foreigner) the gown of a Bachelor of Arts of the University of Oxford (which he has borrowed), and the Registrar nothing at all (except of course his ordinary clothes).[72]

The Joint Court never lived up to the promise of its architectural or sartorial setting. It "proved to be as much a disappointment as the rest of the Condominium."[73] A lack of fluency in French and English, the president's deafness, limitations on the powers of the court, and the backlog of cases were some of the problems, but many other problems that beleaguered the Condominium can be read out of the official buildings themselves.

Problems of the Condominium

Material, cultural, financial, and social problems can be seen particularly clearly through the construction and use of these grand buildings. The problems overlap. For example, lack of "suitable" housing was not just a material and financial problem, but also a social and cultural one; British definitions of suitability and indeed of what constituted a house were expressed and negotiated in discussions about appropriate housing for British officers and in their use of space.[74]

Lack of Infrastructure

The allocation of scarce resources to these building projects meant forgoing alternatives. Money, labor, and the expertise of contractors, carpenters, plumbers, and electricians could have been used to develop the infrastructure of the capital, not to mention the rest of the archipelago. This was a general colonial problem in the Pacific, not just in the Condominium, but the choice to spend so much money

Figure 13. Original Joint Court. From Reece Discombe collection, with permission.

on court buildings rather than on roads, sewers, and electrification was problematic. "I suppose that the 'amour propre' of each nation demanded that these costly buildings should be constructed, but I am inclined to agree with a critic that much of the money spent upon them might more profitably have been used in other directions."[75] Not until the American armed forces arrived during World War II was an oft-discussed, adequate water supply developed. Similarly, the Americans completed a long-delayed electrification project, constructed roads, and built airfields, contributing more to the development of infrastructure in the New Hebrides in a short time than the Condominium was ever able to accomplish.

Housing Shortages

Lack of suitable housing, such as we saw in the case of Romilly, the first British consul, was a recurring problem. It was not a problem arising from the Condominium per se, but it was exacerbated by the need for at least double the housing ordinarily required for colonial administration.

Housing shortages persisted throughout the Condominium's existence. As the history of the Native advocate's accommodation suggests, housing was always a game of musical chairs, a matter of competing for and switching between scarce Condominium, French, British, and private housing (see figure 14). Officials on leave were usually without "chairs" in this game as there was generally someone in need of accommodation waiting to move into any vacated residence.[76] The housing shortages also point to the inefficiency of the Condominium and the ponderous slowness with which it worked.

IN 1922, THE NATIVE ADVOCATE, a Dutchman named Dr. Borgesius who had become a high official of the Joint Court, complained of his accommodation, or lack thereof. Borgesius lived like a hermit crab, moving from house to house, occupying the residences of various court officials on leave. As an indication of the severity of his plight, from a colonial viewpoint, he had to live in housing that was almost on the level of the natives: "[H]e has even been compelled at times to live in a small hut constructed of grass and branches of coconut palm, differing from a native habitation only in that it has a plank floor and a window." Eventually, Borgesius obtained British approval to build a house costing £2,000 or less, to be paid for from Condominium funds. Although the French had agreed, however reluctantly, to pay half the costs of building and furnishing the earlier houses for Joint Court personnel, by 1922 they drew the line. The French resident commissioner balked at paying for the house for the Native advocate, saying his accommodation was not a Condominium responsibility.

British Resident Commissioner King then came up with an elaborate scheme (with which he did not expect the French to agree) first to lodge Dr. Borgesius in the house belonging to the president of the Joint Court, who was on leave. Then he would move into the Condominium house to be vacated by the French police commissioner when the police forces became a national rather than a Condominium concern. The superintendent of works, who had planned to move into the police commissioner's house, would have a house built for him (money had already been appropriated). The French, King suspected, opposed housing the Native advocate for personal reasons and wanted to buy the house for use by French officials, something the British would adamantly oppose.

It is unclear what happened next, but by 1929 the archives record that repairs were made to the public prosecutor's house prior to its occupation by the Native advocate. In 1938, Condominium house no. 3 was referred to as the Native advocate's house. In 1942, the French judge requested to use the house, as his own house was required by Colonel Fassett of the American armed forces.

Figure 14. The homeless Native advocate.

Lack of Skilled Labor and Building Supplies

Precut buildings and architects in Sydney were used because the New Hebrides lacked carpenters and building supplies. It was a challenge, bordering on foolishness, to build public architecture in such a place. How incongruous it was, as well, to have such buildings where there were so few to be impressed by them even within the archipelago. The largest centers of white settlement in the early days of the Condominium were on Epi, Santo, Malakula, and in Mele, outside Port Vila.

In a letter to his French counterpart dated 3 January 1911, British Resident Commissioner Merton King described the classically "Condominial" construction process: "houses (a), (b), (d), and (g) were constructed by a French contractor from material supplied by Sydney; (e) was also built by a French contractor, but from material imported from New Caledonia." All labor contracts had to be tendered in New Caledonia, under terms of the Condominium signed by both high commissioners as well as both resident commissioners in Noumea. Not only did tenders then have to be translated into English, which could introduce errors and misunderstandings, the whole process of tendering was different in Noumea from

the British system.[77] Most building materials came from Australia. Strikes by coal miners in Wales and brick makers in Australia, problems with poor-quality timber and cement, cost overruns due to inaccurate estimates, and the rising price of materials were only some of the problems that delayed completion of the Condominium building projects. The Sydney architects Joseland and Vernon soothed a frustrated King, reminding him of the wisdom of retaining an architect for all aspects of a project:[78] "Of course there is always a lot of business in connection with any building, perhaps more especially with these and always a certain amount of worry—that is why there are architects."[79] This comment was in response to King's complaints about Georges Raveton, the contractor from Noumea who built the post office and signed on to build the British judge's house, the house for the president of the joint court, and the public prosecutor's house.

King's and Vernon's complaints about contractors would seem familiar to many of us in the 1990s: cost overruns, delays, shoddy materials and workmanship. In the end, Raveton took such a long time to complete the British judge's house that he withdrew from building the other two, which passed to M. Julienne, another New Caledonian contractor who also built the Joint Court. M. Julienne's projects, too, suffered from cost overruns and delays. Although the court began meeting in temporary quarters on 5 August 1910, the courthouse was not completed until 21 September 1912, after the builder had obtained repeated extensions of time. The house for the public prosecutor took ten months to complete instead of an estimated five. That of the president of the court was also expected to take five months from 20 October 1909, but in January 1911, Merton King wrote in frustration that the building was still not completed.

One problem was that while the timber for these houses was precut before shipment from Sydney, the houses were not so simple to assemble as a five-month time period for construction would suggest. (Again one sees similarities with today's handyman purchases for which "some assembly required" can mean far more work than expected.) Precut and prefabricated materials were widely available through catalogues and were commonplace in the islands by the turn of the century because of a lack of locally milled building materials and skilled labor. But trained carpenters turned out to be necessary if the precut structures were to be completed even roughly on time.

Tensions between the British and "the other side," as the French were known, prolonged the construction process. For example, the director of works expressed his frustration with French "interference" to the resident commissioner: "Private: There is evidently some interference with French labor from the other side as every time workmen have made arrangements with me to do some work and perhaps have started it they suddenly find they have something else to do."[80]

Cultural Differences in Colonial Space

Some housing controversies were expressed in cultural terms, drawing attention to perceived differences and even literally constructing them. For example, the interesting thing about the French judge's house in terms of colonial space is that it was explicitly different in style from the other buildings. That difference was a cultural marker. The French resident commissioner objected to designs similar to those for the other Condominium buildings, including that for the British judge,[81] because the "bungalow" or "colonial" style of building was "unsuited to French tastes, and, accordingly, he suggested that the design for the French Judge's house, and other arrangements connected with its construction, should be left to him."[82] The design of the house would be altered to meet French ideas of domestic architecture. The British archives do not contain further architectural detail on the resulting French judge's house, but they do contain a brief description of the rooms. The house had a modest number of rooms by comparison with the British judge's: only two bedrooms, a bathroom, a reception room, a dining room, a library, a pantry, a kitchen, and two rooms for servants.

Servants themselves appear in the archives expressing views of cultural difference attributed to them by colonial officers. For example, when the French judge was rehoused in the Native advocate's residence during World War II so that his own house could be used by an American colonel, there were consequences for his servants. The French judge's Indochinese servants would have to share a toilet with the New Hebridean servants of the British judge. The cultural schisms of the Condominium were extended to the servants. In fact, rather than resisting this plan himself, the British judge insisted that his New Hebridean servant would be unhappy with the arrangement: "I have personally no objection, but on mentioning this matter to my boy, he objects strongly. He is a native and the others are Tonkinese. He says he keeps the lavatory scrupulously clean—which the Tonkinese will not do. He and his wife are very clean in their habits and I fear would be very discontented by the proposed arrangements."[83]

Financial Contradictions

Throughout the archives and in my interviews with British ex–colonial officers, British frugality was repeatedly contrasted with the higher pay and better standard of living that the French enjoyed. By the 1960s, one former British district agent told me bitterly, he had earned less than the French district agent's driver. While this may have been an exaggeration, it was certainly true that the British tried to pinch pennies in administering the New Hebrides whenever they could. Jacomb commented summarily that "everything has been sacrificed to cheapness."[84] This tendency, however, was contradicted by the expense of the

British judge's house, which cost nearly twice as much as that of the French judge. When asked to pay half the costs of the more expensive British judge's house, the French objected. A debate ensued about whether the judges' housing and furnishings were Condominium or national responsibilities. Resolving that they were a Condominium responsibility, each nation paid a moiety of the construction and furnishing costs for the judges' houses; but as we have seen, the French then drew the line at paying half the costs of the Native advocate's house.

Another financial conundrum evident in the early Condominium building projects was that local revenue was expected to pay for buildings and services, but no local source of revenue existed except the postal service. No wonder that building the post office was such a high priority. The lack of revenue meant that in effect the two powers were splitting the entire amount of construction costs, not the moiety of the difference between revenues and expenses. Moreover, over the years France and Britain had to pay for expensive maintenance and repairs to these buildings caused by storms, termites, and other effects of the tropical climate.

Finally, grand houses for officers with low salaries was a financial contradiction that made maintenance particularly difficult.

> The provision of a house costing £4,500 for an official who draws a salary of £700 per annum is palpably absurd. . . . It would require a very large staff of servants and constant supervision to keep such buildings in any kind of good order, and it would be unreasonable to expect officials with small salaries to expend them entirely in this way or their time either. And, as a matter of fact, the results are precisely what might have been expected. For the most part the houses look uncared for and neglected, and if the ground surrounding them were not periodically cleaned by a gang of prisoners, they would soon be mere jungle.[85]

Social Problems: Complaints and Arguments about Housing

The financial straits in which junior officers saddled with large houses found themselves was also indicative of social and political relations between Home, in this case the Colonial Office in London, and officers posted to the New Hebrides. The provision of large houses was not sufficient indication that "the authorities at Home" were really interested in getting the best out of colonial servants in the New Hebrides:

> The Administration of the New Hebrides no doubt depends largely on instructions received from the higher authorities at Home, but it depends also very largely on the individual units that go to fill up its ranks. If an interest is not shown by the Home authorities in the welfare of its servants, it cannot reason-

ably be expected that those servants will take any particular interest in their work or make any special effort to fit themselves to perform it properly or to improve themselves. Up to the present—apart from the provision of enormous houses for some of them—no interest has been displayed in the welfare of the junior officers.[86]

By the 1920s, telephones in the court did not work, and the noises from the people using the toilet were embarrassingly audible in the British judge's office. The court president, the Count of Buena Esperanza, wrote to British Resident Commissioner Joy: "I beg to draw your attention on the fact that the room chosen for lavatories is next to the British Judge's office, and the partition is only a single one made of wood."[87]

The furnishings of the judges' houses were as fancy as the residences themselves. Joint French and British approval was needed for frequent repairs and replacements. Furnishings—their acquisition, repair, and replacement—occupied remarkable amounts of archival space, and presumably administrative time, throughout the life of the Condominium. Will Stober observed in his notes to me regarding archival documents from 1949:

> British Residency minuting serves to remind us—though many other files offer numerous examples of the phenomenon—that senior officials occupied themselves with the minutest points concerning the allocation of furniture, to an extent which may appear ridiculous in retrospect unless one appreciates that in the Condominium (or British and French national housing contexts) there had to be either rules—bent though they might occasionally be—or a chaotic free-for-all.[88]

Stober also noted that the archives concerning the house of the president of the Joint Court "open a window on to the nature of things that went wrong in this large house, perhaps the strangest of which was the presence [in 1935] of swarms of bees in a partition and under a portion of the roof making the Acting President's bedroom and office uninhabitable."

In the New Hebrides British Service archive alone, ninety-four other entries address issues of housing repairs, mostly for Condominium buildings. Ironically, the most highly placed Condominium officers, namely the judges, received less satisfaction with regard to housing requests than more lowly officers in the British Residency.[89] The judges' much fancier houses and furnishings were in almost constant need of repair. In part, this was *because* they were fancier; only a judge would need to replace the dust cover for a billiard table: "I have the honour to request that I [be] permitted to procure a new Dust Sheet to cover the billiard table in this house as the

present one is so rotten that it is falling to pieces. Such a sheet is absolutely necessary for the protection of the green cloth from damp and dust."[90]

In part, however, the agitation for repairs was a direct product of the Condominium. Had the houses of high-ranking Condominium officials been national responsibilities, results probably could have been achieved more quickly. The British resident commissioner could have made repairs to the British judge's house a high priority and could have ensured that repairs were carried out. The British judge's house, however, was at the mercy of "the Condominium system, which necessitated the interaction of at least four senior officials (plus subordinates): the British Judge or French Judge (usually obliged to play supplicant or mendicant), the BRC and FRC (who had to agree, even where there were rules to go by) and Public Works Department (cast, justly or otherwise—partly depending on the (in)efficiency of individual holders of this post and of their staff—in the role of villain more often than not)."[91]

Denouement

The complaints and problems evident regarding these early buildings continued throughout the Condominium. In some regards the problems are similar to those in other colonies, for example, regarding levels of housing and leaves. The Condominium, however, exacerbated such problems by involving three providers of official housing as well as trades between them. A 1927 document states: "It would be difficult to exagerate the dissatisfaction among Condominium officers on the housing problem." A list is appended of ten officers awaiting housing, seven of whom are married with children.[92] Ex–colonial officers whom I interviewed in England complained of similar problems in the 1950s, 1960s, and 1970s. In sum, as one official document put it with regard to the whole Western Pacific High Commission area, "Housing causes more hair-splitting and ill-feeling than anything in Colonial Service."[93]

The fancy houses were there, not for the convenience of the administrators, sometimes junior ones, who lived in them. Instead, they were a grand gesture on the part of both Britain and France that reflected the promise of the Condominium as a unique approach to territorial administration. While competitive British and French national pride was expressed in these buildings, their rapid decline reflects political ineffectiveness, a lack of funds for maintenance, and inadequate finances to build an urban or civil infrastructure. The fate of the buildings illustrates the fate of the Condominium as an institution.

The president's house was no longer needed as a residence when the last court

president, Bosch Barrett, retired in 1939. During World War II, the house of the president of the Joint Court was converted into offices and became headquarters for the American Island Command. After the war, it became the Joint Court building, as the original Joint Court was in poor condition. The president's house/Joint Court was rebuilt following hurricane damage in 1987 as the first historic restoration of European origin in Vanuatu. It is still in use as the Supreme Court of Vanuatu. The chief justice resides in a modern house on the site of the old British judge's house, which lost its second story in the 1959 hurricane and was later destroyed. The prime minister occupies a similar home on the site of what had been the French judge's house. The original Joint Court was used for a time as a theater for occasional plays or films, with one floor converted to apartments for junior Condominium staff. It was condemned and finally demolished in 1970.

"Divided authority destroys itself," Jacomb asserted. Consequently, the Condominium "never has worked and it never will work. It might have worked under certain ideal circumstances, but we must not look for ideality in the southern seas, or if we do we must not be disappointed if we do not find it."[94] In terms of colonial space, the quest for ideality in the South Seas continued, if somewhat tempered by the lessons learned in these early days of the Condominium. The British Residency, the British and French District Agencies, the British Paddock, and the other houses used by colonial servants and their families in the period leading up to independence all engage the "ideal" South Seas in built forms that tell financial, political, and cultural tales of the strange colony that was not a colony, the Condominium.

THE BRITISH RESIDENCY

The British Residency was constructed at the summit of Iririki Island in Port Vila harbor during the same period as the Condominium buildings described in chapter 2. Although only about a hundred meters high, the site was such that the Residency commanded a view of the town, in keeping with a long and international tradition of asserting a colonizer's authority. The site was not without its drawbacks. Visitors had to cross the channel, often in the British Residency launch, *Nereid*, then climb 179 steps to the top of the hill. There they entered—or had drinks outside—the home of the British resident commissioner. Today, visitors make the same crossing in a small motorized ferry and arrive at an international resort. The British Residency, heavily renovated, is the manager's house. Tourist bungalows cluster along the shoreline, looking across the generally calm water toward the town. The resort's ferry comes ashore near the site of the British resident commissioner's boathouse. Postcolonial tourism has replaced the Anglo-French administration. Plus ça change, plus c'est la même chose.

Through discussions about the history of the British Residency, its physical form, and the ways in which the space was used, one can glimpse the influence of individuals in negotiating, contesting, and shaping the culture of empire. Its reconfiguration as a resort reveals postcolonial variations on the same theme. The meaning of the site also emerges as culturally constructed. The island-ness

of this tiny island off the big island, the view back toward the town rather than toward the sea, the equivalence of the Residency's site with that of the French resident commissioner, and the siting of the Residency atop the hill—all were important, negotiated elements that contributed to the particular colonial character of the British administration and that even helped to shape the course of independence. Right up to the end, the island gave resident commissioners a distance, a vantage point outside the political scene that may have helped to keep political events literally in perspective. Now it does the same for visitors to Vanuatu, which tourism promoters call "The Untouched Paradise."

Why Islands?

Islands were favored sites for missionaries, planters, and colonial administrators in the early days of colonization for many reasons. They often seemed "empty" as a consequence of diseases, both introduced (e.g., measles) and indigenous (e.g., malaria). Hostile islanders were also a consideration. Island sites offered some protection from attack because one could see the canoes coming. Along with the sense of safety, the view from an island afforded an ineffable sense of power, control, and prestige. Little islands could be domains in microcosm. The attraction for British colonial administrators was almost irresistible, as is evident from correspondence regarding both Iririki and the British District Agency on Venui Island in the northern New Hebrides.[1]

The Presbyterian mission, as mentioned in the previous chapter, was willing to share its land with the British, provided the New Hebrides never fell under exclusive French control. In 1913 a lease was drawn up allowing the British to occupy half the island for ninety-nine years at a peppercorn rent.[2] The Presbyterians prohibited the erection of fortifications and of buildings other than the Residency and accommodations for domestic staff. Special permission from the Presbyterian mission was needed, for example, to construct a boatbuilder's shed for British Residency marine supplies.

The British established themselves literally and metaphorically on the highest ground. This followed a pattern, common in colonial Africa, in which the British constructed rest houses and more-permanent buildings on hilltops that were prone to lightning damage. As an ex–British resident commissioner explained to me, "This siting, in the first stage, enhanced European prestige—'He's not even afraid of lightning!'—up until the time when the house was destroyed and reputations plummeted."[3]

Iririki was no more of a lightning rod than the French Residency at an equally

high and nearly as exposed site on the main island. Both the French and the British enjoyed excellent views of each other's Residencies, of the harbor, and of what became the town. Legend has it that much attention was paid to ensuring that the flags at the French and British Residencies flew at equal height. Having stood at the site of both flagpoles, I suspect that the French held the higher ground. There is no doubt, however, that flags were an important issue, for they occupy substantial amounts of correspondence in the British archives. The flag at the British Residency was not hoisted at sunrise and lowered at sunset, as was customary in British colonies, for the New Hebrides, being a Condominium, was not British. It had grown out of a joint naval commission, so the custom adopted was that of the British Navy and of British representatives in foreign states, namely to raise the flag at 8 A.M.[4]

Captain Rason (1902–1907)

Following British naval custom would have been pro forma for the first British resident commissioner, Captain Ernest Rason (see figure 15 for a list of all British and French resident commissioners). In May 1902, he received a set of specifications for his house on Iririki Island from Alexander Dean and Sons, an Australian building firm. Presumably to reduce costs, Rason asked the builder to omit the proposed verandahs and eliminate eight water tanks. He reduced the strength of the roof and did not want to pay for tie-down bolts, both features that would have increased the building's ability to withstand a hurricane. Nor did he care to have a proper foundation. What he did seem to care about was having strong exterior walls, which would be made of concrete and stone. Quite probably, he feared attack by local natives, even with the protection his island site afforded.[5] Rason's home, built in 1903 or 1904, predated the 1913 Presbyterian church lease that prohibited fortifications, but the house he built would have met the letter of that requirement. Although it was well fortified with strong walls, the building retained a domestic appearance and function. When the Residency was rebuilt in 1959, Rason's concrete walls were very difficult to remove and had to be burnt out.

Merton King (1907–1924)

Rason seemingly did not care a great deal about what most people would consider to be comfort. Merton King took over as the first resident commissioner under the newly proclaimed Condominium on 2 December 1907. He inherited the Residency on Iririki, which had served as both Rason's home and his office.

British Resident Commissioners		French Resident Commissioners	
Ernest Rason	1902–1907	Gaudens Faraut	1901–1904
Merton King	1907–1924	? Amigues	1904
Geoffrey B. W. Smith-Rewse	1924–1927	Charles Bord	1904–1908
George Andrew Joy	1927–1939	Jean-Martin Colonna	1908
Richard Blandy	1939–1949	Charles Noufflard	1908–1909
Hubert Flaxman	1949–1955	Colonna ?	1909, 1910
John Rennie	1955–1962	Jules Martin	1910, 1911
Alexander Wilkie	1962–1966	Jules Repiquet	1911–1913
Colin Allan	1966–1973	Louis Miramende	1913–1921
Roger Du Boulay	1973–1975	Henri d'Arboussier	1922–1929
John Champion	1975–1978	Antoine Carlotti	1931–1933
Andrew Stuart	1978–1980	Henri Sautot	1933–1940
		Robert Kuter	1940–1946
		André Menard	1947–1949
		Pierre Anthonioz	1949–1958
		Marcel Favreau	1958–1960
		Maurice Delauney	1960–1965
		Jacques Mouradian	1965–1969
		Robert Langlois	1969–1975
		Robert Gauger	1975–1977
		Bernard Pottier	1977–1978
		Jean-Jacques Robert	1978–1980

Figure 15. British and French resident commissioners in the New Hebrides.

The resident commissioner's office remained in the house on Iririki for some years, despite King's plans to relocate it to the mainland.[6] There was also a prison, created out of half of the boat builder's shed.[7] In 1907, the British Residency offices "consisted of two small rooms. . . . Any member of the public having business with the Residency had to find his way over as best he could. There was as yet no telephone.[8] Office hours were from 9–noon and 1–4 P.M. except for Saturday afternoons and Sundays."[9]

According to a fellow occupant, the lawyer and assistant British resident commissioner, Edward Jacomb, the Residency was

> in a deplorable state of confusion and disrepair. We had to borrow the ship's carpenter to patch up the roof, and the electrician to fix the bells. The house is [very badly and insufficiently furnished, and] appallingly dirty. Half the "boys" are

leaving almost immediately, and if we do not get an Annamite [Vietnamese] by tomorrow we shall have to cook our own food. As regards furniture, although it was all new when the house was built three years ago, hardly a thing remains sound. Most of the chairs have only three legs, and there are only two beds—I have to sleep on a stretcher. The scarcity of beds is partly explained by the fact that Rason used to sleep on a special contrivance of his own, bare planks and a log as a pillow. . . . As to mosquito-proof doors, it appears that originally they were all properly protected with wire-gauze netting, but Rason's bulldog used to walk through the netting. King says that he does not propose to have them renewed as the damp would destroy them almost as fast as the bulldog, and anyhow that mosquitoes do not worry him—if one bites him it falls off dead. In the meantime they [mosquitoes] are pretty trying.[10]

As impervious as the new resident commissioner, Merton King, may have been to mosquitoes, he did not much like the house either. As described in chapter 2, he retained the Sydney firm of Joseland and Vernon to make an addition to the Residency (designated in correspondence as "Mr. King's cottage") and to construct the other residences and buildings for the Condominium as well as for the British government.[11] A later description of the Residency commented on the

Figure 16. Afternoon tea, Shepherd's Hill. Edward Jacomb (seated, right) and unidentified men. From William Stober's collection, with permission.

"extraordinary design" that resulted from Rason's fortresslike core and the Joseland and Vernon "addition":[12]

> It was built round a central area of 30' by 20'6", the walls of which are solid concrete [i.e., Rason's house]. Rooms were then added round this central concrete structure in all wood construction [i.e., Joseland and Vernon's addition]: two small rooms of 15' x 15' were added on each side of the concrete structure with two larger rooms 23' x 14'6" across the front separated by a passageway. A verandah was added across the back and continued round the sides and front of the whole structure, while the kitchen and servants' quarters were erected a few feet away.

The new wooden Residency encompassed Captain Rason's concrete-walled core. By the end of September 1908, when Edward Jacomb's mother visited the Residency, she found it to be "a beautiful house—large rooms and a broad verandah all round. The dining room is magnificent."[13]

Geoffrey Smith-Rewse (1924–1927)

In 1924 Geoffrey Bingham Whistler Smith-Rewse replaced Merton King as resident commissioner. He was the first commissioner to be accompanied to the New Hebrides by a wife. Domesticity introduced a new set of expectations with regard to accommodation. Smith-Rewse's complaints bring to mind June Knox-Mawer's observation that, for new arrivals throughout the Pacific, "[h]ousing itself was often a disappointment, described architecturally as Early Antipodean."[14] A letter to the secretary of the treasury on behalf of the secretary of state for the colonies states, "It will be seen from the correspondence that very little expenditure has been incurred on furniture for the British Residency for some considerable time during which the Resident Commissioner was a bachelor, and that steps are now in progress to properly equip and maintain the building with necessary articles at no great expense."[15] "No great expense" seems to have been the operative phrase throughout the history of the New Hebrides British administration. Poor Smith-Rewse was caught in his own trap. He created a Board of Survey to account for and revaluate the furniture in British government houses, including his own, then was unable to provide invoices for numerous items acquired at the Residency. There is an extraordinary amount of correspondence in the archives concerning topics such as missing soup spoons. One wonders how much time Smith-Rewse was able to devote to other administrative matters. In an August 1926 letter,

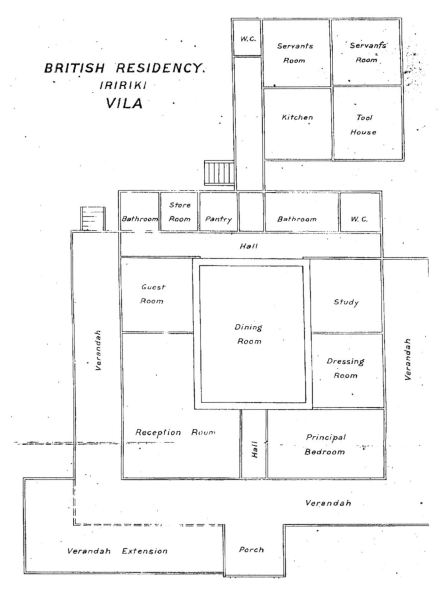

BRITISH RESIDENCY.
IRIRIKI
VILA

W.C.

Servants
Room

Servants
Room

Kitchen

Tool
House

Bathroom

Store
Room

Pantry

Bathroom

W. C.

Hall

Guest
Room

Dining
Room

Study

Verandah

Dressing
Room

Verandah

Reception   Room

Hall

Principal
Bedroom

Verandah

Verandah   Extension

Porch

Figure 17. Floor plan of British Residency with proposed verandah extension. NHBS 227/1908.

Smith-Rewse expressed exasperation when queried about the value of linoleum in the Residency. There is only one piece, he responded, and it is under a leaky hallway roof. About a year later, Smith-Rewse was dead—whether of a heart attack, overindulgence in alcohol, a fire caused by knocking over a lamp, or all three remains a matter of debate.

George Andrew Joy (1927–1939)

His successor, George Andrew Joy, had been assistant resident commissioner under Smith-Rewse. Joy served as British resident commissioner for twelve years, from 1927 to 1939. He organized repairs to the Residency and requested authorization in 1935 to spend £100 to widen the eastern verandah from ten to twenty feet. His rationale for this request suggests the degree to which Joy sought to integrate the seemingly isolated, insular residency into Vila social life:[16]

> Apart from other forms of entertainment it has been my practice for many years to give a garden party at the British Residency every second month throughout the year as well as a Ball at Christmas time. I have never favoured a "social wall" around the Residency believing as I do that it is very necessary to encourage a democratic spirit amongst small communities and thus open the way to a closer understanding between its members on the one hand and the Administration on the other.

These parties were attended by "a relatively large number of the British and French community," totaling "rarely less than a hundred." Joy's request to extend the width of the verandah can be seen as an attempt symbolically to expand the semipublic space of the Residency, to reach beyond the limits not only of the building but of the island toward a more inclusive social world.

Richard Blandy (1939–1949)

The coming of thousands of American troops to the New Hebrides in 1942 opened up social life far more than the resident commissioner ever could have, introducing, for example, outdoor cinema. The American presence also placed increased demands on the Residency to accommodate visitors. The resident commissioner who replaced Joy in 1939, Richard Blandy, arrived with a wife, a grown daughter, and two smaller children. With such a family in residence there

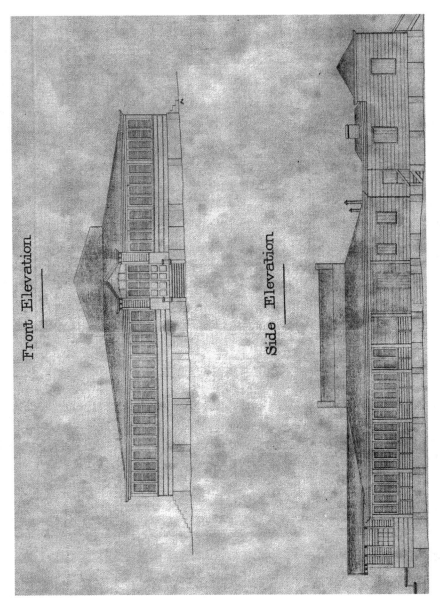

Figure 18. British Residency, front and side elevations by Joseland and Vernon. NHBS 227/1908.

was no room left over for guests, so Blandy had an annex built next to the Residency during the war. Materials for the annex were salvaged from an old cottage that had been demolished. From these bits and pieces, local carpenters constructed two guest rooms and an office.[17] Blandy described the annex as a contribution to the war effort; it would "supplement accommodation for the large number of official military and civilian visitors, such available accommodation having become very greatly restricted owing to military requisitions."[18] Although not yet an international resort, the Residency was on its way to feeling like a hotel.[19]

Hubert Flaxman (1949–1955)

From before World War II until the mid-1950s, the archives narrate a story of the increasing dilapidation and structural weakness of the British Residency, whose ability to survive future earthquakes and especially hurricanes was progressively in doubt. Sir Harry Lukes on his first visit to Port Vila "condemned the appearance and state of the building in no uncertain manner and told Mr. Blandy that its replacement would have to be estimated for in the near future."[20] The war intervened and the matter was dropped until 1946, when the high commissioner was reminded again of the poor condition of the Residency. This reminder seemed to have little effect, and the Residency deteriorated for a further nine years.

Hubert Flaxman secured advice about the condition of the Residency as he was leaving office in 1955. He received a report from Newcastle (Australia) architects Hoskings and Pilgrim indicating that the existing Residency was beyond repair.[21] Only the concrete walls and floor timbers, then serving as the dining room at the center of the building, were judged to be still sound. These were Captain Rason's original cement and stone structures.

John Rennie (1955–1962)

John Rennie arrived in Port Vila at the end of 1955. Negotiations about the new Residency took several years and are well documented in the archives. This detailed correspondence reveals much about what was negotiated regarding suitability, affordability, comfort, and the relative proportions of semipublic and private space. Hotly debated were such basic issues as whether the new building should be a bungalow like its predecessor or have two stories. Initially, the resident commissioner proposed a two-story building with a floor area totaling

approximately three thousand square feet.[22] In the end, however, a smaller bungalow design was chosen, partly to reduce costs and partly because it was deemed to fit in better with the rest of the town, which still consisted largely of single-story structures.

The secretary of state for the colonies in London sent a telegram refusing to approve the initial Australian architects' plans for the Residency. The reason given was that the cost was too high, but Rennie himself was unhappy with the plans. He had written a personal letter to Geoffrey Atkinson, an architect whom Rennie had met in Africa. Atkinson was by then employed in the Colonial Office Liaison Unit, which made use of the U.K. Building Research Center resources. The Colonial Office architects seldom became involved in such specific projects in the territories, but Atkinson and other architects in the unit agreed with Rennie. The Australian plans were rejected, and Atkinson drew up alternate plans.[23]

The original design was wasteful of space; in addition, the ventilation in the bedrooms was inadequate, and "if the Resident Commissioner is to conduct business in the study, this should not be placed next to the children's play room. I am advised that there are great merits in separating the 'official' and 'private' parts of Government Houses entirely."[24] Concern with the zoning of public and private space was matched by a desire not to overspend on the building. In Rennie's words, the Residency was not to be an impressive government house. It had to be a *machine à habiter* in Le Corbusier's sense, and indeed that boxlike modernist simplicity was evident in the final building.[25] The British resident commissioner and his wife were young, not yet forty, and they remember having no pretensions to grandeur. The Colonial Office telegram rejecting the original design went on to say that the best way to ensure a separation of dwelling and official spaces would be for the resident commissioner and his family to have living quarters separate from those used for entertaining and business, but that this would probably exceed the funds available. The Colonial Office then provided a sketch of Atkinson's alternate to the Australian plan for the Residency. Notable is the encouragement of the flexible use of space; male visitors, however, have a bathroom dedicated to their own use, while female guests "can use one of the guest or family bathrooms."[26] This can be seen as favoring male guests or as allowing female guests deeper into the domestic space of the Residency.

Both the Australian and the British architects were participants in the ensuing debate, as were the Rennies; the Western Pacific high commissioner, John Gutch; and others. Should the new Residency be on the island at all? In a 1955 telegram to the secretary of state for the colonies, Rennie observed that "ample accommodation is required for entertainment, in view of the nature of the administration of the Group, and for guests, in the absence of any suitable alternative." The

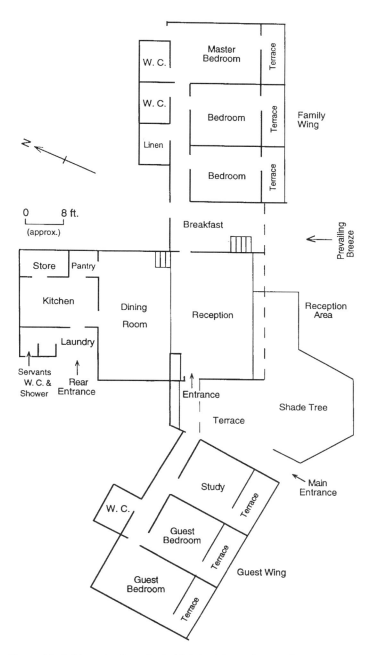

Figure 19. Atkinson's plans for British Residency, home of BRC Rennie. Archival. Carol Randall, Cartographic Office, Department of Geography, York University.

higher cost of land in Vila on the "mainland" would have to be weighed against the economies and increased convenience of living in town. In Rennie's view, "There would be many advantages in moving to the mainland and I am in favour of the alternative site behind the British Office provided the land can be obtained."[27] The Australian architect, Maxwell Hoskings, disagreed:[28]

> On my last visit to Vila, I had the opportunity of examining several proposed sites for the above Residency. After due consideration I recommend a site on the Island situated to the right of the landing stage of the present Residency. This site is fairly level, well treed and requires little or no clearing, and water, electricity, and telephone services are available. It faces East and South-East and receives the full advantage of the prevalent South-East cool winds and is sheltered from the West by a cliff at the rear. As opposed to the other sites, it faces away from the Western glare off the Harbour and overlooks the Township and activity of Vila. It is about 12'0" above the water level and eliminates the climb and distance of the present Residency from the landing stage. *We feel the siting of the Residency on the Island is more in keeping than on any of the other sites.* The inconvenience of the short water trip can be minimized by an awning and motor on the present boat at small cost, and is more than compensated for by the *advantage of privacy.*

Interestingly, the site on the island that the architect recommended is exactly the one that Iririki Island Resort selected and developed for tourism. The resident commissioner and higher administrators were less convinced that this was the perfect site for the new building. They accepted the idea of building on the island for a variety of reasons. Although Rennie favored building the Residency in the British Paddock, he wrote me that his first priority had been to expand British efforts in such areas as education, health, and cooperatives, with a view toward political development. This expansion required that additional housing be built to accommodate staff in the area of the British Paddock on the main island, leaving not enough room to build the Residency there. It then seemed best to rebuild the Residency on Iririki Island. This site was also most "in keeping," to use the Australian architect's phrase, with whatever it was—the isolation, the insulation, the vantage point, the relative position vis-à-vis the French—that made an island feel appropriate as the home for British rule overseas. But greater privacy was attained, and a symbolically powerful gaze expressed through a view from the heights, by rejecting the architect's recommendation in favor of rebuilding the residency on the top of the hill. The Western Pacific high commissioner, John Gutch, wrote Rennie on 4 June 1957, listing five good reasons against "siting the new Residency half-way down the hillside instead of on the top."[29] None of these

Figure 20. British Residency circa 1965. From Wilkie family photo album, with permission of Margaret Wilkie.

reasons mentioned the nursery rhyme "The Grand Old Duke of York," but one wonders if marching halfway up to the top of the hill could have been far from the minds of those engaged in the debate.

Ultimately, the new Residency took far longer and cost far more than expected. It was not completed until March 1959, with finishing touches extending into April. The original estimate was £23,000, but the final cost was at least £28,500.[30] Although the form of the house changed little from the time it was rebuilt in 1959 until it was abandoned at independence in 1980, the guest lists for Residency functions changed tremendously.

Alexander Wilkie (1962–1966)

The Wilkies followed the Rennies as the next occupants of the British Residency. I interviewed Margaret Wilkie at her home near Tunbridge Wells in July 1994. Will Stober and I arrived hours late for our meeting, as was all too often the case. Mrs. Wilkie graciously served us tea and cakes anyway, the tea in cups so fine they were translucent in the fading sunlight. Her views on her life in Port Vila as resident commissioner's wife convey a sense of the way entertaining at the Resi-

dency was intertwined with, and expressed, the British agenda in the early to mid-1960s. It was a time when "getting on with the French" was fun and almost natural, while an increasing awareness of Melanesians in social life suggested the growing emphasis on development and long-range plans for independence.

Alexander ("Sandy") Wilkie served as British resident commissioner from 1962 to 1966, dying in office of a heart attack at the age of forty-nine. He had served in the British Colonial Service as financial secretary in Kenya before meeting Margaret in England, where she was employed as a social worker. They married, and Wilkie hoped to return with her to Kenya. To their surprise, he was posted instead to the Solomon Islands as financial secretary. This was at best a sideways move in the Colonial Service, but he had been away from his post in Kenya for two years dealing with his dying father in England. The person who had replaced him in Kenya was doing a good job, so Wilkie was sent elsewhere.

During their six years in the Solomons, Margaret Wilkie gave birth to a daughter and three years later to fraternal twins, a boy and a girl. With three children, the Wilkies felt it was important to establish a home base for themselves in England. She felt strongly that making a house into a home overseas was a measure of a woman's self:[31]

> About making a home, I think [it] totally depends on the person you are. If you're determined to make a home for yourself, you will make a home for yourself wherever you are. And we saw that particularly in the Solomon Islands, where basically the housing was similar for everybody. If you were more senior, you were expected to put people up, and therefore you would have a bigger house and more bedrooms, but the basic settee, armchairs, dining room table, tables, beds, chest of drawers, it was the same for everybody. You didn't have anything grander because you happened to be financial secretary, or whatever it was. Basically, things were the same. Now, some people made their houses absolutely charming, and some people, their houses were deadly dull and boring. It all depended on the person themselves and what they made of it.

Margaret Wilkie had made what she considered to be a welcoming home for her family in the Solomons, but things were different at the Residency. It was a comfortable place to live, but its purpose, Margaret Wilkie felt, was to serve as a venue for entertaining. The Residency was in effect more a public place than a domestic one. Thus it was not a home that she could alter at will in any but superficial ways.

While the Wilkies were committed to a life in what I have called houses far from home, they still, like many others in the Colonial Service, wanted to create a

"home" in England as "something familiar" for their children to come back to. Margaret Wilkie stayed behind for a few months to finalize the purchase of a house near Tunbridge Wells when Sandy was promoted to serve as British resident commissioner in Port Vila. She then came out to the New Hebrides with an Egyptian nanny for the children. They chose to travel out on a French steamer because Mrs. Wilkie liked the idea that the British resident commissioner's wife and children would arrive by a French boat. Upon arrival in the New Hebrides, the nanny fell in love with a divorced Catholic Vietnamese French *ressortissant* and apparently spent more time looking after his children than her Wilkie charges. Mrs. Wilkie reluctantly sent her home. She was relieved to hear some time later from the nanny's mother that the young woman had turned to anthropology instead of marriage to fulfill her cross-cultural interests: "Dear Mrs. Wilkie, I think too much happened to her too soon. . . . You'll be pleased to hear she went to Nottingham University and read Anthropology. She did extremely well, she's now decided the last thing she wants to do is go back to the New Hebrides and marry."

Margaret Wilkie took the shift from Kenya to the Solomon Islands and then the New Hebrides in stride. After all, she told me when I interviewed her in 1994, it was better to go to the Solomon Islands as her first experience overseas than to be sent there from someplace with better accommodations and servants, such as East Africa or Hong Kong.

> I think that was a very great advantage because I'd nothing to compare it [the Solomons] to. I had no particular expectations. I was so amazed when you went into the post office in Honiara and asked for a stamp, and the girl knew what you meant. I mean, I thought everyone would be up trees, you know? So it was helpful, whereas I think some of the wives who'd come from more advanced territories found it very hard. And I remember Lady Trench saying, "It's hard. My husband is now high commissioner. He was chief secretary [a lower rank]. When I was in Hong Kong I had all the staff and everything. Now I'm a high commissioner's wife, but I have to spend my afternoons cooking for the parties." Well, you could see how she would find that was hard to take.

Mrs. Wilkie's rationale includes some social evolutionary assumptions that I heard from many of the people I interviewed in England. These suggest a hierarchy of progress in which some colonial territories such as Kenya were more "advanced" than others, such as the Solomons or the New Hebrides. It is not that she had *no* expectations, as she claims, but rather that her expectations for her standard of living in the Solomons were low. Consequently, she was not disappointed, as were many wives of high-ranking colleagues.

Margaret Wilkie's expectations elided class and race. Just as Solomon Islanders were simpler than Kenyan tribesmen, so were the people she helped as a social worker compared to her own background. She felt that her work experience prepared her rather well, in an unanticipated way, for her career as a colonial officer's wife. Her French counterpart, the wife of the French resident commissioner, could not work up the courage to address a group of Melanesian women assembled at a public gathering, but Margaret Wilkie had no such hesitation: "To me, the Melanesian women had so much in common with sort of East End mums and people I've mixed with [as a social worker], rather simple people who were interested in their families. It didn't worry me talking with them, or talking to them, or thinking up some sort of little speech."

In small, symbolic ways, Margaret Wilkie felt that she and her husband shifted the balance toward Melanesians. She knew that some of these were mere gestures. They acquired a carpet for the Residency living room with a zigzag pattern that was vaguely reminiscent of patterns on New Hebridean mats. Mrs. Wilkie collected shells to display at the Residency. Her husband insisted on retaining the Rennies' New Hebridean chef, Marcel. Mrs. Wilkie remembers Sandy saying, "I would not be resident commissioner in the New Hebrides and not have a New Hebridean cook." In contrast, the French relied on Vietnamese cooks and, in Mrs. Wilkie's words, "They had planters' wives who used to be imported for occasions to help cook." Mrs. Wilkie acknowledged that New Hebridean cooks probably could not meet with the requirements of French cuisine, which even in the islands reached extraordinary standards. Spectacular dishes were often paraded around long dining tables, each invariably covered with a white linen cloth. She remembered one dessert paraded around the table at the French Residency to celebrate the opening of a bridge. It was "an enormous sponge cake all iced and modeled like a bridge."

Rather than try to compete with such spectacular meals, Margaret Wilkie preferred to surprise her guests. They all expected roast beef and Yorkshire pudding, she thought, so she served American dishes from her Boston Cooking School cookbook or tried something completely different. As an example, she told me of a party she and Sandy hosted to which they took the radical approach of inviting whomever they chose, not because of who the guests were but simply because the Wilkies liked them. They enjoyed knowing that many of the guests would spend the evening trying to puzzle out the logic of the guest list.

On another occasion, the Wilkies held a farewell party for their French counterparts, the Delauneys, a couple with whom they had a friendly social as well as official relationship. Rather than try to serve the kind of meal they might have expected at the French Residency, Margaret Wilkie organized a "sort of"

Melanesian feast. It was an explicit attempt to put Melanesians, or at least their cuisine, front and center. Yet it was only "sort of" Melanesian because the shelter in the garden built for the occasion was covered with tarpaulins, not thatch; because the roast pig was cooked in "Fijian or Tahitian style" on a piece of wood that gave it flavor; and because the pieces of "lap-lap" (New Hebridean mashed, steamed pudding of taro, yams, manioc, etc.) were very small, as the dish, Margaret Wilkie acknowledged, "is very heavy" to English and French tastes. Finally, although the idea of Melanesian cuisine was celebrated, the guest list consisted largely of prominent people in the French and British administration, not islanders.

There were usually a few Melanesians at Residency events. Mrs. Wilkie made an effort to include them. The challenge, in her view, was language and culture. French women, she said, inclined toward discussing infectious diseases in one corner, while the men were in another corner talking about politics. Seating arrangements required careful attention to avoid such polarization and to encourage other conversations. Place cards were deployed strategically to situate a French speaker who didn't speak English next to someone who could speak French. Margaret Wilkie explained to me, "And someone who didn't speak Pidgin English would have somebody else there who could carry on the conversation so that they could mix. It was terribly important." When Lady Foster, wife of the high commissioner, visited the Residency, Margaret Wilkie decided to invite "all the women whom I thought did things that were worthwhile in the town." These included an Australian woman who was secretary at the golf club, missionaries' wives, and some French women. The guest list also included Mrs. Kalkoa, mother of George Kalkoa, a New Hebridean who would go on to become a leader in the transition toward self-government. Margaret Wilkie commented, somewhat tentatively, "Do you know, she'd not been invited to tea at the Residency, and I think probably she was a little surprised to get this invitation asking her if she would come and meet the high commissioner's wife. And she came over in a little canoe and she brought fruit as a present, and she came up [to the Residency]. I think she was delighted, I think, to be asked. She was an awfully nice soul."

While the New Hebridean cook, Marcel, was, in the Wilkies' view, quite wonderful, other tasks that servants might have done elsewhere in the British empire fell to the British resident commissioner's wife. She told me that one visiting male member of the British Parliament asked her to give some of his dirty clothes to the laundress with special washing instructions. Confident that her staff could not deal with the subtleties of drip-dry nylon shirts and cold-water delicates, Mrs. Wilkie washed them herself. She then asked a friend, a more junior wife, to explain tactfully what the situation was in Port Vila:

And the next morning I had a rather embarrassed visitor who came and said, "Mrs. Wilkie? I gather that it was you who did my laundry." So I said, "Yes." He said, "And tell me, when I was in the Gilbert Islands, was it my hostess who did my laundry?" I said, "I'm sure it was." And he said, "When I was somewhere else, would it be—" And I said, "Yes." He said, "You know, I had no idea." You see, they think you've got staff, and you clap your hands and everything is done. And maybe, if you were in India or if you were in Hong Kong or whatever, it would be so.

Colin Allan (1966–1973)

Colin Allan, who had been serving as assistant resident commissioner, took over as acting resident commissioner when Sandy was ill and then served after Wilkie's death as resident commissioner from 1966 until 1973. He was a New Zealander and a "Pacific Man" in terms of his colonial service career, not, as some put it, an "Africa Retread" such as Wilkie and many others. He had served as assistant British resident commissioner in the New Hebrides since 1959.

Figure 21. Wilkie children descending the 179 steps from the British Residency on Iririki Island (about 1965). From Wilkie family photo album, with permission of Margaret Wilkie.

He and his wife Betty organized a major renovation of the Residency kitchen and replaced the wood-burning stove with more modern equipment. One can surmise that their Solomon Islands cook, Silas Maqu (pronounced "Mangu"), was pleased. By the time Colin Allan became British resident commissioner, Maqu had worked for him for twenty years. Silas Maqu stayed on to serve the remaining three British resident commissioners, so well entrenched in his position as to be somewhat intimidating to newcomers. He went on to be chef at a hotel in the Solomon Islands after Vanuatu independence.

Patricia Stuart, the last British resident commissioner's wife, told me that Maqu was "a total rogue." She had once made the mistake of reprimanding Maqu's son:

> I caught his small son in the kitchen, taking stuff from the fridge when we first arrived, and just severely chastised him. Maqu came in and said "I'm resigning, I'm not going to have my son talked to like this." So Andrew [the British resident commissioner] chastised me for doing it, and [apologizing] was the worst thing I did because actually if Maqu had gone it would have been a very good idea!

Colin Allan's attention to detail is evident in the twenty-one-page document about the Residency that he prepared for his successor, Sir Roger Houssemayne du Boulay. It includes everything he thought du Boulay should know. Details are provided on maintenance of the Residency garden that his wife had "considerably developed," including a kauri tree from Vanikoro that Mrs. Allan planted in 1960.[32] (It was a big tree when I visited in 1995.) She had cultivated numerous indigenous orchids from which a Royal Society expedition had taken samples for Kew Gardens. These were heavily looted by expatriates after independence. Allan's document described the lease arrangements with the Presbyterian church including details about the Residency's herd of cattle. Du Boulay was advised that the bull belonged to the Presbyterian mission and, although ten years old and in need of replacement, could not be removed "for technical reasons" until a Presbyterian Charolais bull calf (later called Golden Boy) grew to maturity. The cows were to be milked each morning by the sailors attached to the British resident commissioner's launch, *Nereid,* and by the gardeners, in turn. The old flagpole had been damaged in the 1972 hurricane season, and Colin Allan had ordered a replacement. Du Boulay should be aware that its erection might occasion French reaction: "It is slightly higher than the present one because the trees have grown up in past years. I can find no record that the French and British flagpoles have to be the same height. It will be interesting to see if the French make a political issue of it."[33]

Colin Allan warned du Boulay that "the main rooms can be unbelievably hot," that the electricity and telephone connections to the main island were unreliable, and that the staff was insufficient. The Colonial Service assumption that an officer's wife was unpaid staff was borne out in Allan's statement that forty-hour weeks for the staff were only achieved with the contribution of the British resident commissioner's wife's unpaid labor—in other words, "by one's wife doing a very considerable proportion of the entertainment cooking and cooking the two main meals when there are neither guests staying nor visitors."

Roger du Boulay (1973–1975)

Sir Roger du Boulay and his family live in Anstey House near Buntingford. In late July 1994, I set out on my own while Will tended to business matters in Birmingham. Driving to the interview with Roger du Boulay, I was determined to be on time for our 3:00 P.M. meeting, as Will and I so often had been late. I did not know where du Boulay's house was so I stopped for directions in the Anstey Pub. I went on to find the house easily. It was set back from the road about fifty yards, behind a wrought-iron gate. The gate was closed. On it was a sign that read DO NOT ENTER WHEN GATE SHUT. DOBERMAN LOOSE. I considered entering. My father had taught me how to deal with dogs, and I am not often afraid of them. I am also not completely foolhardy. So I stood outside the gate debating what to do. What had gone wrong? I had written from Canada, phoned from Birmingham; and du Boulay seemed to be happy to meet with me. Just then, the man from the pub who had given me directions drove up. He was on his way home and wanted to see how I was getting on. I asked if he thought the sign was serious: was the dog dangerous? It was. He said he would phone du Boulay and tell him I was at the gate if I gave him the phone number. Sure enough, five minutes later, a large, black-and-tan dog was called and put inside; then du Boulay came striding down the driveway and opened the gate, full of apologies. There had been confusion about the time of our appointment. I had thought it was for 3 P.M. He had thought I was coming at 3:30.

Fortunately, things improved considerably after this. I sat on a sofa in a comfortably casual living room that had a huge dog bed in the corner. Sir Roger showed me family photo albums and talked about what he had seen as his mission to get the French on side for independence in Vanuatu.

Despite Colin Allan's detailed briefing document, du Boulay was not prepared for what he found at the Residency. He told me, "The basic concept of having your own island of forty-odd hectares was marvelous. Your own boat.

And your own people. And the house on top of the hill should have been wonderful, but it was all wrong." Du Boulay seemed a confident man, but he said, "I was pretty humbled by it, this damn house."[34]

Du Boulay had described himself in a letter to me as

> a professional nomad, son of another (Royal Navy), and grandson of two others (Army and Indian Service), so early on I had a choice—was "home" to be where I was or where I came from? My wife and I decided, at the penniless outset, that "home" would very definitely be England, for our own sakes as well as the children's, and that all our residences abroad would be in the nature of "holidays" or "aberrations." . . . So we bought this [Anstey] house and it has been the hub of our universe ever since . . . : abroad never was home.

The Residency was far from home indeed. To the du Boulays, the small bedrooms were concrete boxes, and the house as a whole, he wrote, "was intrinsically pretty contemptible. It even turned its back on the finest view in the world."

Like its predecessor, the new Residency that Rennie had built faced eastward toward the town and the main island. It is true that the house on Iririki turned its back on often spectacular sunsets over the sea to the west, but Rennie had been critical of orienting the house to the western view. He suggested that I should have been, too, in a paper on the Residency I delivered to the American Anthropological Association. As a symbolic statement, turning one's back to the sunset was one thing; turning one's back on the capital of the place one was charged with administering was quite another. Rennie wrote me,[35]

> Turning away from Vila would have been rather offensive (I can imagine what you would have said in your paper) and I dare say the French—and no less a person than De Gaulle on his visit—would recall the sulphurous exchanges between Churchill and De Gaulle on the eve of D-day, when Churchill said he would always opt for the open sea (meaning the USA, whose President Roosevelt, incidentally, was adamantly opposed to the restoration of its Pacific colonies to France), a statement that was to reverberate for twenty years or more and delay the entry of the United Kingdom into the European Common Market.

The du Boulays, in any event, had little choice but to put up with conditions at the Residency, which they regarded as a "missed opportunity" to take advantage of the incomparable site. They did add a west-facing balcony to their private suite at the northern end of the bedroom wing that later occupants also appreciated. In our interview du Boulay said, "Well, we found it perfectly adequate, practical to

live in, and to entertain a limited number of guests in, and on the whole we only did, one couple at a time, you see." Reading this sentence later, du Boulay clarified that he had meant one "grand couple" such as a visiting head of government, cabinet minister, or the like.[36] For such visitors, there was only one suitable bedroom suite initially, and two by the time the du Boulays left. The Residency could seat twenty-four for dinner, and many more could be accommodated at a buffet-style meal. Du Boulay estimated that they entertained some three thousand people a year.

In February 1974, they entertained an especially grand couple, Queen Elizabeth herself and Prince Philip, as well as Princess Anne, Lord Mountbatten, and others in the royal party. Du Boulay went from the job of British resident commissioner to a position in the queen's household (as vice-marshal of the Diplomatic Corps), so the visit must have gone rather better than described in his interview with me. The du Boulays moved out of the Residency into the annex so that the main house could be given over to the royal party. The most anxious moment, he told me, was when a house girl gave one of the plate-glass windows a final polish and put her hand right through the glass:

> [She] cut herself quite badly, and I remember my wife grabbing her by the arm, holding her arm, and saying "You can't bleed in here!" And taking her outside, and getting her down to the hospital and stitched up. I had to take a hammer and I knocked all the glass out of the window, because there was no question of replacing it, so we just had no glass in the window in that room for her visit.

Another incident suggested the rather informal way the Residency operated compared to what one might think royal visitors would expect. Du Boulay recalled that "when the Page of the Presence [the royal butler] came up just before tea [to prepare things for the queen] he said, 'Can I get the tablecloths?' or something, and I said, 'In the sideboard there.' He opened the drawer and went 'Hoo!' There was a cat and six kittens in the drawer, and we didn't know about it."

For all the excitement of the queen's visit, du Boulay's explicit mandate was to "get on with the French." In du Boulay's words, "There was so much detailed groundwork to be done that with the best will in the world on *all* sides, the countdown to self-determination could not responsibly have been much shorter than it turned out to be. But the French were eventually persuaded to see, as I believed all along, that their interests as well as ours and those of the locals lay in taking the quickest possible steps to self-determination, which meant of course independence."[37]

Getting on with the French had been the goal in various ways throughout the history of the Condominium, and of the Entente Cordiale, but it took on new

urgency as indigenous political movements strengthened in the 1970s. The British wanted to move toward independence for the New Hebrides, but both they and the French, who were less than enthusiastic at the prospect, seemed unable to move with the speed that the radical leaders of the New Hebrides National Party wanted.

John Champion (1975–1978)

John Champion served as the penultimate British resident commissioner, from 1975 to 1978. This was a very tense period politically. The first indigenous political party, the New Hebrides National Party, led by Father Walter Lini, who went on to be the first prime minister, emerged in the early 1970s. In 1977, it became the Vanuaku Party (or Vanuaku Pati). Other, mainly Francophone, "moderate" parties began to emerge at about this time, partly in response to the perceived radicalism of the New Hebrides National Party and the threat it seemed to pose to French-language education. Further, the Nagriamel, which had begun as an agrarian movement in the 1960s, gained momentum as a political movement in the 1970s. Nagriamel's leader, Jimmy Stephens, came from a settler family on Santo (see chapter 7). His movement particularly opposed the expatriate alienation of customary land.[38]

Elections for the first Representative Assembly in November 1975 were inconclusive. Father Lini's party won seventeen of the twenty-nine universal suffrage seats, but there was considerable grumbling about election fraud. Meanwhile, Jimmy Stephens announced that the Nagriamel would soon proclaim independent territory. His secessionist bid came to naught at that time, but it presaged events to come on the final resident commissioner's watch.

In February 1977, the Vanuaku Party lost a vote in the Representative Assembly calling for all seats to be elected, not appointed. Party supporters then walked out, boycotting the Assembly and making its continuation impossible. Independence still seemed a vague and distant goal. The French and British sought to ensure a Representative Assembly with moderate views and a gradual progression toward self-rule. At the London ministerial conference in July 1977, the French and British agreed that there should be an entirely elected Representative Assembly with a Council of Ministers based on it. By this time, however, the Vanuaku Pati had boycotted the Assembly.

New elections were called for November 1977, but the Vanuaku Party refused to participate. Instead, Father Walter Lini announced the creation of the People's Provisional Government. Throughout the islands, but especially near

Figure 22. Will Stober and BRC's wife, Olive Champion, at her home, Farmore, Hereford-shire, 1994. Author's photo.

Lini's home in the north, traditional chiefs began to join with young politicians in shirts and trousers to raise the new flag of the Provisional Government. The Provisional Government had a greater effect on the lives of some rural islanders than the centrally located Condominium had ever exerted. Building on linkages in the Presbyterian and Anglican churches, in some areas Vanuaku Party supporters organized and administered a pass system, implemented their own village codes of law, and occupied plantations claimed by European settlers. The Condominium government had neither the wherewithal nor the will to counter the Provisional Government effectively. Eventually, the Vanuaku Party gained enough concessions to dissolve the People's Provisional Government and participate in an interim Government of National Unity.[39]

As Will Stober drove me in the red Citroen from Birmingham to Herefordshire on a bright summer's day in 1994, I asked him to describe Olive Champion, the woman we were going to interview. Her husband, John, formerly a resident commissioner, had died earlier in the year from Creuzfeldt-Jakob disease. Will replied, "More than many colonial wives, Olive stands out as a *person*. She was in no sense an appendage to John." He went on to say that she and John had seemed to enjoy each other's company a great deal and that they enjoyed walking tours in places such as Nepal.

I interviewed Olive Champion at her home in the Herefordshire countryside,

where I also had the opportunity to meet three of her children, Peter, David, and Sally. Their home, an old rectory, felt full of life and energy, with barking dogs and the sound of sheep reaching my tape recorder across the open fields as we talked. Olive Champion spoke little about the political difficulties that characterized their time in the New Hebrides, with independence less than five years away. She did show me the family's photo album from the New Hebrides as we talked about her life in the Residency. The album included several photos of her husband posing with Jimmy Stephens, in colorfully innovative "customary" regalia, but none of Champion with the less dramatic Father Lini. We spoke about the Residency, and in the course of our conversation about the house, the source of some of the difficulties facing resident commissioners in this period became clearer.

Like du Boulay, Olive Champion felt that the house was not well suited to the tropics. Knowing little of the Residency's history, she felt that it must have been designed by someone who did not understand the requirements of tropical houses. The house was at odds with its environment. The air conditioning was so ineffective that the Champions tended not to use it, and the bedrooms lacked cross ventilation. In contrast to du Boulay, however, she believed that the view was secondary to practical considerations. Importantly, the house's eastward orientation provided some protection from hurricanes, which tended to be worst when they blew in from the open sea to the west.

The Champions, like many other colonial appointees including the Wilkies, had not expected to be posted to the New Hebrides. Nor had they expected the political turmoil that greeted them there. John could not have been less of a "Pacific Man." The Champions had spent seventeen years in Uganda (from 1946 to 1963), then been posted to Iran and to Jordan. They were looking forward to Afghanistan as their next post when John, who spoke French and had colonial experience, was suddenly chosen to fill the top British position in the New Hebrides.[40] Although their African experience had some relevance in terms of familiarity with a tropical environment (see figure 23), the differences were significant. Their house in Entebbe, for example, had been more commodious, less modern, more dependent on servants, and considerably more comfortable than the Residency in Port Vila. Did she feel this promotion was in fact a lateral move, I asked? Olive Champion's reply surprised me, for it addressed differences between Africans and Melanesians, rather than between the two jobs or between the houses in Uganda and Melanesia (see figure 24). Olive Champion and Will Stober struggle to define their colonial categories and to convey the nature of the differences they perceived, constructing the categories and differences anew in the process. The assumption that Melanesians should be like Africans because they are black is at once a racial stereotype and a colonial one, for both were sub-

---

Avocados at Large

From Mr J. S. Champion

Sir, In paying tribute to the versatility of the avocado pear your recent correspondents (May 1, 4) appear to have overlooked its military applications.

When I was employed in the Colonial Secretariat in Entebbe 30 years ago, there was a fruitful avocado tree in our garden, windfalls from which provided an arsenal of ammunition for the rival gangs in which our own children and those of our colleagues used to play their games.

Indeed the gang based on the other side of our garden fence was fittingly known and respected as the Mighty Pear-Balls.

The over-ripe, rotten avocado pear is singularly well adapted for use as a projectile in juvenile gang warfare. It is not lethal; it is exactly the right size and weight for throwing; its large stone provides the requisite solidity and mass; and in the event of a direct-hit its explosive potential is spectacularly satisfying.

Yours faithfully,
JOHN CHAMPION,
Farmore,
Callow, Hereford.

Figure 23. "Avocados at Large." The (London) *Times*, 11 May 1989.

ject peoples and so were expected to behave in similar ways. Where Margaret Wilkie had found similarities between Melanesians and East End mums, Olive Champion and Will Stober found differences between Melanesians and the people in their African posts.[41] I repeatedly heard nostalgia for Africans. Colonial officers and wives preferred to deal with the seemingly easygoing Africans, who were as quick to laugh as they were to anger, than with Melanesians, who were "not nearly so forthcoming." Perhaps the higher rank and thus relative isolation of Champion's position as British resident commissioner also made the contrast between Uganda and the New Hebrides even more apparent to Mrs. Champion.

For her, domestic comfort was not a matter of housing but of dwelling. How she lived was shaped by an interplay between house design and servants. In Uganda, where there were fewer modern conveniences but a greater number of highly competent servants, the Champions lived more comfortably than they did in Port Vila with more modern appliances and a smaller staff. The houses they occupied in Uganda had been built in about the 1930s. They were modeled on Indian bungalows, raised on pilings, with verandahs all around and a corrugated iron roof. The lack of modern appliances increased the colonial families' dependence on servants. Cooking on a wood stove, shopping every day at markets because there was no refrigeration, ironing without electricity—all made servants indispensable. The servants worked mainly at the back of the house. The dining room was generally at the center of the house with bedrooms on the sides and a

OLIVE CHAMPION: The thing about it was, having got used to Africans, Melanesians weren't quite right. . . . they should have been the same but they weren't.

WILL STOBER: I know what you mean.

MARGARET RODMAN: Why do you say they should have been the same?

O.C.: Well, because they were *black*. [But] they *weren't* the same as the Africans. They were just totally different.

M.R.: What were the differences?

O.C: Gosh, apart from the fact that they looked completely different. (Pause) Well, the Africans were much blacker. (Pause) They were just totally different. (Pause) There was a lot in Melanesians that was in fact Polynesian, I think. . . . But Africans are just totally different, aren't they, Will? (Chuckles)

W.S: Well, I think my first impression was of the relative shyness of the Melanesians.

O.C: Yes, that's right, they weren't nearly so forthcoming. . . . And they hadn't got the same sense of humor. Africans . . . had a very good sense of humor. They might lose their tempers and sort of hack you about a bit, but then they'd say "sorry" and laugh. . . . You had to sort of work away at Melanesians to get them to laugh.

W.S: Having said that, East Africans are rather less effusive than West Africans. Even so, by contrast to Melanesians they were pretty outgoing.

O.C: Yes, . . . they were outgoing. Now I don't know whether Melanesians were so affected by what was done to them in the nineteenth century by the missionaries, by being given measles, and by the "blackbirders". . . .

W.S: I sometimes wondered the same thing. But then of course as you got to know Melanesians. . .

O.C. (interjects): Well, yes, but you see in our position, we never really *did*. John met quite a lot and got to know people like John Kalsakau and so forth. But we were always a bit remote.

Figure 24. Why Melanesians Are Different.

kitchen reached by a raised walkway at the back. Many of the older Port Vila houses followed a similar plan, as had the old Residency, replaced in Rennie's day by the modern house that made Olive Champion yearn for "[t]he older, more dilapidated, and less technical houses, [which] were much better suited for the climate."

The Champions inherited the staff of three servants from du Boulay, who had in turn inherited at least two of them from Colin Allan. Maqu, whom Olive Champion described as a "splendid fellow," was very loyal. He was, however, also very opinionated about what should be served at dinner parties and had a rather limited repertoire. Olive Champion remembered that he could make only

three desserts. Frequent entertaining meant considerable repetition, particularly for the Champions and long-suffering, frequent guests such as the French resident commissioner, whose cook had a wider range.

Olive Champion found it difficult to adjust to the Residency. She described an odd house disconnected from its past but not adequately connected to the present. She spoke of this disconnection in terms of water, but knowing the Residency's history one can see the issue that exasperated her in broader terms. A rainwater catchment system of cisterns including a large in-ground tank had supplied the old Residency. By the time Colin Allan wrote his instructions on the Residency to du Boulay, however, it was no longer possible to connect to the Residency's cisterns. Instead, the Residency was supplied with town water through an underwater pipe that carried the water from the main island to Iririki. This pipe was at risk from ships in the harbor, high winds that rubbed the pipe against the coral sea bed, and corrosion. If a break occurred the town had to be notified promptly or the entire municipal water supply could drain into the harbor.[42] Soon after the Champions arrived, the water main broke. Olive found it frustrating that there was a perfectly good water supply in the tanks next to the house that they could not get into and a broken pipe under the channel that would take weeks to repair. She remembers threatening John that she would go home to England immediately if the water wasn't restored by the next day. Repairs were carried out with lightning speed, and she did not have to carry out her threat.

Andrew Stuart (1978–1980)

Andrew Stuart, the last British resident commissioner, served from 1978 to 1980. He and his wife, Patricia, told me that they invited "everybody" to official functions at the Residency. Who was "everybody"? New Hebrideans from across the entire political spectrum. Shaping a Government of National Unity out of diverse Anglophone and Francophone political interests was a challenge that, surprisingly, Iririki Island itself helped to meet.

Elections were held in November 1979, and this time the Vanuaku Pati participated. The French sought to ensure a better performance from Francophone candidates, known as the Modérés. But the Vanuaku Pati swept to victory, gaining majorities throughout the islands and winning 62 percent of the vote.

According to Stuart, meetings were held at Iririki, not at the French Residency or at the British offices on the main island. Although Iririki was the essence of British space in some ways, its geographical location also made it a place to retreat from the rest of the world. The boat ride was crucial, for it took people

Figure 25. Margaret Rodman with the last BRC, Andrew Stuart, and his wife, Patricia (left to right). Photo by Will Stober, with permission.

away from Vila. The idea was to get everyone "away." Away from what? "From everything," Stuart said. From everything except British influence, the French might have added. Although Stuart's French counterpart, Inspector General Robert, was a participant at these meetings, it was widely assumed that the British were pushing more strongly for independence than the French.

Once the Government of National Unity was a reality, meetings were no longer held only on Iririki. Seemingly, the participants no longer needed the liminal space the little island had provided. Nevertheless, the island played a leading role in the independence celebrations. British customary practices had developed in association with independence in former colonies. Indeed, there were by 1980 ample precedents in the Pacific as well as in Africa and elsewhere. One such practice was to lower the Union Jack and raise the new country's flag at midnight on the eve of independence. According to Andrew Stuart, the French were not interested in making a major social event out of the lowering of the French flag, so the midnight ceremony would be quite low key. Stuart, therefore, decided to have a flag-lowering ceremony at sunset at the British Residency on Iririki the day before independence. This was a major social occasion to which many New Hebrideans as well as British residents were invited. It initiated the independence celebrations, which continued with more flag ceremonies at midnight outside Parliament and the next day outside the British government offices on the mainland.

In 1995, I interviewed Jimmy Meameadolu, an islander who grew up on Iririki, where his father was the head boat man. Meameadolu went on to be general

manager of Tour Vanuatu, one of the largest tour groups in the country. He remembered the excitement of the last days of empire in Vanuatu. He watched the future prime minister of Vanuatu and other indigenous political leaders make the crossing and climb the hill to meet with the resident commissioner. The concrete boat man's house on Iririki was bulldozed after independence. Just as Jimmy Meameadolu, whose home it was, has risen to the top of a career in tourism, so the entire little island has become a tourist site.

Iririki Island Resort

At independence, the British Residency was abandoned. Unlike his distant predecessor, Smith-Rewse, Andrew Stuart never had to account for the disposition of any items at the Residency, much less the soup spoons. A British official sent out from Hong Kong to assess the furnishings at the Residency concluded that there were only a few pieces of value. Stuart took custody of a chest that had belonged to the first captain of the Residency ship, MV *Euphrosyne*, and some silver plate presented to the British resident commissioner by the Americans in the Second World War. He handed everything else over to the new government. His children, who stayed in the Residency briefly after the Stuarts left with the royal guests at independence, reported that there was virtual looting of the house and garden, not by islanders primarily but by Australian residents. Maqu, the chef, stood at the door of the Residency handing out tokens of the colonial era.

The building stood empty for three years while the Ifira islanders, to whom the land reverted at independence, decided what to do with it. In 1983 they leased it for development as a resort. Peter Nicholson, the developer, chose the site that had been recommended to the resident commissioner in 1959. In addition to the qualities cited by the architect at that time, the beachfront location seemed the most desirable place to put the resort. Several tiers of bungalows were built, some on stilts at the water's edge, all grouped around a restaurant and swimming pool with a magnificent view of the town. The manager lived in the Residency until 1987, when hurricane Uma took off the roof. Rick Graham, the manager in 1995, told me that they were surprised to find that the roof of this modest showcase of empire had not been securely bolted down. Perhaps Captain Rason's original cost-cutting measures also applied when the Residency was rebuilt in 1959. Following Uma and a later hurricane, Prema, the front wall of the Residency was rebuilt with cement block, and new, storm-proof windows were installed. Otherwise the building remained structurally unchanged when I saw it in August 1995.

The island, once the domain of the resident commissioner, the Presbyterian

Figure 26. Iririki Island resort, 1995. Author's photo.

hospital, and their collective herds, has changed far more than the Residency itself. The shifting boundaries between public and private point to interesting similarities and differences in the spatial forms of colonial and touristic experiences on Iririki.

First, the public is now invited into many of the areas that once were private, although not into the Residency itself.[43] Now the island is marked with mowed walking trails so that tourists can explore what are designated as historic sites from the colonial past. What was the house of the Presbyterian doctor is marked with a plaque as a historic site, although it dates only from 1949. When I visited the island in August 1995, the resort was allowing a Presbyterian missionary to live rent free in the old doctor's house, partly to deter vandals and trespassers and partly as a gesture of goodwill toward the Presbyterian church, which had occupied that part of the island for so long.[44] All the older hospital buildings were gone. Foundations and other ruins were indicated on the walking trails. The hospital crematorium served as the resort's incinerator.

Second, to some extent, the Residency always was a hotel. The wives, especially, thought so. Now the boundary of the "hotel" is just larger, encompassing many bungalows and a restaurant as well as the house and grounds.

Third, as in the days of the Condominium, the isolation Iririki provides is experienced as both positive and negative. Tourists, like resident commissioners,

find it both charming and inconvenient. The island affords a wonderful view, a sense of getting away from "everything" while panoptically having everything within one's gaze. Now those who enjoy this privileged position are tourists, the colonizers of a postcolonial world. In some sense, however, the gaze is now returned. Islanders in town watch with some amusement, and probably some resentment, as tourists parasail and wind surf. For some islanders, tourist antics are money in the bank; the resort pays its rent to the Ifira Islanders Land Trust. A final irony of the history of colonial space on the island is that the tourists, coming from the late-modern world, spend their holidays in fake native bungalows.

Iririki Island is a good example of privileged space without fancy architecture. Although the resident commissioner's house eventually became a comfortable place to live, it was never up to the standard of similar accommodation in most other British colonies. Resident commissioners who went to the New Hebrides from Africa found it, sometimes appealingly and sometimes appallingly, unpretentious. One of the wives who had lived there told me that she had heard that the Iririki Residency had an elegant colonnade; she arrived to find instead what looked to her like a budget motel. The site, not the house, made the place special; but the house, as we have seen, allowed officials to tell unofficial stories that shed light on the course, and the culmination, of the Condominium.

PRISONERS IN GRASS HOUSES

On 29 May 1908, Edward Jacomb, a tall, lean lawyer in his early thirties who was serving as assistant to the British resident commissioner in the New Hebrides, wrote to his mother, describing a "most interesting trip" he had just made to the island of Ambrym to apprehend an alleged murderer named Berk. The trip was long: two days on a packet-boat from the capital, Port Vila, to the island of Paama; a weekend with the Reverend Maurice Frater, a Presbyterian missionary who had reported the murder; an abortive trip to the wrong part of Ambrym; and finally four and a half hours rowing a whaleboat across a glassy sea to the accused man's village. Jacomb went on:

> On entering the village I found the object of my search without the slightest difficulty. My arrival seemed to astonish the inhabitants pretty considerably. The village is about as primitive as it is possible for a village to be; the huts are low and can only be entered on hands and knees; the natives are practically naked, and most of them were strolling about smoking clay pipes charged with black plug [tobacco], and with Sneider rifles at full cock over their shoulders. There were a number of piccaninnies [children], pigs and fowls roaming about in the mud. I must confess I did not care for the environment, my only weapon being a pencil. However I made the best of it and sat down on a tree trunk and

spent half an hour questioning Berk as to the alleged shooting of his wife. He
made no effort to deny it, but I failed to discover his motive.[1]

Jacomb arrested Berk, traveled with the confessed murderer back to Port Vila,
and handed him over to Captain Edwin Harrowell, who was in the process of
training the first British colonial police force. Once again, Jacomb asked Berk
why he had killed his wife. The Melanesian "wrinkled his face, and the wrinkling
soon turned to an engaging smile: 'Mi no savvy,' he said."[2]

"Mi No Savvy"

Berk's punch line, "mi no savvy," is shared with two other stories Jacomb
recounts earlier in his diary for 1908. In one, his manservant is apprehended in
the act of trying to pluck a chicken before killing it, inverting the "natural" order
of events. In the other, Jacomb, saddle sore and weary, arrives in a native village.
His traveling companion suggests a whiskey, which Jacomb downs with alacrity,
only to discover that a female villager has provided seawater rather than fresh
water for the drinks. On both occasions, when asked why they made such foolish
mistakes, the servants replied, "Mi no savvy."

   In British eyes, then, Melanesians neither deny their guilt nor understand
why they perform culpable acts. While Jacomb feels uneasy, his only weapon being a pencil amidst rifle-toting, nearly naked Melanesian men, he apprehends the
murderer "without the slightest difficulty." The primitive quality of the village,
spatially evident in the low huts, sets the stage for Jacomb. Is this a real crime?
Is the perpetrator too naive to be a danger to a white man? Ironically, the criminal, though guilty of the act, is innocent of the crime. Because he does not know
why what he did is wrong, he is not really responsible for his actions.

   For the Melanesians caught in these stories, "Mi no savvy" had other meanings. From the research that Bill Rodman and I conducted in the islands over the
years, it is clear that crimes punished by the colonial government were not necessarily crimes against local customary law; even killing one's wife could be
justified, although probably not without payment of compensation to her kin. By
the same token, offenses against customary law meriting a penalty of death
might not be considered a "real" crime by Europeans. Although sorcery was a
punishable offense in the Native Code that the British and French district agents
could enforce, they rarely did so.[3] In part, the problem was that the Europeans
didn't believe that this was a real crime. Moreover, the islanders hardly ever
handed over a sorcery case to the government for resolution; they just did not

think that the Europeans would understand how to deal with such a case.[4] So "Mi no savvy" could mean "I don't know how to explain this to you" or, in the cases of the chicken and the saltwater, "I don't know what you thought I was do-ing"—"I pulled some tail feathers out as I chased the chicken; I wasn't plucking it alive" or "I brought this saltwater up to cook vegetables in and you silly men drank it." Yet another possibility is "I didn't know how to do this strange Eng-lish thing you asked of me."

Why were Europeans not afraid of people like Berk? The answer is not so simple as Jacomb's anecdotes suggest. Europeans had learned at their peril to ig-nore the threat that Melanesians could pose to their lives. John Williams, the first London Missionary Society missionary to the islands, had been martyred in 1839. For the next twenty-five years, missionary activity in the New Hebrides was a "tale of tragedy, martyrdom and clergical persistence."[5] Only a few months after Jacomb's encounter with the docile murderer on Ambrym, the mur-der on Santo of a settler, Peter Greig, and his two daughters shocked the Euro-pean community in the New Hebrides.[6]

Jacomb's diary records his certainty that Greig had not provoked the mur-der and his initial desire to blame labor recruiters, especially the French. Ja-comb's comments about the primitive "Man Santo" also resonate ironically with the cruel justice that would be imposed by the supposedly civilized colonial gov-ernment (passages he deleted in the final text are shown in square brackets):

> I had never met any of the Greig family, but from all I had heard they seemed to have been quiet, inoffensive folk, unlikely to have done anything to have pro-voked their native neighbours. Their murder was probably an act of reprisal for wrongs done to these neighbours by other white men. [At and prior to that time and for some time after, numerous outrages had been committed particularly by French subjects who had forcibly kidnapped able bodied youths and maidens, their victims having either died or been detained indefinitely on plantations with scant hope of ever seeing their homes or friends again.] "Man Santo" was still a very primitive human and considered all white men as belonging to the same tribe, and thought that by attacking the nearest available whites he would avenge his dead, missing or captive relatives.[7]

Greig, however, did not prove to have been "inoffensive." The murderer, who was apprehended on the third punitive expedition along with seven others deemed to have been accomplices, was Ifurer, a Melanesian from an interior vil-lage who had worked for Greig and not received the pay he was owed. When Ifurer had asked Greig for his wages, the planter had refused to pay. As well, it

was possible that islanders believed that Greig, and another murdered settler before him named Sawers, were blocking the route that cargo, or wealth, would follow if and when it arrived for the inhabitants of the interior. The eight prisoners, including Ifurer, were taken off to Vila, where presumably they were housed in the French prison, as there was not yet a British facility.

Producing the Prison and the Police

The construction of the prison and introduction of a police force were closely linked in the colonial New Hebrides. Neither existed on the British side before 1907, when Captain Harrowell was appointed commandant of the British Division of the New Hebrides Armed Constabulary.[8] He lived with Jacomb and Resident Commissioner Merton King in the British Residency on Iririki Island. Jacomb, who never liked Harrowell, described him as "a fine figure of a man, with a magnificent moustache but, unfortunately, a balding head."[9] In 1907, Harrowell was about thirty-eight years old, "a bachelor, a teetotaller, a heavy smoker of pipes and cigars, a non-reader even of newspapers, and devoid of any interests outside his as yet non-existent police force."[10]

The first policeman was a "West Indian named Alcide," whom Jacomb "found derelict in Vila and handed to Harrowell as the nucleus of his future police force."[11] By the end of the year, Jacomb had recruited nine more policemen; the resident commissioner found another four, and by 7 May 1908 there were sixteen British policemen. Harrowell set to training them and within a month had "worked wonders with the very raw material available."[12] A large grass house was built to accommodate the police on Iririki Island near the British Residency.

There were at that time no British prisoners, and no provision for them. In late January 1908, Jacomb writes, "we were suddenly made aware that we were short of a prison, and had nothing to serve as a temporary substitute." Four months before Jacomb apprehended Berk, a Melanesian man accused of having shot a local woman was brought in from the north. The case could not be heard until the end of the hurricane season, so the resident commissioner "invoked for him the hospitality of the French gaol which was readily granted as they thereby got an unpaid laborer for some months."[13] Plans were made to house the police in a more permanent structure and to build a prison. According to architects' drawings from 1909, both were to be housed in similar structures.[14] Both the barracks and the prison had cells. Policemen and prisoners were to sleep on raised platforms along the length of the walls of their respective accommodations. The main difference was that the barracks had more porous boundaries,

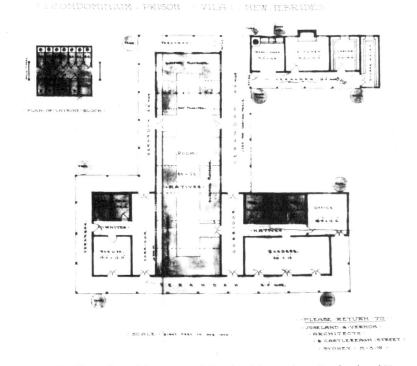

Figure 27. Floor plan of the proposed Condominium prison, Joseland and Vernon Architects. NHBS 227/1908.

such that the policemen could sleep on an open sleeping porch at the front entrance if they wanted. Whites, whether prisoners or policemen, would dwell separately from Melanesians. As the drawings indicate, there was to be a French wing and a British wing of both the police barracks and the prison. This separation reflected the structure of the Condominium.

In theory, they were the British and French divisions of the New Hebrides Armed Constabulary and therefore divisions of what was designed to be a more or less unified force, but in practice they were separate. This separation was evident in the fact that neither the joint prison nor the joint police barracks were constructed, despite the drawings prepared by Joseland and Vernon, the Sydney architects who oversaw the construction of the other Condominium buildings between 1907 and about 1911. The French retained their own prison near other administrative buildings on the bluff overlooking the town and the harbor. By 1912, the British had requested permission from the Western Pacific High Commission

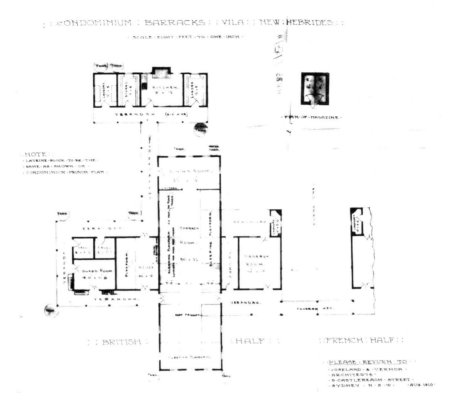

Figure 28. Floor plan of the proposed Condominium barracks, Joseland and Vernon Architects. NHBS 227/1908.

to convert half of the boatbuilder's shed near the British Residency on Iririki Island to a jail.[15] The British police continued to live in their grass house on the island.

Eventually, the prison, the police, and the British offices relocated to the main island (Efate), creating the British Paddock on a block of land adjacent to and south of the French government buildings. The prison and the police barracks were built to specifications that the resident commissioner obtained from the Western Pacific High Commission before 1924: four cells (10'8" x 10'4" x 12') to accommodate a maximum of six prisoners each. Prefabricated galvanized iron buildings were available by mail order from Australia at that time. The same building could be ordered as housing for labor, as a police barracks, or as a prison. The only difference was how many people could be put in a room/cell. British regulations concerning native labor required 300 cubic feet for each adult, but the prison, if it were full (which it never was), would allow only 220 cubic feet per

inmate.[16] The interchangeability of housing for police and prisoners was especially evident later, as prisons became established in the three outlying administrative districts (Southern, Northern, and Central District 2). At some point in the 1950s, the police in the Northern District even switched quarters with the prisoners, preferring the solidity of the prison to the less substantial protection against the elements afforded by their own grass houses.[17] As we shall see, however, the British administration took the decision to allow prisoners to live in grass houses more cautiously than did the Melanesian policemen in the Northern District.

Prisoners in Grass Houses

The minuting in the New Hebrides British Service archives is often ruminative. Running commentary on correspondence and other contents begins on the inside covers and often fills the front pages of a file. Handwritten or typed, terse or loquacious, minuting was the email of its day, a way of thinking about things in a less formal discourse than even demi-official correspondence. It is always self-conscious, as if the writer were aware that, in spite of the informal appearance, minuting was a matter of record. As Will Stober has commented,

> Typically, minuting, whether initiated from the top or the bottom of the official ladder, is hierarchical in nature, and normally revealing of the processes of reasoning leading to a decision or to agreement on the text of the documents, such as a letter to the French residency or a draft Joint Regulation. At least the outward courtesies are preserved towards a senior officer, not least the Resident—their absence would be unthinkable—while on the other hand subordinate officials, if occasionally complimented, may suffer immortalised rebuke, sometimes severe, from the Resident or other senior official.[18]

Because of these qualities and because it is by definition a multi-vocal, inscribed conversation, minuting can be a window into contested issues, individual differences of opinion among colonial officers, and the practical workings of empire.

This is particularly evident in an exchange from October 1935 about prisoners and grass houses. In brief, the exchange, explored in detail below, is this: When the Presbyterian mission doctor brings sanitary conditions at the British prison to the attention of Resident Commissioner George Andrew Joy, the commissioner is moved to consider the kinds of prisoners housed in the jail; he proposes that a "suitable grass house" be built for some prisoners. Conflict arises with the commandant of police, who fears that British prestige will suffer. The

doctor agrees that additional ventilation is required, but by the end of the exchange, sanitation is a secondary issue to questions of categorization, containment, and the definition of both prisoners and homes.

A bit of background about the three protagonists may provide useful context. The commandant of police, Ernest A. G. Seagoe, at forty-nine, was ten years older than his boss. He was the nephew of the first resident commissioner, Captain Rason, had arrived in the New Hebrides with his uncle, and had served at the age of sixteen as Rason's secretary. He stayed on after his uncle's departure in 1907 and visited often at the Residency during the period when Captain Harrowell was recruiting and training the first British police.

Joy himself was no newcomer to the islands. His first post in the New Hebrides was in 1924 as assistant to the new British resident commissioner, Geoffrey Bingham Whistler Smith-Rewse, who died in office in 1927. Joy replaced Smith-Rewse as resident commissioner. Both Seagoe and Joy had returned from six months' leave in June 1935.[19] One can assume that they were still relatively fresh in October.

The third participant in the exchange, through correspondence rather than minuting, was young Dr. Alexander S. Frater. The son of Maurice Frater, with whom Jacomb had stayed on his trip north to arrest Berk, Alexander Frater had recently completed his training as a doctor and a Presbyterian minister in Glasgow. He arrived in the New Hebrides with his wife, Lorna, only a few months before the exchange with Joy and Seagoe. His job was to take over Paton Memorial Hospital, which shared Iririki Island with the British Residency. While he was familiar with life on the island of Paama from his childhood, he was inexperienced in his new position and had been away from the New Hebrides for some years at the time of this exchange.

In the course of his medical duties, Dr. Frater visited the prison, not to inspect prison conditions, but to treat a sick man; nevertheless, he had noticed that his patient was sleeping on the floor and that the air was very stuffy. He recommended to the British government that the prison be better ventilated and that prisoners not have to sleep on the concrete floor.

On 1 October 1935, Joy minuted to Seagoe:[20] "I shall be glad if you will take an early opportunity of discussing the matter [of sanitary conditions at the British prison] with Dr. Frater and put into effect the recommendations he considers necessary on grounds of health."

Joy continued:

There is another aspect of prison accommodation I should like you to consider carefully. We have at Vila three classes of prisoners (1) those tried and convicted by a Court of Law. (2) those who have had no trial but who have committed

offences against the person such as murder. (3) those who have had no trial and are held on administrative grounds only—differing from (2) in that it is questionable whether they would be convicted even though legal machinery were available.

I do feel that a distinction ought to be made between natives tried and convicted and those mentioned in (2) and (3). The latter are not incarcerated as a *punishment*—they are held at Vila simply because trouble would arise if they were not taken away from their villages.

I should like to see a suitable grass house made for these prisoners. [Joy doubts they would run away, and thinks the risk of escape worth taking]. Such a house once erected could be kept in order by the prisoners themselves. [Joy concludes by observing that there is "now plenty of money" for such a project.]

A week later, Seagoe responded in four typed pages to Dr. Frater's recommendations. He observed that Dr. Frater had failed to notice the prison's amenities: each cell had an open window and two open ventilators that allowed stale air to escape at the top of the walls. Further, each prisoner was allotted a portable bunk; "[p]risoners *do not* sleep on the concrete floor except perhaps when the fit takes them, but there is no necessity to do so." Seagoe then suggested that additional ventilation could be obtained "by piercing the galvanized iron ceiling with a number of holes to allow the top air to get out via the interstices in the galvanized iron roofing."

Seagoe trod carefully with regard to Joy's suggestion about the grass house. First, he presented "statistics"[21] in an attempt to show, through the power of orderly enumeration, that the numbers did not justify separate accommodation for unconvicted prisoners. Indeed, based on Seagoe's table, the grass house would have to accommodate most of the prisoners, and the prison would be almost empty. Second, he expressed concern about British prestige. Any distinction between kinds of prisoners "should take such form as will not affect the prestige of the Government and that of the officers" responsible, namely Seagoe himself. Natives, according to the commandant of police, are unable to make the fine distinction between detention and conviction; a separate grass house would carry the distinction "a shade too far, and I think would create a bad impression among the natives."

Finally, Seagoe suggested a solution ("with all deference"). He argued that the prison was better than a grass house; "the prison accommodation is far superior to that of any native house excepting perhaps that of the more advanced missionized natives." While confinement and regular work were irksome, "both of these for the ordinary native, and more especially for the untrammelled heathen, are such radical changes in his everyday life as to constitute a hardship." Work, Seagoe concluded, was "essential for health"; he did not mention, but Joy would have

known, that prison labor was essential to the maintenance of the British Paddock, and indeed to the sanitation of the town. This left only confinement as a possible undue hardship for unconvicted prisoners. Rather than changing the form of the prison by, for example, building a grass house for detainees and keeping only convicts in the "real" prison, Seagoe proposed to alter other spatial and temporal boundaries. The doors to the prison should be left open "and the inmates allowed to come and go as they choose within the prison compound." A handwritten note from the assistant British resident commissioner suggests that all prisoners be locked up at dusk; "this gives [the detainees] reasonable liberty in daylight and a privilege over the others." In fact, at that time, *all* natives were required to be off the streets of Vila by sundown, and their movements were restricted at night.[22]

Seagoe still worried about the consequences of such leniency for surveillance and for "evasion": "I think that advantage will undoubtedly be taken of what the natives will construe as slackness and weakness on the part of the Administration, therefore, whichever system you may adopt (grass house or open cells), I submit with all deference that I should not be asked to accept responsibility for the safe custody of prisoners who are unconfined and unguarded."

One might expect that Seagoe's anxiety came in part from what he had seen, and what British Resident Commissioner Joy had missed. Joy and Seagoe had both returned in June from six months' leave. It had been Joy's first since 1931. On that earlier leave, he had been out of the New Hebrides when the first and only execution by guillotine had taken place in Port Vila. Six Tonkinese had been executed under French law for killing their French manager and another worker.[23] Seagoe, in contrast, had been in the New Hebrides at the time of those executions and at the time of the Clapcott murders in 1923, an event similar to the Greig murders and not far from their site in South Santo.

Although fear of violence directed against whites would seem reasonable given such experiences, there is no sense conveyed in Seagoe's (or anyone else's) writing that prisoners were dangerous. What Seagoe feared, as did Joy, was less what the natives would *do* than what they would *think*. The next section explores the dual nature of this fear and fearlessness. Why were the British afraid of what the New Hebrideans might think but not afraid of what they would do?

Producing the Prisoner

One of the categories debated in the exchange between Joy and Seagoe concerns the difference between kinds of prisoners: should these be acknowledged, and if so, spatially or temporally? Seagoe was right, though for the wrong reasons, in

claiming that the islanders did not generally recognize a distinction between detainees and convicted prisoners. Both were simply "prisoners" to the Melanesians. Whether they were treated differently in Port Vila did not matter; the point was that they were gone from their home islands. Often, Melanesians (and missionaries or planters) wanted a fellow islander removed to rid the community of a nuisance, a threat, or a disturbing presence. For example, in one New Hebrides British Service file from 1934 headed "Dangerous Lunatic," the Anglican priest on the northern island of Ambae (then called Aoba) requests the British resident commissioner to remove a Melanesian who was "mentally deranged with murderous intent." The priest notes, "I do not like the idea of removing him to Vila, but I can see no other way of controlling him."[24] Similarly, a French and a British district agent, on a rare tour together, took into custody an alleged "poisoner" (really a sorcerer in the view of the French district agent) to protect the man from villagers as well as the villagers from the suspected poisoner.[25]

Even when Melanesians had clearly committed what would have been crimes under British law, they might be brought to prison only as detainees. It is unclear to what extent Melanesians recognized how limited the colonial government's jurisdiction really was. In the 1930s there was "no law to prevent one native killing another in force any further north than the island of Paama" where, not coincidentally, Dr. Maurice Frater was based. Few such killings were even brought to the attention of the colonial government; and when they were, the government intervened, possibly detaining the accused, mainly to maintain its prestige.[26]

The distinction between detainee and convicted prisoner is an important one in the colonial record because of the questions it raises of liberty and of the transformations of individuals.[27] Seagoe and Joy debated the deprivation of liberty, the former arguing for temporal adjustments and the latter for spatial adjustments to the restrictions on prisoners' liberty depending on whether or not they had been convicted of a crime.

Notice that the matter is resolved by altering the physical structure of the existing prison in the name of sanitation. Literally punching holes in the ceiling opens the building to the outside air and also "opens" it in a weak symbolic sense. Although ventilated as a grass house might have been, the building is clearly still a prison. Thus the grass house, as an alternative for those who were prisoners but were not criminals, was eliminated as a potentially hybrid space. It would have been too anomalous next to the prison. A grass house would look like "home" when it was clearly not home but prison. What is more, the prison, in Seagoe's argument, is virtually homelike, more comfortable than all but the most advanced native house. How could accommodation of the least guilty in the most primitive dwelling be justified when the prison was such a clear step above the grass house on the social evolutionary ladder of housing?

The practice of creating prisoners out of people who had not committed a prosecutable crime under colonial law benefited both the Melanesian and colonial establishments. For Melanesian elders, the colonial government provided a valuable service, removing difficult and dangerous local men. The accused usually came willingly, as Berk had done, and, in later years, often spoke fondly of their time in prison. They learned skills, met new people, ate white man's food (rice and beef stew or fish), and worked for the police, who were less demanding than many planters. For the colonial government, prisoners provided the unpaid labor that was essential to the maintenance of spatial order in the colonial headquarters.

It is interesting to note that French prisons were more secure, more prison-like, and larger; indeed, the French prison became the official jail after independence in both Port Vila and in Santo. I found no record of the French wanting more prison labor, as the British did, perhaps because they had often had more prisoners than did the British. Further, the French colonial project was always better funded than the British, and, at least until 1963, the French could draw on the large pool of Tonkinese labor for gardening and other maintenance work.

The British came to rely increasingly on prison labor. By 1911, it was recommended that prison labor be used for refuse disposal. Prisoners kept the jungle at bay: "For the most part the houses look uncared for and neglected, and if the ground surrounding them were not periodically cleaned by a gang of prisoners, they would soon be mere jungle."[28] By 1928, British Resident Commissioner Joy could report to the high commissioner that prison labor was used to keep the town of Port Vila in "such sanitary condition as is possible under present arrangements."[29]

Much later, in the late 1960s, British District Agent Darvall Wilkins cleared the government station at Lakatoro (Malakula) with a team of police and prisoners. He came ashore with his wife and children, three policemen, and an assortment of prisoners "recruited" on Malakula and Santo. Initially, they all lived in the one building on the premises, the old plantation house. The Wilkins family had two rooms, the prisoners had two rooms, and the police had one. As Jerry Marston, an ex–assistant British district agent and admirer of Wilkins, put it, "At night they'd all eat together and the prisoners would play—a couple of prisoners would get their guitars out and play. . . . That's how they spent their time. In the morning they just go and cut a bit—just extend the civilization of the station about another twenty feet, until lo and behold one day they got up and found that they had a station."[30] Ironically, then, the creation of docile prisoners, most easily achieved among those who had not committed a crime, was necessary to the establishment of other kinds of disciplines, those of sanitation and civilized places. The Lakatoro station came to rely especially heavily on prison labor to maintain the grounds. Wilkins kept many of the large trees, and it was very difficult to mow the grass under and around the trees with power equip-

ment. Queen's Birthday celebrations in June, for example, prompted the "re-cruitment" of prisoners. Jerry Marston recalled that for such occasions

> the place [had] to be looking really good, [so] we used to go out hunting for [pris-oners]. There were very large numbers of cases [that could] be heard, it was a question of whether people were prepared to give them to you. So around April and May of every year, we'd go out and recruit prisoners. We'd intensify our interest in misdemeanors in and around the islands and bring back loads and loads [so] that we had the work force to clean the station up.

Marston recalled how readily New Hebrideans reported for imprisonment.

> You had to make it clear to them they didn't need to come right away, otherwise by the time you're onto the next case, . . . often . . . they'd have rolled the mat up, got their few belongings together, said their farewells, and were standing by the beach waiting to get onto the boat. And you'd say "No, no, no. We've got another three or four days of touring to do, make your own way there."

Had prisoners *not* given themselves up willingly with the support of their communities, the colonial officers would have had a very difficult time arresting them. In short, most detainees were in prison only because local island elders, missionaries, and district agents agreed that prison was the place for them and because most of those sentenced or detained did not really mind being impris-oned. British prestige, then, was crucial to maintaining colonial authority espe-cially given the improbability of mustering British force. It is therefore not surprising that Seagoe and Joy were so concerned about what the natives would think of British actions with regard to incarceration. Joy was worried that the British would seem unfair if they continued to treat two different categories of prisoner as if they were the same kind of criminals. Seagoe was worried about conveying signs of weakness. Their concerns suggest a fear of seeming to lose or abuse control over New Hebrideans.

Docile Axe Murderers and Other Oxymorons

In interviews with ex–colonial officers, their wives, and children, I always asked about their sense of security in the New Hebrides. Although concerns about theft and sexual assault increased around the time of independence in 1980 and con-tinued to worry some people in the 1980s and 1990s, residents from earlier peri-

ods were almost uniform in their responses. By and large, they did not lock their doors. They did not even know where the keys were, if indeed there were keys issued with their houses. They walked in the evening. Some women even collected shells on the reef at night. If they worried at all, it was about the Melanesian gaze, the sense that you might be watched in the bath or, in later years, the knowledge that a teenage boy was watching your video through the window.

Material on prisoners almost always came up in the course of discussions of security. Again the responses ran to a type. Prisoners were described as docile, with tendencies toward depression rather than violence, and many were seen as more intelligent than the average New Hebridean. They found training and often subsequent employment in the British offices. For example, a triple murderer from Ambae worked in the British Residency offices for many years. He had killed three men out of jealousy, assuming, rightly or wrongly, that they had been lovers of the local woman with whom he was obsessed. One colonial officer said he "took a lot of interest in the case because we considered it a problem—we didn't want to keep him in prison forever, [but] we were beginning to understand that it would be dangerous for him to go back to Ambae."[31]

I knew from personal experience that many of the most successful leaders and entrepreneurs on the island of Ambae in the 1970s and 1980s had served their time in prison for such offenses as adultery and chicken theft. When my husband and I had first arrived in the New Hebrides in 1969, we stayed in the rest house in the British Paddock (the official residential area) near Luganville, on the island of Santo. Through our bedroom window on the day of our arrival, I was surprised to see a New Hebridean man with a large bush knife. He was, of course, cutting the grass. He turned out to be from the Longana district of Ambae, where we were headed for fourteen months of anthropological research. He was in prison for what he thought of as a self-financed loan, which the British construed as embezzlement from the local council. He became a key informant for us on legal matters, a leader in his mature years, and is still our friend. It is hard to overemphasize how common it was to serve time in prison. Once, when my husband gained access to court records from Santo in the 1960s, he concluded that every politician who was worth his salt had served time in jail.[32]

Not that prisoners always stayed in jail. It was never difficult to escape from Vila prison. Jimmy Stephens, leader of the secessionist rebellion at independence, did it with style in 1982. He claimed to have used magic to make himself invisible to the prison guards, then made his getaway in a glass-bottomed boat. Stories abound in the interviews about prisoners who came and went as they pleased. For example, there was the prisoner who announced that he would not be taking his weekend pass on Friday. "What weekend pass?" the policeman asked. "You've

never had a weekend pass." It seems the prisoner had been in the habit of going home on the weekends and returning to prison Sunday nights. No one had noticed. By the 1980s there was a well-worn path from a peeled-back portion of the prison fence to the Tropical Market across the street.[33]

The people I interviewed repeatedly emphasized the harmlessness of prisoners carrying machetes or bush knives. They brought this theme up with such regularity that it seemed to me they protested a bit too much. The sight of docile prisoners with bush knives fascinated and amazed them, as well it might. Some even told of lending a prisoner the family bush knife and a file to sharpen it.[34] Perhaps talking about how harmless the prisoners were allayed anxiety that these armed men might one day slit their throats. It seemed absurd to the people I interviewed to imagine such a turn of events in the New Hebrides. Yet some colonial officers in the New Hebrides had served in Kenya and elsewhere in East and Central Africa. They knew that even faithful servants could turn against their masters. Not one adult said they felt unsafe around prison laborers, although there were clear, enforced rules about not having prisoners as workers inside the house, rules that were as symbolically loaded as they may have been practical.[35] Most of those who had children in the New Hebrides remembered them playing with the prisoners. One mother recalled that it had been quite some time before she and her husband discovered that their son and a friend were making prison visits in the 1970s: "Gerard and his eight-year-old friend had been chatting to one of the prisoners who said, 'Have you got any comics?' They said, 'Yes.' [Soon] the lads were going up to the prison and the prison warden would be letting them in, and they'd be sitting in Kan's cell, swapping comics." What was Kan's crime?

He'd murdered his wife, or something, sort of a family murder. And it was a long time, a long time before I knew. It was just quite casually Gerard said something about "That nice man gave me a new comic today," or something. He and [his friend] had been visiting quite regularly. So I said he started his social work career at the age of eight. But I mean, *you knew that they were safe*.[36]

The exception, however, may prove the rule. For one boy, prisoners were not safe. Edward Leaf had lived in the New Hebrides between the ages of eight and ten in the early 1960s. At that time his father was a British colonial officer (legal adviser) and his mother was active in the Red Cross and training track and field athletes.[37] Edward had plenty of time to play with his friends—other English boys, one girl who was a tomboy, and a number of New Hebridean children. They were intrepid, setting off cherry bombs under the offices where the English fathers worked and visiting Chinese stores and fantasizing about stealing (though he said they never carried out their plans). Leaf described himself as having "gone native." By the time he

left for boarding school at the age of ten, he spoke better Bislama than English and
could hardly fit a pair of shoes on his feet. What follows is an excerpt from a conversation that Edward Leaf, and Will Stober, and I had.[38] At the time of the interview, Leaf was about forty years old, a lanky, former Royal Air Force pilot working
on a book about photo interpretation in World War II. It was never clear to me how
many children he had; there were four or five playing in a wading pool in the back-
yard during the interview. His eyes never strayed from them as he talked to us:

> RODMAN: Do you remember prisoners around?
>
> LEAF: Yes, God yeah.
>
> STOBER: Why do you put it like that?
>
> LEAF: Because they used to bother us as children. Well, they were let out with no
> supervisor or one policeman, unarmed policeman, and there were these guys
> wandering around with bush knives.
>
> STOBER: They bothered you. In the sense that you were worried.
>
> LEAF: Yes. We used to keep away from them. Threatened by them, I think you
> felt threatened by them. Yes, because you'd see them come out in the morning,
> and there'd be sort of, probably, five, six of them? All with bush knives, they'd
> be out clearing grass somewhere or something like that, and I think that when
> you're a child you think a prisoner's done something bad.

Was it because he saw himself as more part of a New Hebridean world than
an English one that Edward Leaf found prisoners' presence so immediate and
disturbing? Was it that his own pranks made him feel on the edge of petty crim-
inality himself? Was he aware of his father's legal position and did this heighten
his awareness of crime and its dangerous implications? We have no way of
knowing, and even Edward may no longer be sure. What *is* clear is that this boy
"saw" the prisoners, and they saw him. He saw them in a way that British adults
and other children uniformly did not, perhaps because they could not bring
themselves to look. What he saw were adult Melanesian men, many guilty of
some "bad" and often violent deed. He saw them walking virtually at liberty inside the inner sanctum of colonial space, the British Paddock. He saw them carrying large, sharp knives. And he saw them looking at him. The question then
arises: Why weren't the others afraid?

The Lack of Fear

The answer to why prisoners were not scary to anyone but Edward, I conclude,
is fourfold: (1) others did not want to, or could not, see what Edward saw; (2)

they could not afford to; (3) they did not have to; and (4) prisoners did not want them to. "The New Hebrideans weren't sort of really prisoners, were they?" observed a former British district agent who had served in many parts of the group. "In Vila there was a semblance of sort of a prison regime, but on the islands, they were just—the lads would cut the grass, and they became members of the family."[39] Paternalism was a comforting position, and perhaps it was the only viable one for the British to adopt. The colonial government could not financially afford anxiety about the presence of prisoners cutting grass around officers' houses. As we have seen, unpaid prison labor was integral to the colonial project of creating and maintaining spatial order and sanitation.

Ultimately, the irony is that prisoners, whether convicted or detained, guilty or innocent, were essential to the physical creation and maintenance of the order that the British worried they might not achieve without them. Not only could the British not afford financially to change the practice of using prison labor, they could not afford it symbolically. The oxymorons of the gentle murderer, the prisoner with the bush knife, the colonial officer armed with only a pencil, and the guilty man who did not know why he committed his crime provided discursive spaces for laughter, for discounting danger, for relieving anxiety. In this sense, prisoners stood comfortingly between the British and their fear of disorder.

This may explain why it was important that prisoners not be seen as scary, but it does not explain why the British so readily accepted the idea. After all, Jacomb, armed with plenty of bravura despite his "only weapon being a pencil," does not report that he was really afraid of Berk and his fellow villagers back in 1908, before there was any British prison or prison labor. There were, I conclude, two additional and equally crucial elements in this colonial equation of docility with armed prisoners. The first has to do with the belief system of British colonial culture. The second concerns the agency of New Hebrideans.

While British officers, their wives, and children no doubt all had individual views on how safe they really were around prisoners, there was a consensus of belief expressed in the material on which this study has drawn. That consensus assumes that those resident in the New Hebrides mutually constructed a number of relatively separate worlds. There was, of course, the separation between French and British spaces, and the separate worlds of the planters and of the missionaries. There was the world of Vila where the greatest semblance of colonial order was evident in, for example, prison regimes.[40] The British stations on the outer islands, such as Santo where the police switched accommodation with the prisoners, also were spaces of colonial order, maintained through more casual, and often more intimate, relations with prisoners. Then there was "the bush." From the bush came murderers of white settlers. By and large, however, New Hebrideans were seen to be dan-

gerous to each other, not to colonial officers who had few dealings with them except when missionaries, settlers, or the islanders themselves initiated such contact.

British officers tended to believe that New Hebridean "poison," sorcery, and magic could not harm them. One former assistant British district agent posed for me with a sign he had fearlessly removed along with a taboo leaf during conflict with a Santo group in the late 1960s. The obverse of this conviction that they were immune to the magical thinking in New Hebridean spaces made prisoners safe to be around. Men who had committed crimes against customary law, who were detained as exiles for their own safety, and even those who had killed other islanders were no more dangerous to British people in British spaces than were New Hebridean sorcery and taboos. New Hebridean and British colonial spaces were so separate that New Hebridean crimes were not real crimes and prisoners were not real prisoners. So, even armed, they were not scary—unless, like young Edward, you really looked at them.

A close scrutiny of the situation suggests a final point: the viability of British colonial beliefs with regard to prisoners hinged on the complicity of the New Hebrideans themselves. As I have shown, the system of prison labor, and especially of detention, benefited island communities. It appealed to elders trying to maintain order of their own and to young men who were agreeable to leaving the island and working elsewhere, in this case prison, for a while. The colonial practice of recruiting prison labor would have been jeopardized if islanders had acknowledged the distinction between detainees and convicts, to which Joy pointed in 1935, and if they then had objected to detention without trial. Further, if prisoners had failed to comply with the British stereotype of the docile axe murderer, the system could have ended abruptly. That prisoners seemed to perform their roles so well for so long indicates their acceptance of a practice that any one of them could have brought instantly to an end with one swipe of a bush knife at a little English girl.

Ultimately, then, the prisoners created their own gentle image. Their potentiality may have frightened a naughty boy, who saw what they, and he, could be. Joy and his commandant of police, for whom this potentiality went without saying, were wise to be concerned about what the natives would think. What the natives thought was crucial; so was what they did or, rather, did not do. Prisoners did not give British officers cause to reconsider their calm acceptance that incarcerated New Hebridean men were not dangerous. One could understand, describe, and deal with them armed with only a pencil.

■ CHAPTER 5

THE WHITE HOUSE AND THE BRITISH PADDOCK

3 0 July 1993—Independence Day. My daughter Channing at thirteen is the same age as the country of Vanuatu. A few months older actually. She was born in April; Vanuatu became independent on 30 July. Today Channing and I set out with a video camera, like many other tourists. We walk with the crowds into town from the south. It is as if the table has tilted and the entire population has slid into one corner, Independence Park. Smells of baby powder and soap and wood smoke are in the air, smells of clean people and cooking, holiday smells. It is a crowd only by Port Vila standards. Like traffic in what we have come to think of as rush minute rather than rush hour, this is a brief period of intensity in a usually quiet town. The crowd consists almost entirely of ni-Vanuatu families. Bigger children carry smaller children. Teenage boys and girls walk swinging each other's hands—boys with boys, girls with girls, boys watching girls, girls giggling and making eyes at the boys. Men in shorts, flowered shirts, and flip-flops. Women in Mother Hubbard dresses. Like Hawaiian muu-muus, Mother Hubbards were introduced by missionaries to cover up bodies, but ni-Vanuatu women subverted them, adding ruffles that swing with the hips, letting ribbons trail from the sleeves, and appropriating them as the national dress for mothers. There is a contest for the best dress on Independence Day.

Channing and I walk past a lofty thatch and bamboo structure on our right. Known as the Chiefs' Na Gamal, it is a meeting house that honors traditional leaders and provides a place for customary procedure in what used to be Colardeau's plantation and is now nearly "downtown" Port Vila. On our left is the new Parliament, opened a few months earlier. Its red roofs are vaguely Chinese in style, a reminder of the source of aid money that helped finance the complex. This is no stranger, I think, than the British and French architecture so characteristic of the colonial period, which is also a reminder of who paid for what. The parliamentary complex filled in the last fields of a plantation belonging to the Colardeaus, one of Vanuatu's oldest settler families. A fence used to demarcate the boundary and keep Colardeau livestock separate from the horses grazing on the British Paddock. Now there are no livestock left to fence in this urban area. The Paddock referred most generally to the area containing the multipurpose green space of the paddock proper as well as the offices and housing facing that space. The British Paddock now is Independence Park, with Vanuatu government offices in the former British offices and government ministers living with their families in the houses where British officers and their families once lived. The reviewing stand is set up overlooking the cricket pitch. Cricket continues postcolonially as if nothing ever changed. Except today, Independence Day, the Vanuatu Mobile Forces Marching Band will play before the cricket match begins.

The band is loud. We decide to listen to it from the best seats at the back of the house—atop a cliff that has a panoramic view of the Paddock—the site of the former French Residency. We climb fifty meters up a muddy, well-beaten track to the north of the British offices. In 1985, Channing used to run down this trail with her friends to take a shortcut to Vila Central Primary School where she was in class 1. They would wave at the guard outside the big house at the top of the cliff. In those days the big house was home to the president of Vanuatu. Before that it was home to the French resident commissioner. But by 1993 it is in ruins, the roof ripped off by a hurricane, vines growing through the windows like Sleeping Beauty's castle, with graffiti adding a chill to the fairy-tale feeling. We look down at the Independence Day celebrations, imagining the eye that the French resident commissioner could have kept on the English beneath him, as well as on the British resident commissioner's home on Iririki, clearly visible across the "English Channel." We wonder if it is true that one hard-drinking French resident commissioner used to have trouble parking his car at home after parties and from time to time his vehicle had to be towed from its landing spot in the British Paddock.

The view we have of Independence Park, so full of people, with boys in the branches of every flamboyant tree, shows how the picture, and the viewer, have

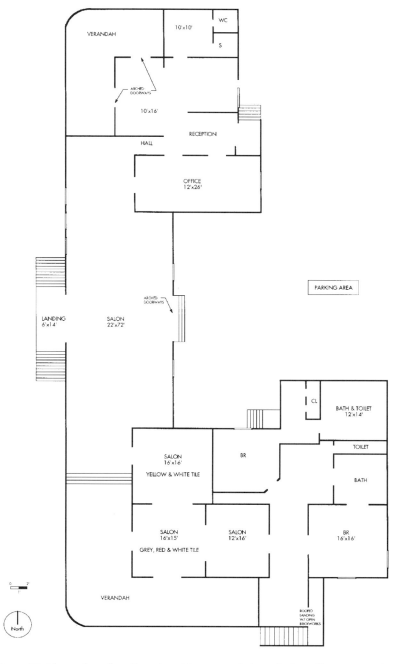

Figure 29. Floor plan of ex–French resident commissioner's, later Vanuatu president's, house. Drawn by Wins Bridgman from author's sketch.

Figure 30. Ex–French resident commissioner's house in ruins, Reece Discombe saluting, 1995. Author's photo.

changed. This is now a ni-Vanuatu place overlaid on British and French places and practices, like parades, marching bands, *petonque,* and cricket. This is exactly what most of the retired British colonial families I interviewed expressly wanted. It is what they had worked for. It is why many of them made a lifetime out of living in houses far from home and why others went on special assignments to the Southwest Pacific.

Memories about the Paddock recounted to me during the research with colonial families who had returned to the United Kingdom ranged from major decisions about the fate of the Condominium to kissing someone else's spouse in the kitchen. The Paddock had become a repository of colonial memories, invisibly compartmentalized according to when they were in the Paddock, where they lived, and with whom their memories were shared. In an almost archaeological sense, I could date when someone had served in the New Hebrides by whether they remembered the British Paddock as a horse pasture, vegetable garden, or golf course. Everyone knew his or her own slice of time and space, with little awareness of the Paddock's significance in other people's memories. For example, everyone living in the Paddock in the 1960s knew certain houses by the names of stations on the London Underground: King's Cross, Swiss Cottage, Parson's Green, Mile End, and Hendon. No one I spoke to who was living in the

Paddock in the 1990s knew any of those names. The ni-Vanuatu elite who were living there just looked at me funny. The London Underground? Here?

Some memories of the Paddock, however, were American, and not all the British knew that either. Some told me that the White House, a notable exception to the London Underground naming principle, was painted white, hence the name. Not so. It was white, all right, but the nickname came from the Yanks.

The New House

In May 1941, the British needed some new housing for an officer, Peter Colley, arriving from the Solomon Islands. British Resident Commissioner Blandy wrote to Burns, Philp in Sydney requesting plans and quotations for "a suitable ready-cut dwelling." This was basically the same kind of request that the first British resident commissioner, Merton King, had made some thirty years earlier, a request that led to the construction of large buildings from precut timbers, including the post office, the Joint Court, and its associated residences. By 1941, there still were housing shortages for government personnel in the New Hebrides. The relatively large numbers of administrative personnel who made up the British, French, and Condominium government were one part of the problem. The general lack of nongovernmental housing stock with even modest amenities was another. The quality and quantity of local building supplies were still very limited. Builders were nearly as scarce in the New Hebrides as they had been in 1910, and most were still notoriously inefficient. In short, very little had changed regarding the provision of housing.

With the war against Germany under way in Europe, it was not exactly business as usual in the Western Pacific territories. But the problems that the war posed for the British resident commissioner at that time were on the same scale as a Welsh coal miners' strike that had impeded progress on the earlier houses: both the strike and the war had meant slower service and higher prices. Burns, Philp's reply to King's inquiry about a ready-cut house noted that timber costs were subject to variation because the Australian price commissioner was reviewing them: "We beg also to point out that the [Australian] Defense Department require the full capacity effort of all such houses, which naturally acts against prompt quotations being received."[1] Nevertheless, Burns, Philp supplied two plans and quotations from George Hudson Pty. Ltd. British Resident Commissioner Blandy opted for the less expensive plan number one. It is not in the archives, but plan number two is there. The main difference between the two plans seems to have been the inclusion of the kitchen within the main house in the

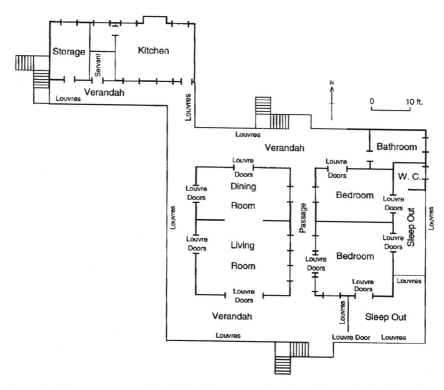

Figure 31. Hudson plan no. 2 for White House. Archival. Carol Randall, Cartographic Office, Department of Geography, York University.

cheaper plan whereas it is a separate structure connected by a verandah in plan two (see figure 31).

The first batch of materials for the new house arrived on 7 November 1941. There was no rush to unpack them, pending the arrival of the rest of the shipment. But by the time the second shipment arrived on 17 December, everything had changed. The war had already been a nuisance and a worry for Blandy; but his problems increased exponentially once the Japanese bombed Pearl Harbor on 7 December 1941. A Japanese invasion now seemed a real threat. Evacuating women and children and mounting a defense effort, including the creation of a New Hebrides Defense Force, assumed top priority for the British and French.[2] It was a month before Blandy even found a moment to write Burns, Philp and acknowledge receipt of the house. Still another month passed before the new British works officer, Mr. Johnson, checked the shipment. By that time, "owing to exposure to the weather, a considerable amount of the fibrous plaster had been

rendered useless." A proper accounting for the house never was made, an irregularity that by itself suggests what unusual times these were.

Approaching an understanding of the effect of World War II on the British administration in the New Hebrides through its effect on colonial space is a bit like focusing on a needle being buried by a haystack. There is so much more to the haystack than its effect on the needle, but for the needle it is a cataclysmic event. In this case, inasmuch as the needle was British colonialism, the effect is well documented, if not all that easy to find.[3]

The first few Americans had arrived on a reconnaissance mission to Efate from New Caledonia on 17 March 1942. The mission followed a meeting of President Roosevelt and the Joint Chiefs of Staff on 5 March. There Admiral King had urged, "Hold Hawaii, support Australia, drive Northward from the New Hebrides."[4] On 4 May, the day the battle of the Coral Sea began against the Japanese in New Guinea and the Solomon Islands, 6,400 additional army and navy troops sailed into Port Vila harbor. At its peak, the American presence on Efate numbered about fifteen thousand. A much larger military presence was established on Santo beginning in August 1942.

Efate became "Rose's Island," or III Island Command. Brig. Gen. William Rose was in charge of a military effort that was almost Condominial in its attempt to forge unity from the diversity of the U.S. Army including the Air Corps, and the U.S. Navy including the Marines. In many ways, the U.S. wartime experiment in joint action worked better than the Condominium. The various administrative units were able to get things done, including some things that the Condominium had never managed to complete. They built the first airfields, bulldozed a road around Efate Island, constructed hospitals, and literally electrified Port Vila, completing a project that had been in the planning stage for years. Lt. Col. Ritchie Garrison, who served on Efate, reflected, "We were not used to working together under an officer from one of the services in charge of a 'joint' force. We were not used to providing Army supplies for the Navy and vice versa. Our methods and administrative procedures were not uniform. Here in the South Pacific there was a quick change in thinking—in a remarkably short time—all of the units were 'pulling together.'" In Garrison's opinion the New Hebrides experience made it possible, indeed "inevitable," to establish the U.S. Defense Department as a umbrella administrative unit for all the armed services after the war.[5]

Why was Rose's Island so much more successful as a joint effort than the Condominium? The answers are not hard to find. Whatever football fans might say, the cultural differences between Army and Navy are much smaller than those among the French, British, and ni-Vanuatu. There was no hybrid body cre-

ated in between the existing military units, in contrast to the Condominium. Not least, the United States had vast amounts of money, technology, and manpower. At Base Buttons on Santo alone the U.S. Navy spent more than $36 million in two years.

The White House and the Americans

The British were having trouble finishing the new ready-cut timber house. A local builder, M. Anger, was hired in January 1942 to assemble the house. By May he was making little progress. A Japanese invasion seemed imminent. The Americans were in a hurry to provide temporary hospital space in anticipation of thousands of wounded as well as to treat soldiers suffering from tropical diseases. The Navy Seabees took over from Anger and completed the new house in only two weeks. It was to serve as one of the temporary hospitals and was called, in honor of its U.S. construction, "the White House." The Seabees followed the basic Hudson plan number two but added many more light fixtures as the house was now to be a hospital.

The White House, along with the Presbyterian church across the street from the British Paddock, served as temporary hospitals to supplement the Presbyterian hospital on Iririki, the French hospital in town, and a temporary hospital in the Joint Court building until the completion of the base hospital at Bellevue, a plantation on a ridge east of Port Vila. In only a week, a coral-surfaced airfield was constructed below Bellevue.[6] (Resurfaced and upgraded, it was still in use in 1995 as the only runway for the international airport.) Once the base hospital opened in September 1942, planes could bring soldiers wounded in the heavy fighting in the Solomons practically to the doorstep of the new medical facility.

Although the White House was not needed for long as a hospital, it remained in the Americans' hands for two years. From the archival record it seems that British Resident Commissioner Blandy talked tough to his own people about how he would refuse to give up property to the Americans, then about how he would reclaim it from them. But face to face with the U.S. military, he was unwilling or unable to stand his ground. For example, the White House was to have provided housing for Peter Colley. He was a "Pacific Man," an administrative officer new to the New Hebrides but with nine years' experience in the Solomon Islands and several years' service prior to that in Fiji. He understood the Americans' need to use "his" house as a temporary hospital but wanted to reclaim it for the British as soon as possible.

In June, a month after the house was completed, Colley sent Blandy a gentle

reminder. "When I first arrived in Vila [in April]," Colley wrote, "you spoke to me on the subject of the new quarters, which you stated that I would be allowed to occupy when finished. Your Honour also spoke on the question of forming a mess, for economic reasons, of British Service officers, using these quarters." Colley and the other officers were keen "to move into the house as soon as it is vacated by the United States medical unit now in possession, and form an Officer's Mess for British Service only."[7] In formal terms, Colley also asked Blandy if he could move the billiard table from the British judge's house, then serving as a club and residence for higher-ranking officers.[8] The point of moving the billiard table, Colley wrote, "would be the formation of a self contained unit, Officers thus being able to obtain relaxation in their own quarters, thus obviating visits to the Club in the town for that purpose." The letter concludes with a rumor, sure to get Blandy's attention, "that the Officers of the US Marines and Army are proposing to take over the house as an Officers Club for their own use when it is no longer needed as a hospital."[9]

Blandy minuted his reply: "I approve in principle, and shall resist the taking over of the new quarters by U.S. I think it is an excellent plan." He questioned Colley about the number of men to be accommodated in the officers' mess and about whether the floor could bear the weight of the billiard table.[10]

When dealing with the Americans, however, Blandy seems not to have pressed for Colley's proposal. Instead, in a meeting with Major Mandl, Blandy emphasized his willingness to cooperate with the Americans. "When the United States forces started coming here we immediately did everything we could to give them what they wanted and we shall continue to. We've already given them every government building it was possible for us to spare."[11]

Mandl's response was to emphasize that "you have subjected yourselves to the protection of the military forces of the United States" and in so doing Blandy had to accept their judgment regarding what additional space might be required for military purposes. It was a military necessity that the United States "continue the occupation of these houses."[12] In a similar vein, Peter Colley reported his "casual conversation" with Lt. Comdr. William Hepburn. Colley asked Hepburn when the White House would be available for the British to use. Hepburn replied that he would not consider vacating the house, which he shared by then with Captain Porter, until the proposed officers' huts for Service Command, headquartered in the White House, were erected on the British Paddock. This, he said, was a low priority.

Hepburn apparently went on to tell Colley that "he was not going to be inconvenienced and that if anyone was it would have to be the civilians. He pointed out that 'there was a war on' and that the forces had, or should have, first

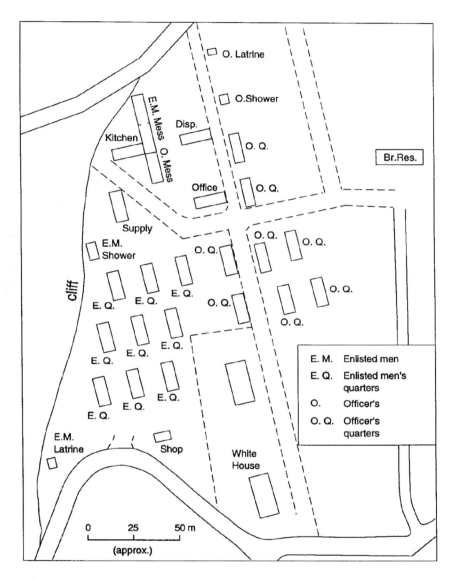

Figure 32. Plan showing U.S. use of British Paddock. NHBS 50/3, 1942.

preference." Colley did not argue, "as it was a matter for Y.H. [Your Honor]." Blandy minuted in return: "We are not in a strong position as there is nothing on paper (I shan't be caught again!) and I have no doubt he could under the circs make a fairly good case. It is no good fighting for the sake of fighting. . . . [W]e must first see if we can make other arrangements." He then laid out plans for doubling up to accommodate the arrival of more British district officers and others from the Solomons. "I should like to 'arrange' matters if possible, as though H [Hepburn] is in many ways an unpleasant fellow, he has been quite obliging in other ways.[13]

Neither Colley nor the British officers ever moved into the White House. Whether the billiard table ever left the British judge's house is unknown, but it is certain that the British judge himself had to move out.[14] Judge Egan moved into the British Residency with British Resident Commissioner Blandy. This proved to be something of a trial for both men. Egan complained frequently about the quality of his accommodation when he lived in the British judge's house. He continued to complain about it in absentia, claiming that the Americans had confiscated or broken a great deal of expensive furniture. By February 1943, Egan was willing to accept any housing at all if he could only move out of the Residency. Blandy urged the French resident commissioner to agree to let Egan take a house soon to be vacated by the Marine Corps and to supply him with furniture.[15] The French resident commissioner agreed, but only if the French judge was treated comparably to the British judge.

The Americans were unwilling to give up any of the buildings they had commandeered, including the White House. By late 1942, they had taken over all usable French, British, Condominium, and mission space in Port Vila. There were tents in the British Paddock, and navy troops camped on Iririki; and yet the United States, with a seemingly insatiable demand for space, needed more. In response to an American notice that additional housing would be required in the near future, Blandy, ever the optimist, minuted that the notice "was meant solely for [FRC] Kuter because he [General Neal Johnson] knew he had *one* empty house near GHQ." It would not apply to the British, Blandy felt sure: "I got the impression that [this notice] will never be acted on—in any case he's not intending to interfere with *us*."[16]

The Paddock

The paddock itself was the public plaza of British colonial space, a place for organized and casual recreation as well as for ceremonial displays of British colo-

nial authority. Houses faced the paddock rather than the sea, turning in toward the green lawn that was the center of British space. Not surprisingly, the British regarded the idea of Americans leasing the paddock with horror, although the troops were welcome to use it as part of a kind of gentlemen's agreement.

When Major Mandl proposed a lease for the paddock in June 1942, Blandy and his staff strongly objected. Blandy penciled "I agree 100%!" next to a minute in which his assistant said, "I am of the opinion that no lease should be entered into. Let them have the use of the paddock for recreation etc. (there is none other available) reserving the right to use the football ground when required."[17] Blandy insists that "a spot of resistance to them . . . will do no harm. . . . Any agreement I make will leave me in full control." Blandy wrote Major Mandl on 25 July: "To save time I will say at once that I will not make a lease."[18] Famous last words. He softened his tone by adding that he would do everything possible to cooperate with the Americans regarding their use of the paddock. He invited Major Mandl to visit him on Iririki Island, where Blandy was immobilized by sciatica, and to discuss the matter over a scotch and soda.

The next thing Blandy knew, he had signed the lease with the Americans that he had insisted he would never sign.[19] Nor was he in full control. A year later, the Americans were so much in charge of what had been British space that they ploughed the paddock to plant a garden. British Residency staff arriving for work were horrified to discover that the paddock was being turned into a garden, and at first assumed the ploughing was a mistake. Blandy met with Captain Riser, who was responsible for the ploughing, only to learn that one of Blandy's own men had authorized Riser to go ahead and make a garden on the paddock. Acting Assistant Resident Commissioner Leembruggen explained what had happened in a handwritten minute to Blandy (see figure 33). Seemingly, Yankee informality clashed with British culture in this exchange. Leembruggen assumed that casual agreement was not authorization, and Riser, given an "OK," climbed on his tractor. (Or, probably, ordered someone else to do so.) Riser's friend, Ritchie Garrison, with whom he had shared a stateroom on the journey from San Francisco, reported that "our gardens provided excellent corn. In fact our corn was so famous that Air Corps C-47 transports would arrive from other islands to get corn."[20]

The Americans vacated the White House on Monday, 28 February 1944. The war effort had wound down gradually on Rose's Island as the Americans shifted their attention to the larger Base Buttons at Santo in 1943. Civilians, including women and children, returning to the islands moved back into the houses the Americans had used. At the end of the war, Blandy was as short of accommodation for British staff as he had been at the beginning. In addition, he had a new problem: accommodating female staff.

THERE HAS EVIDENTLY BEEN some misunderstanding: my recollection of the conversation is as follows: At the White House on the afternoon of the 31st August I happened to be talking to Lieut. Lançon about the supply of empty [44 gallon] drums for the *Santa* [illegible; a ship] when Captain Riser came in. We asked him about the drums and he agreed to supply them. Captain Riser then said he was thinking of starting a garden near the American huts and wondered whether it would be OK. I told him I thought there would be no objection. I cannot recall the exact word used but both his query and my reply were in the nature of casual conversation and I certainly did not gather the impression that Capt. Riser was getting an "authority" from me as A/ARC to go ahead with ploughing and fencing.

Heard nothing further from Capt. Riser regarding the matter and gave it no more attention until the other morning when I was surprised to see the ground being ploughed up.

Figure 33. Leembruggen's defense of the garden. NHBS 52/2, 24 September 1943, ARC Leembruggen to BRC Blandy.

Women in the White House

Before the war, the British Residency had employed only male staff. The Civil List shows a staff of eight officers and three clerks, all male "Europeans," for 1941. By 1950, there were still eight officers but no male clerks. Instead, the wife of the office assistant and three unmarried women were working as temporary clerical assistants, and two native clerks had been hired.

The clerks, George Bule and James Liu, came from Vureas High School on Ambae. They were allegedly told by the Anglican bishop, "Now, you must pack your things, because you have got a very important job to do, you are going down to work for the British resident commissioner. You are going to be part of the British Residency." Their first assignment was to do an inventory of the White House.[21]

From 1945 to 1950, the British Residency employed a series of female, white temporary clerical assistants. Even before Pearl Harbor, male clerical staff were unobtainable in the Colonial Service because of the needs of the war in Europe. But for British Resident Commissioner Blandy to hire female staff, he had to be able to house them, and the old question of "suitable housing" again became an issue (see chapter 2). Female staff could not be expected to share a house with men. As part of his plans to hire two female staff in 1941, the British resident commissioner leased a house called Larba, or Labra, from Burns, Philp and arranged to have it appropriately furnished. In early 1942, the Americans arrived, and Larba was used to house a Lieutenant Bullock and later some American marines. Some of the furniture, including crockery, was removed for "safe-keeping." The British, while pressing Burns, Philp to replace the furniture, kept paying rent of £9 per month for a fully furnished house, which they in turn were renting to the Americans, rather than giving the house back to Burns, Philp and losing control over it for postwar accommodation.

Racial attitudes, as well as gender issues, are evident in correspondence about this house, exacerbating tensions between the British commercial and administrative sectors. From Bullock's departure until the marines' arrival the house apparently was left in the care of a ni-Vanuatu house girl. Stan Jones, the manager of Burns, Philp in Port Vila, expressed shock that there was no "European supervision."

> We are given to understand that this woman made full use of kitchen utensils, etc. and while we did not approve of this, in view of the fact that your administration was renting the house we could voice no objection.
>
> However, it was always understood that the house was to be occupied by Europeans and we would appreciate it, if in future it remains unoccupied, that no native be permitted to live on the premises and have access to household utensils.[22]

The ni-Vanuatu woman's ability to look after the house is not questioned, nor is breakage or misuse of the utensils an issue, although these kinds of doubts about ni-Vanuatu were raised in other contexts.[23] What seems to concern Jones is the polluting of domestic space; the house was explicitly European space, not native space. A ni-Vanuatu woman should never "live" there. While she would normally be allowed in the kitchen, even expected to be there, she should only prepare meals for white residents and should never use the white folks' utensils to prepare food for herself.

It is highly unlikely that Blandy could have reclaimed the house from the United States, but he later insisted as part of an argument with Burns, Philp about the house that Lieutenant Bullock's tenancy was "solely on the condition that he would vacate it when my female staff arrived, or if I required it for other purposes."[24] In June 1943, he renewed his efforts to hire temporary female staff, but the Americans would not give up Larba, and there was nowhere Blandy could have put them. By 1945, the British resident commissioner's needs had increased from two temporary female staff, whom he had never hired, to four. He planned to put two women in Larba and the other two in the White House, where some of the furnishings from Larba had ended up.

There was consternation at the British Residency when Burns, Philp pressed its claims to Larba and took it back in 1945. At first Blandy, as was his wont, just said no. But in the end, as seems so often to have been the case, he lost the battle. All the female temporary staff would have to live in the White House. Moreover, they would have to return the furnishings borrowed from Larba. There had already been considerable turnover among the female staff. The current residents, Miss Daly, Miss Lewis, and Miss Harrison (one other already had left), were

already unhappy about the inadequate furnishings at the White House. Mr. Blackwell, the assistant resident commissioner, had unwisely promised them fully furnished accommodations, so they had brought only their personal effects from Sydney. When they found, for example, only two cups and three saucers in the White House, they felt they were victims of false advertising. All three wrote letters of protest but because, except for Miss Daly, the women had received only oral, not written, assurances of fully furnished accommodation, they were told that they were "in error," and that was the end of the matter.

From the White House to Another World

By the time Kath Pattrick arrived as a temporary clerical assistant in 1946, the quality of life in the White House had improved. "The White House was fully furnished down to linen and china," she writes in her memoirs.[25] Kath had found work with the British Residency through Burns, Philp. Her future husband, Bob Paul, was offered a job running a trade store in the New Hebrides through his brother-in-law, Reg Johnson, who worked in the British Residency.

After their marriage, Bob and Kath Paul planned to establish themselves at Pango Point south of Port Vila. In 1946, the British Residency completed a "beach hut," an indication that, although all but the clerical staff were still male, there was now a need for family recreational facilities beyond the paddock. When Bob and Kath Paul married in November 1947, they were offered the use of the beach hut while Bob built a house behind Pango village. The Pauls felt that British Resident Commissioner Blandy was good to them. He gave Kath away at the wedding, drove the couple to the church in his Daimler, and hosted the wedding reception at the Residency on Iririki.

Although the connections between the Residency and the English-speaking traders and businesspeople were close, they were not always as cordial as the Pauls' relations with Blandy. The exchange of letters over the Burns, Philp house, Larba, suggested some of these tensions. Bob Paul experienced others when the Ambrym volcano erupted in 1951. Peter Colley (the same man who had once hoped to move into the new White House) asked Bob Paul to join in the evacuation effort. Paul took 701 people on board, heavily loading his 120-foot boat at the insistence of the district agents supervising the evacuation, and took them safely to Epi Island. The ship's engine was badly damaged from the volcanic ash, but he was able to limp back to Vila. Paul was shocked that instead of receiving thanks, he was chastised for taking so many people on his boat (see figure 34).

Bob Paul's sister had married a British official, and Kath Paul worked for the

> BOB PAUL: When I tied up in Vila the then British Resident Commissioner came striding down the wharf and I thought he was going to thank me for a job well done. But Flaxman said "Is it true you took 701 people on board?"
>   "That's right," I said.
>   Flaxman roared, "How dare you!"
>   And that was all the thanks I got. I was absolutely staggered! The government had asked me to go because no-one else could, or would, and I'd acted at Ambrym and Epi entirely on instructions from the two District Agents. Yet all I received was a rap over the knuckles. And the government never paid me a penny for the charter.

Figure 34. Bob Paul's reward. Dunn, *Pandemonium or Paradise* (Crawford Press, 1997), 107.

Residency. Even so, the Pauls concluded that the British administrators lived in another world, one with very limited horizons. Their opinion of the British was widely shared. Virtually everyone I spoke with outside administrative circles made a similar point: "Officials inhabited another world. Members of the administration were on a posting to the New Hebrides and rarely became part of the place. For the traders and planters the New Hebrides was home."[26]

Home and Away

Was the New Hebrides "Home" for British officers and their families? Perhaps, as Bob Paul suggests, they did not become "part of the place," but sometimes the place became part of them. The kinds of responses to my question "Where is Home?" ranged in a pattern familiar to people in foreign services, business, or the military who spend their working lives in a series of overseas posts. People got confused: "Was this the New Hebrides, dear?" "Oh, no that was Tanzania!" Or Uganda. Or the Seychelles. Home for career colonial officers and their wives was, in one sense, always England. In another sense, it was wherever they were posted at the time. Lady Patricia Garvey, who was the daughter of a British doctor in Fiji and spent most of her life overseas, retired to Britain with her husband and stayed there after he died. I asked her why she had retired to Britain. At first, I thought she did not answer the question. She told me, "Well, you see, my husband was English, and I was only twenty-one when I married him. I went everywhere with him, so I left [my parents' home in] Fiji almost immediately, really. And, as I say, we were lucky enough to move to the house in the Caribbean as well, in Belize, and so I was very lucky. Very lucky. And I loved them all."[27] Then she told me how hard it was to leave the post in Belize when Garvey was recalled to Fiji. She had set up a soup kitchen and become very friendly with Belizean

> LADY GARVEY: Well, they all were completely different, all the places we went to. And the funny thing was, so many of them were islands. [We went to Africa, but soon it was] "Back to the bloody old coconuts," because we were going to the West Indies. Then when Ronald retired we went to the Isle of Man, which is a tiny little island between England and Ireland. You know, humanity is the same the whole world over, and these darling people would say to me when I was going to make a speech or anything, "Do you like this island?" And I used to say to Ronald when I came home, "I just closed my eyes and I said 'I wonder which island this is.' And then I opened my eyes and said 'I love it.'"

Figure 35. Close Your Eyes and Think of England.

women. The only way to explain the move, she said, was for Garvey to broadcast on the radio that they had to go home to her birthplace, Fiji. On reflection, I think she was saying that she retired to England because she was a loyal wife, used to following her husband anywhere. Home was Fiji, where she had lived until she married. A remarkably adaptable woman, she was happiest living on islands (see figure 35).

Many of the people I interviewed explained that England was Home because they owned a house there, or conversely, that they owned a house there because it was Home. At the same time, everywhere they lived, including the New Hebrides, could be home in a different sense. The presence of a spouse and often children made postings to the New Hebrides by the 1950s at least a temporary home, when contrasted to the bachelor postings more common in the early days. The presence of "one's things," the possessions that made a house a home and that made home to some extent portable, was crucial for some but not others. Some brought oriental carpets from the United Kingdom, others brought artifacts from earlier postings in Africa. Many decorated their houses in the New Hebrides with paintings by local European artists, especially Brett Hilder in the early days, then Ola Reeve, Robert Tatin, and, continuing into the 1990s, the Russian Michoutouchkine. For a few, house and home just were not very important. I visited one woman who held this view, and she seemed to have the same attitude to her place in England. Gardens were another matter. Some who cared deeply for their house in the islands gave up trying to garden there because they couldn't grow anything familiar. Others concentrated on the garden rather than the house, growing bougainvillea, poinsettia, oleander, and numerous varieties of hibiscus.

British Children's Worlds

The climate in Vila agreed with British children. There was little malaria in town, and Port Vila was cooler than any of the postings in the New Hebrides except

Tanna. I interviewed Camilla Turner in London in 1995. She had spent about ten years of her childhood in the New Hebrides. My husband and I had been captivated by Camilla and her two older siblings when we met them in 1970 on Santo, where her father was the British district agent. A family picnic with Chris and Irène Turner convinced us that if we could have children like theirs, then having children was a good idea. The Turner children clearly loved living in the bright freedom of the islands. Camilla grew up to be a barrister, wife, and mother. I stayed in her renovated old house in Holland Park, which made exquisite use of light and space. She remembered her experience of the contrast between Britain and the New Hebrides:

> England for me was really a very unattractive country. Of course England also meant boarding school, and boarding school [meant deprivation] in terms of the quality of life. It was very cold. The food was appalling. We thought everybody in England lived like we did in boarding school, you know, they all ate bread and jam and they were cold. You couldn't have a bath every night or shower, because in those days when I was at boarding school [in the 1970s] you had to rotate, and each child had a bath three nights a week or something like that, and you didn't change your clothes every day. Also, traveling from the school to the New Hebrides, you would arrive at Charing Cross Station, go across grimy London, or go to Victoria, and we really regarded England as absolutely anathema compared to the New Hebrides.[28]

Children seemed to develop deep attachments to the New Hebrides. The islands were a wonderfully free environment for them. They never had to wear heavy clothes, and it was safe to wander, even among the prisoners armed with machetes.[29] Alys Stober, Edward Leaf, Camilla Turner, and others spoke to me of a nostalgia for the places they had lived in Vanuatu. Many of the grown children took a trip back to see their birthplace in the islands or to see where they had played on school holidays.

Paradoxically, though Port Vila was a perfect place to raise children, it was culturally impossible for British children to stay there. To be well-brought-up, they had to be well-educated, and to be well-educated, most thought, they had to leave the New Hebrides after primary school. By the mid-1960s, the British Primary Schools in Vila and Santo provided basic education to expatriate children. These schools did admit some ni-Vanuatu, but only after filling all the places required by expatriate children. Expatriate teachers followed a New Zealand curriculum, making no concessions to the needs of ni-Vanuatu students. The missions continued to provide nearly all of the schooling for islanders, who, like

the expatriate children, had to leave the country for secondary education. English-speaking islanders were sent to schools in Fiji, the Solomons, Norfolk Island, and, less often, New Zealand or Australia. French speakers generally went to Noumea or France. The British children generally went all the way to the United Kingdom. British parents felt that only in Britain could their children be sure of receiving the education that would give them the best chance of success later in life.

The British government became involved in education with the creation of the post of education officer in 1959.[30] Establishment of Kawenu Teachers' Training College was the first project, followed by the British Secondary School (later Malapoa College), which opened in 1966. These schools were explicitly not open to European students. "The aim was to increase the number of secondary educated New Hebrideans, which at the time rarely if ever exceeded six a year, in order to proceed with the localization of posts in the British National Service."[31] So British children continued to make the long journey back and forth to school in England. These journeys were a lark for the children (and a worry for their parents), as they traveled in a group of "unaccompanied minors." I heard tales of smoking cigarettes at the age of eight, of bouncing on the beds in hotels in Fiji and San Francisco. One of the best stories involved the son of a resident commissioner stuffing his British passport down the toilet of the aircraft, and the chaos that ensued.

Despite the hazards, or pleasures, of the journey, British children were dutifully sent Home to school. I was told that the few families who did not follow this practice found that their children suffered scholastically. Camilla's mother, Irène, was born and raised in Goa. She recognized how important the right schools in Britain were to her children's future. We had a few moments together at breakfast before Camilla and the others joined us. The conversation turned to a meeting I had had the day before with a couple who had left the Colonial Service because they wanted their children educated in Britain but did not want to be separated from them.

Irène's comment seemed to me to come out of the blue. "I am not English," she said; "I wanted to be sure my children were raised to be as English as possible."[32] I had first met Irène twenty-five years earlier, and I had never in all that time thought of her as not English—Indian, yes, but always English. She, however, was very conscious of the subtleties of race and culture in the United Kingdom. The girls went to a Catholic convent school in England. From Irène's point of view, going to the right schools was essential to being accepted at Cambridge or Oxford, getting jobs, and settling in England, all of which she wanted very much for her children. (They did not disappoint her.) She told her children as little about her own background as possible. They knew that she looked different, that her parents were Indian as well, and that she cooked different food, but

little more. Now that they are grown and have children of their own, they are curious about her background, and she is willing to tell them more, perhaps because they are now safely English.

The World of British Adults

For the British staff, the New Hebrides had, and had to have, aspects of both home and away. People had to create a separate world, as the American military had done in its turn. There was, however, a fundamental difference. The United States had no colonial project in the New Hebrides. The military forces had come not to stay but to fight, and then go home. For the British and French, the purpose was more complex. The colonial mission involved a commitment to stay in the New Hebrides, among islanders but apart from them, until islanders were prepared for independence through education, such as the British Secondary School and Kawenu College provided, and through work experience in the New Hebrides British Service. Equally important, the British wanted to ensure that the islands' political future would not be a standoff between the British and the French. By the late 1950s, many of the officers posted to the New Hebrides had a sense of purpose, a mission, such as the one John Leaney summarizes in the next chapter on Tanna. The challenge was not so much to bring civilization to savages, a goal similar to the missionaries' message of salvation. Rather, British administrators sought to prepare the ground for independence, partly through institutional development and personnel training, to provide skills deemed to be necessary for self-government. Native clerks were hired, ni-Vanuatu began to be trained as assistants to the district agents, and an advisory council, foreshadowing a parliament, was established in 1957.

Some certainly recognized the insularity of the British administration, not so much with regard to isolation from settlers as from ni-Vanuatu. Keith Woodward, who served in the New Hebrides longer than anyone else in the British Colonial Service, from 1953 to 1978, commented in an interview for this project:

> We in Vila—the expatriate officials of the British Residency, to talk only about my immediate colleagues—lived in a manner which was more or less cut off from the Melanesian people of the islands. Although physically we were only a few kilometers from the nearest villages, we were really, as regards our way of life and lack of any consistent social contacts with Melanesians, quite cut off from the Melanesian population and the way in which they led their daily lives. There is no getting away from that basic fact.[33]

Nevertheless, the Melanesian staff were beginning to live less on the margins, as prisoners and police had, and more in the midst of British colonial space in preparation for an independence that still, by 1960, was a long way away.

New prefabricated Braybrook housing from Australia was constructed in the 1960s to cope with the expansion of British administrative staff. Most of the new housing was on the eastern edge of the Paddock and across the road from the back of the Paddock, in what was known as the Colardeau Estate. It had been part of the Colardeau plantation, from which part of the Paddock also had been carved. The subdivision faced rue Colardeau, which runs south along the crest of a ridge and of houses extended down the far side of that ridge toward Erakor Lagoon. Although some of the houses had a view of the lagoon, most faced the Paddock, which they could not see as it was over the crest of the hill. In effect, what they faced was the road. The new streets in the little housing development were given English names: Cumberland, York, Kent, Gloucester, Edinburgh, and Cornwall. Additional concrete quarters for ni-Vanuatu staff were constructed along rue Colardeau directly opposite some of the expatriate quarters.

The increase in housing did not reduce tensions about accommodations. To the contrary. As elsewhere in the British empire, there was by that time in the New Hebrides an "establishments" officer in charge of British personnel and their conditions of service (pay, leave, etc.), including specifically their housing. Alex Mitchell was a financial secretary who had experience in housing, "wearing various hats" in the Sudan and Solomon Islands before being posted to the New Hebrides. He explained to me that by the early 1960s housing was allocated by a housing committee, composed of both expatriates and local people. I asked if he ever served on that committee. "Not if I could help it." he replied; "I think I did from time to time, but the subject of housing raised so many vexations and so much acrimony."[34]

General Orders, applicable to all British colonies, provided the basic structure of housing allocation in the New Hebrides. Of course, this applied only to British housing. The Condominium and the French each had a totally different system of housing allocation. For example, the Condominium provided "free" housing whereas rent was deducted from the somewhat higher pay of British staff. French housing was based on rank rather than salary. Mitchell explained that for the British there were seven or eight grades of housing: "The grade one house was the sort of thing a resident commissioner had. A grade two house was for the senior officers, grade three was for the general run of the professional and middle ranking, grade four was for more junior expatriates. Grade five was the single officer's house, such as a secretary might have. And grade six was [for] the senior local civil servants."[35]

Although Mitchell described the housing categories in terms of position, actually base salary rather than position determined one's housing grade, with a couple of exceptions. The White House and a newer, large concrete house next to it in the Paddock called Monument were "tied" houses. They were tied to the positions of financial secretary and assistant resident commissioner, respectively. The Residency on Iririki was a grade one house. The White House and Monument were grade two. Most of the rest were grade three, with the prefabricated houses in the new York Road subdivision mostly grade four. The assignment of housing according to basic salary effectively ensured residential racial segregation. This could be maintained only so long as the local ni-Vanuatu officers who were entering the ranks did not reach a basic salary that was the same as that of an entry-level expatriate. The system also ensured that only the new educated elite among ni-Vanuatu would ever become neighbors of their British counterparts.

By the mid-1960s, the British had two housing commissions—one for junior staff and one for senior staff. David Dale, who had been Establishments officer at the time, told me that "the New Hebrideans had their own separate allocation of houses. Allocations were based on points which were given for length of service, seniority, number of children, et cetera. If a chap lived in an out-island he got a considerable number of points. If he lived in Ambrym and was working in Vila, *we* had to accommodate him. He had to have priority." Hardly any Efate islanders had staff quarters; "they lived all about." Only the ones from "outside" had quarters. Doctors were the exception. Assistant medical officers were given quarters because they had to be on call. They had senior-level staff quarters, which, Dale opined, "weren't all that bad. Although they weren't all that brilliant compared to the expatriate housing." Will Stober's rejoinder to Dale was, "So this is where the sort of discriminatory element comes in. A fairly typical British colonial situation."[36]

The persistence of clear distinctions between local and expatriate housing contributed to a lack of socializing between the races. There was, in contrast, plenty of socializing among the expatriate staff within the Paddock. The new houses in the Colardeau Estate were generally considered to be dismally bland. Hannah Dale, David Dale's lively Polish wife, called the subdivision Shepherd's Bush by-the-Sea. The houses were small, with their backs to the view. They were, in a word, boring. George and Kathleen Bristow decided to liven things up. They enlisted their friend, Ola Reeve, an artist and expatriate resident of the New Hebrides, to paint a mural on their living room wall. Ola in turn organized other British friends, George laid on drinks, and the painting session became a New Year's party.

Rosemary Leaf remembered the occasion. She was an active member of the

British community, worked at the British Secondary School, and was proud of the fact that she had trained a girls' relay running team to meet the qualifying time for the Mexican Olympics. Her husband (now deceased) was on the Residency staff, and their son, Edward, whom I also interviewed, grew up in Port Vila. Rosemary told me that the Bristows' house was quite small:

> It was not very well planned, and the main, long wall of the sitting room had absolutely no window on it. It was totally bare. One New Year's Eve—George and Kathy were renowned for their parties anyway—George said, "Look, let's do something with this wall because it's awfully boring!" They had got a copy of *Country Life.* On the cover was a picture of Stourhead, the gardens, you know the famous picture with the lake and the little pavillion in the foreground. So George suggested we could do Stourhead on the wall, and we did. It took all night to do it. It looked absolutely stunning. Ola [Reeve] sketched it all out and we did the whole thing! The only person who wasn't very amused was [British Resident Commissioner] Colin Allan a few weeks later when he found out. We had a complete vista of Stourhead and it looked stunning. It was still there when we left.[37]

Edward Leaf, who had been a child of about eight at the time, remembered how drunk everyone was:

> Yeah, the mural, yeah, that's right. I remember the adults being absolutely legless, truthfully. They painted this mural, it was very good painting, I remember that. [And] I remember [British District Agent] Dick Hutchinson—they had a basset hound called Beastley, and there was a big party, an all-day party, and Dick Hutchinson fell asleep, and everybody decided to make him up with all this makeup. He sat there slumped in this chair, and he'd got these daisies for eyes and this sort of thing, but Beastley the basset hound was still on his lap. It really was quite amusing.[38]

Back to the White House

Throughout the 1950s, the White House was the residence of various high-ranking British officers, generally those in charge of finance. Alex Mitchell drew a plan for me of the White House as it was when he, his wife, and three daughters lived there in the 1960s. To retain the guest room and dining room, which seemed essential for entertaining, they put their three daughters in one bedroom. The three little beds in a row each had a mosquito net suspended above it. By this time

the two bedrooms on the eastern side had been enlarged to enclose what had been the "sleep-out" on the verandah. The Mitchells' photographs give a clear view of the verandah that was relatively unchanged when I took photographs from the same angle in 1995.

The Turners lived in the White House in the 1970s. They were transferred to Efate from Santo, where Chris had been the British district agent and where my husband and I had visited them on a break from fieldwork on Ambae. They were disappointed to find that they had been allocated a modern bungalow in Port Vila. Soon they were able to make an informal exchange with the occupants of the White House, who admired the modern bungalow for its cleanliness. Camilla told me,

> We looked at this large sort of dismal wooden structure and thought this is what we would like. All it needed was a little bit of love and care. It was one of these wooden structures with the solid hurricane shutters, which you used to lift up with poles. They had very short poles, so the whole house was very dark and dingy. So Daddy got Public Works to make [the poles] an extra four feet long. That would pull the shutters up away from the house, all the light came in, and we also took the mosquito netting [window screens] down as well because we took the view that it made the house so dark.[39]

Some aspects of the house just could not be improved. It was not clear whether the U.S. Navy or the British resident commissioner was to blame, but the house, like so many others including the British Residency, turned its back on the view. One could catch a glimpse of the sea from only one window, the kitchen.

Chris Turner told me in 1995 that he thought the house walls were made of some sort of compressed sugarcane. It was probably just as well that neither he nor I knew at that time that the materials delivered from Sydney to build the house included fibrous asbestos to cover the walls. Much of the asbestos plaster spoiled on the dock, so perhaps sugarcane was part of the mix in the end. At any rate, it was easy to renovate. The Turners told me they removed some walls, but the floor plan in 1995 was very similar to the one that Alex Mitchell drew for me. Although the rooms were the same, the uses of the space were somewhat different; the dining room, guest room, and second sitting room had been turned into bedrooms.

Plus Ça Change

I visited the White House in August 1995, fifty years almost to the day from the Japanese surrender that ended World War II in the Pacific. By 1995, the White

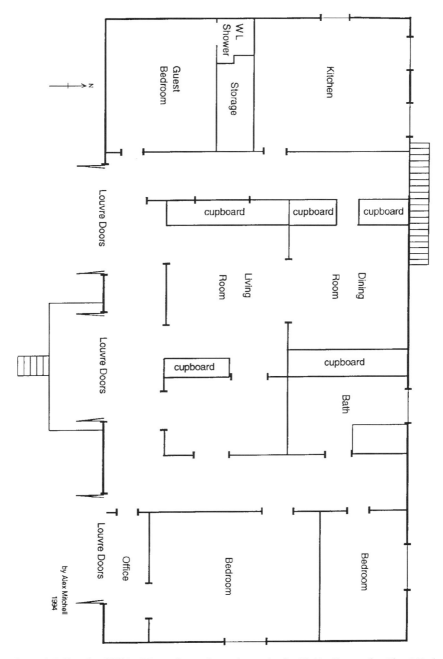

Figure 36. Sketch of White House floor plan as it was in the 1960s. Drawn by Alex Mitchell, 1994, with permission. Carol Randall, Cartographic Office, Department of Geography, York University.

Figure 37. Entrance to White House, 1995. Author's photo.

House was home to the ni-Vanuatu minister of transportation and his family. Regine Battick, my counterpart from the Vanuatu Cultural Centre, and I paid a visit there to list the building as a historic site in the registry we compiled as part of my service to the country, a quid pro quo for issuing me a research visa. We glided up a long, covered flight of shallow terracotta tile steps, a bridge really, reaching from an embankment across to the raised main floor of the house. Regine knocked on the door. After a pause and the sound of bare feet walking across tile floors, the door opened. A ni-Vanuatu house girl greeted us. Regine explained our business and the house girl let us in. She showed us the living room (with two television sets), verandah, and dining room. She told us that there were five bedrooms, two showers, two toilets, and two sitting rooms including the verandah. We entered the kitchen to find a surprised-looking lady of the house, the wife of the minister of transportation. I explained why we were there and the woman, still looking somewhat shocked at the intrusion, agreed that, yes, it was an old building but they found it liveable. She and her husband had added an outdoor earth oven for traditional cooking with hot stones.

She was the most recent link in a long chain of administrators and their wives. They came from somewhere else, another island, one near or far. They made the houses in the British Paddock feel more or less like home by changing this or adding that. For the minister of transportation and his wife, their colonial

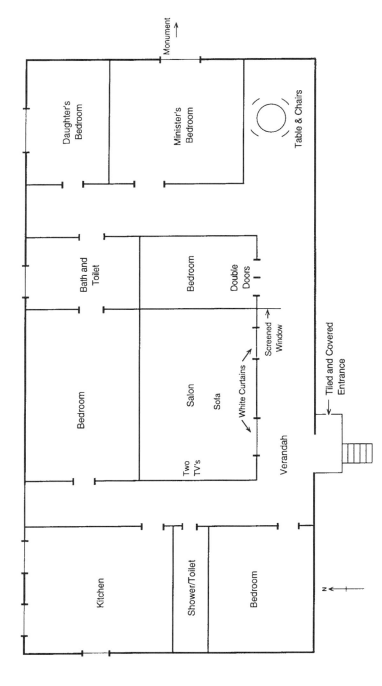

Figure 38. Author's sketch of White House floor plan, 1995. Carol Randall, Cartographic Office, Department of Geography, York University.

predecessors, the American military, and even the American president and first lady who live in the real thing, the White House could not be home. The White House in the British Paddock could be reasonably comfortable, prestigious housing in a place where such housing was, and still is, in short supply. But it would always be a house far from home, except for some of the children for whom it remains, in memory, a home far away.

THE TANNA HOUSE

In Tanna, all stories start with rumors and end as myths.

The bloodstains on the floor were a worry. Everyone I interviewed about the Tanna district agent's house spoke of them. Allegedly, the blood of a young British district agent, Basil Neven-Spence, stained the floor when he committed suicide in 1948. He was not the only one who lived in the house to die tragically. Another British district agent had been run over and killed by his own driverless jeep in 1944. In 1970, the wife of a British district agent died in the bath of asphyxiation from a gas water heater. The blood stains testified to the "heaviness" of a place that some found too much to bear.

The old wooden district agent's house on Tanna is no longer there but the ghosts probably are. The roof blew away literally over the heads of John Wilson and his family in hurricane Carlotta in 1972.[1] Damaged beyond repair, the house was replaced with a Japanese-designed prefab that was used by subsequent British district agents' families and is now occupied by the head of the TAFEA area government, who says he sometimes hears an uncanny knocking on the door in the middle of the night.[2]

Memories of Tanna were some of the most emotional that I encountered in my research. No one remembered it as a neutral place, the way Port Vila could be for many British families. Houses in Vila were remembered as just houses; there was nothing remarkable about most of them. Tanna was different, and

people gave particular significance to their time there. Some loved it, even the spookiness of it; others found the island oppressive and the house depressing. The Tanna house told multiple and sometimes contradictory tales. Stories of the house, told through archives and memories, reveal the changing spaces of *kastom,* of Presbyterianism and Catholicism, and of the British and French agents of the Condominium. These stories point to how different life was for expatriates as well as islanders outside Port Vila.

Descriptions of the Tanna house told me a great deal about people's degrees of comfort and control in shaping a colonial space that was more precarious than most in the New Hebrides. Tanna was the easiest post in the group in terms of climate, and probably the hardest in every other way. Some Tannese at certain times saw the government variously as their salvation or their archenemy. At other times and in other parts of Tanna the Presbyterian church was alternately loved and loathed, appropriated and rejected. A complicating factor was the rise by 1940 of what is often called a "cargo cult" based on the mysterious figure of John Frum and the conviction that American knowledge and wealth were on their way to Tanna.

The fragments of memory and records about the Tanna house, from its construction in 1925 to its stormy end in 1972, confirm an ironic adage: "Haunted places are the ones people can live in."[3] They are peopled places, ones that evoke memories of what used to be there, or used to happen there. "What can be seen designates what is no longer there" when it comes to many places in Vanuatu including Tanna. My family joined me for a visit to Tanna in July and August 1995. We found that the offices of the French and British District Agencies had been replaced, although a huge banyan tree mentioned in early documents was still there. The hospital at Lenakel was no longer the old wooden one, and only cement foundations remained where the missionary's house had stood. I poked about in the underbrush with our guide, deciphering inscriptions on tombstones from the 1930s.

Time travel still seemed possible when I glimpsed the old Presbyterian church in a nearby hollow. I had seen a drawing of this very church in a catalogue of buildings that could be ordered from Sydney in the 1920s and 1930s, complete with wooden buttresses. The cross-shaped layout and a few stained-glass, arched windows reinforced the building's identity as unmistakably a church. The cool shade of this large building was a welcome contrast to the hot sun on that Independence Day, 30 July 1995. My family lingered there, my daughter and sister-in-law sketching, my husband and son chatting quietly in one corner. I moved about taking photographs, entranced by the exterior wooden buttresses and, from the inside, by the way the pale wooden doors framed green views. It was easy to imagine the patience and conviction of those who structured this space.

PREPARATION OF TIMBERS. The frame and roof timbers are cut, tenoned, morticed, fitted, and marked ready for erection. Floorings, weatherboards, linings, etc., are not cut, but sufficient is sent to complete the building, ample allowance being made for lap and unavoidable waste in cutting.

JOINERY. On all these Island buildings the doors, windows, fly screens, etc., are fitted and hinged to the frames with suitable hardware, all parts are then numbered, taken apart if necessary, and securely packed to withstand rough handling in transit.

Figure 39. Excerpt from Saxton Island Homes Catalogue (circa 1938). Enclosed in NHBS 291 1938).

The church, like so many other buildings in the New Hebrides in the 1920s and 1930s, including the Tanna British district agent's house, was sent as a pre-cut kit from Sydney. This church was the top-of-the-line model, called Peter in the catalogue for Saxton Island Homes. Other, more modest, church models were Paul and Manna, which I found examples of in Santo and Malakula.

Saxton claimed to have supplied everything from boat sheds to bandstands for people in the islands. In addition to churches, the company sold bungalows, cottages, official residences, barracks, hospitals, schools, and more. All of these standard buildings could be modified to suit the owner's needs. Moreover, all were supposed to be easy to construct without benefit of skilled labor or technical advice. The catalogue (see figure 39) promised that "complete plans, specifications and instructions" were included with each building ordered.

Figure 40. Tanna church. Author's photo.

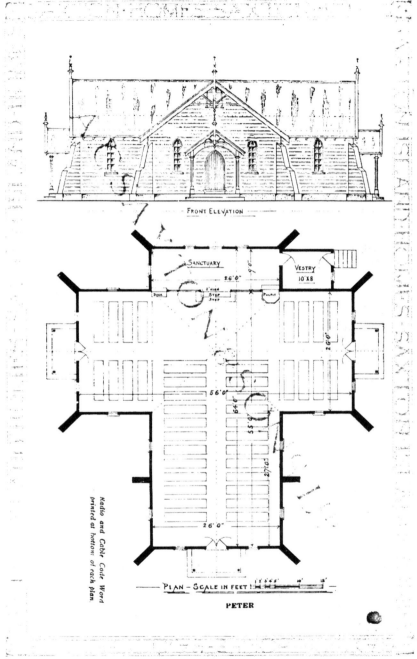

Figure 41. Design of church from Saxton catalog (circa 1938). Enclosed in NHBS 291
1938.

The company prided itself that "[o]ur long experience in supplying clients overseas enables us to thoroughly understand the particular needs of Island traders, missionaries, and residents." This would have been a remarkable accomplishment, for island traders, missionaries, and residents often did not understand each other.

Settlement and Space

By the late 1860s, one trader, Ross Lewin, had settled on Tanna, where he planted cotton, corn, and coconuts on nearly two hundred acres purchased from the islanders at Lenakel.[4] Other planters and traders settled near White Sands. Lewin's "coral stone house overlooking Lenakel Bay was guarded by dogs; his dutiful employees were recruited on other islands so they would not think of leaving." At first the Tannese were tolerant, but soon they became disenchanted with the "white kings." Lewin, who was notorious for his violent treatment of islanders, lived and died by the sword, or rather the gun. In 1874, a Tannese warrior killed the planter when Lewin was having a siesta under the verandah of his house. The murder was in retaliation for Lewin's having shot a Tannese who he thought had stolen bananas. The British investigated but concluded that Lewin had deserved his fate, and no reprisals were made against the Tannese. By the following year, no whites remained in the area. The French cultural geographer Joël Bonnemaison, who wrote extensively about Tannese *enracinement,* or rootedness, described the ephemeral quality of white settlement on the west coast. In a translation of Bonnemaison's romantic French: "The horses of White Grass have multiplied into wild herds since they were introduced by the English; there are also some abandoned cotton plants, and a few memories that the Tannese did not care to turn into myths, so insignificant was this episode in their eyes."[5]

The early years were also grim for the fundamentalist Scots Presbyterians who struggled to establish space for themselves on Tanna. By 1859 there were no converts on Tanna, despite hard-won success on the smaller, neighboring island of Aneityum. Then, when a measles epidemic struck Aneityum in 1860, spreading to Tanna and Erromango, converts died, and the unconverted, blaming the whites for the disease, killed the missionaries or drove them out. Presbyterian missionary John Paton fled Port Resolution on Tanna, fearing he would be killed by islanders. He came back with guns blazing in 1865. To get even with the pagan majority that had forced him to leave, Paton returned on the British navy warship HMS *Curaçoa*. The ship fired on the bay, then landed 170 British soldiers who pillaged the area, setting fire to villages, canoes, and cash crops.

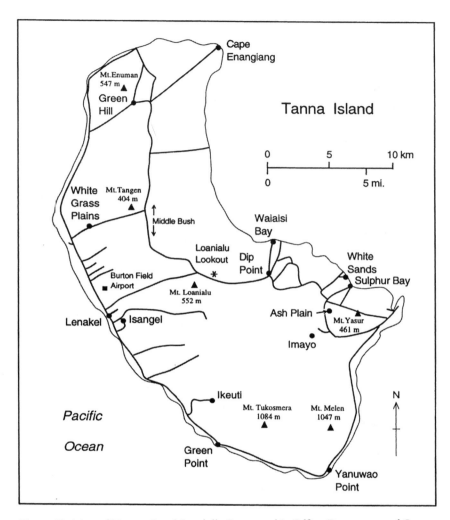

Figure 42. Map of Tanna. Carol Randall, Cartographic Office, Department of Geography, York University.

This episode was heavily criticized in the Australian press. Laying siege to a place because its residents would not convert to Christianity was a rare and unpopular occurrence by that time. Not surprisingly, Paton avoided Tanna, settling on the more tranquil island of Aniwa, known today for its delicious mandarin oranges. Although the Tannese were awed by the firepower of the *Curaçoa*, the experience reinforced their opposition to missionization. Other missionaries did

settle on Tanna but converted virtually no one until late in the century. A measure of the difficulties they encountered was that the missionary Neilson was unable even to build a house at first because the islanders threw the precut wooden beams and boards into the sea as fast as they could be off-loaded from the ship.[6] Meanwhile, Paton went on to make a great deal of money for the Presbyterian cause through his publications and fund-raising. This gave the mission, by 1890, an "air of opulence that could not fail to impress converts."[7]

The Presbyterians sought to reorganize islanders' social and physical space, as well as to change their spiritual beliefs. "Houses with walls, carefully aligned, replaced customary wall-less women's houses and menstrual huts and also men's kava houses."[8] Converts lived in houses on or near the mission station, attended school and church, their days structured by the ringing of a bell.

In the next few years, many Tannese at last began to convert to Presbyterianism. Large Christian settlements developed at Sydney (Isini) near Lenakel on the west coast and at Waisisi and White Sands in the east; the Tannese population that continued to live inland became labeled "pagans." The missionaries deputized local converts as "chiefs"; these men soon became political leaders on an unprecedented scale. They imposed "Tanna law," the eradication of *kastom* in favor of Presbyterianism enforced through the establishment of local courts and police.

Bonnemaison believed that this "wrong move" by the missionaries transformed resistance from a religious into a political domain and that it led inevitably to a "reaction of rejection" by those who had joined the church as well as those who had stayed outside it.[9] At first, however, there was little opposition to Tanna law. On Tanna, as elsewhere in the New Hebrides, people were fed up with warfare, which had escalated and grown more lethal with the increasing availability of guns.[10] Missionization at least promised peace, and islanders found peace very appealing by the turn of the century. Nearly two-thirds of the population of Tanna converted soon after 1890.

Kapman I Kam: The Arrival of the Government

Saxton and Company, purveyors of precut housing, may have understood its diverse clientele, but there was little understanding among islanders, traders, missionaries, and resident government officials. This lack of understanding was apparent when the very first Condominium agent, an Englishman named Wilkes, was appointed to serve on Tanna in 1912. He took issue with the Presbyterians' methods of evangelism. Tanna law, he said, was not a legal manifestation of the Condominium. The missionary doctor, Nicholson, was illegally imposing fines and jail

sentences. Worse, Dr. Nicholson had taken to shooting at recruiting vessels to enforce his prohibition on islanders leaving Tanna to work on plantations. The recruiting ships were mainly French, and there were no French residents at the time on Tanna, a condition that only aggravated matters. A great deal of antagonism existed by this time between Presbyterians and the community of *colons*, Francophone settlers, elsewhere in the New Hebrides. One publication of this community, the *Néo-Hébridais* newspaper, called Nicholson a "religious charlatan," "dishonest business man," and "the worst enemy the settler could ever have."[11]

Condominium Agent Wilkes was on the scene when the French warship *Kersaint* called at Tanna in November 1912. Nicholson terrified his flock of missionized Tannese, shouting that "the devil" was about to arrive in the guise of the French navy. The converts fled into the bush. The pagans, on the other hand, regarded the French as a possible resource in countering Tanna law. They came down near the shore, enthusiastically dancing and chanting a welcome. Condominium Agent Wilkes tried in vain to mediate between the missionary and the French visitors. Dr. Nicholson flatly refused to allow the French sailors to cross his land, which was the only way they could reach the dancing islanders who wanted to welcome them. Mounted on his horse and waving his gun, Nicholson must have been quite a sight. He threatened to put a bullet in the head of the first French sailor to enter his property.[12] The French commander backed off, but not before freeing Nicholson's prisoners and leaving a letter of support for *kastom* dancing and plantation labor. In recounting the story of Nicholson's intransigence, Bonnemaison noted: "A distinctive phenomenon associated with Tanna was already present, namely, that whites staying on the island for too long become somewhat deranged."[13] There was, as we shall see, a good bit of truth to this statement.

Condominium law had to challenge Tanna law for the joint administration, through its single agent on Tanna, to establish its authority. In 1913, Wilkes banned the Christian courts that imposed Tanna law, replacing them with native courts. Only he, the Condominium agent, could impose fines or jail sentences. Wilkes was convinced that the Presbyterians' efforts to extinguish *kastom* were purely political and that there was nothing wrong with dancing and kava drinking. By 1914, he had obtained a joint letter from the British and French resident commissioners allowing islanders to resume these *kastom* activities. But in 1915, Wilkes was recalled from his post in Tanna. The British resident commissioner, Merton King, had given in to pressure from the Presbyterian church to have Wilkes removed. Disgusted, Wilkes left the New Hebrides, never to return, and became an officer in Europe during World War I.[14] Dr. Nicholson left the following year, also to participate in the military.

Wilkes (initials unknown)	Condominium Agent	1912–1915
James Nicol	Condominium Agent	1916–1922
James Nicol	British District Agent	1922–1944
Gordon White	British District Agent	1945–1946
Basil Neven-Spence	British District Agent	1947–1948
Len Barrow	British District Agent	1948–1950
George Bristow	British District Agent	1951–1953
Mike Townsend	British District Agent	1953–1954
Michael Challons	British District Agent	1954–1955
Richard Angeloni	British District Agent	1955–1956
Michael Challons	British District Agent	1956–1958
Darvall Wilkins	British District Agent	1958–1962
Bruce McCaig	British District Agent	1962–1962
C. L. J. Leaney	British District Agent	1962–1964
H. G. Wallington	British District Agent	1964–1966
David Dale	British District Agent	1966–1966
H. G. Wallington	British District Agent	1966–1970
Gordon Norris	British District Agent	1970–1971
John A. S. Wilson	British District Agent	1971–1972
Gordon Norris	British District Agent	1972–1974
David Browning	British District Agent	1974–1975
W. E. Stober	British District Agent	1975–1976
Gordon Norris	British District Agent	1976–1977
David Browning	British District Agent	1977–1977
R. C. Wilson	British District Agent	1977–1978
Job Dalesa	British District Agent	1978–1979

This list is partial as it includes only some of those who served as relief appointments for district agents on leave (e.g., Dale and Stober).

Figure 43. British district agents on Tanna.

White Sands

The replacement for Wilkes would spend the rest of his life, nearly thirty years, on Tanna. James Marshel Nicol (1881–1944) was of Scots background like many of the Presbyterian missionaries with whom he had to deal. For his entire time on Tanna, Nicol would be the only full-time Condominium agent; the first French district agent did not make an appearance until 1926, and then only briefly.[15] The subsequent French agent, Dr. Legrosdidier, served simultaneously as a resident doctor and insisted that he would not be involved in politics.

Nicol was a practical man whose prior experience with the Condominium had been as engineer on *Euphrosyne,* the resident commissioner's steam yacht. He was considerably more sympathetic to the Presbyterian cause on Tanna than his predecessor, Wilkes, had been, but Nicol did not wholly support Tanna law. He insisted that courts, fines, and jail sentences were the prerogative of the Condominium. Yet he ordered that all of the numerous magical stones on Tanna be cast into the sea, a requirement that helped the Presbyterians in their (ultimately unsuccessful) fight to extinguish *kastom.*

When Nicol arrived on Tanna in 1916, he established himself, as Wilkes had done, at White Sands. This was a British bastion, using English pounds as currency and English as the language of education. There was strong anti-French feeling at this time on Tanna, to which both the Presbyterians and traders contributed. The French stronghold was farther north in the islands. The French in New Caledonia were particularly eager to establish a foothold in Tanna, as the southern islands were the closest to them. It is easy to detect an unspoken determination to deter the French from this goal between the lines of British archival correspondence with regard to relocating the government agency.

The prosperity of White Sands, where missionaries, converts, and traders gathered, posed a threat to government space. On 20 December 1922, Mr. Shrubsole, then owner of the land on which the government buildings sat, gave notice that he was terminating the Condominium's lease: "White Sands has become such an important centre of late that I find the drift of trade all tends to that centre and my own trading station [at Loelakas] is no longer within the best commercial area." Shrubsole added that he had tried to buy another piece of land for himself at White Sands, but the natives "appear to have adopted a policy of 'no further land for the white' so the only alternative was to resume my own piece."[16]

Not only was the lease up, the British government had concluded, perhaps as sour grapes, that the site at White Sands was not a good one anyway. It was too close to Tanna's active volcano, which emitted corrosive and dangerous ash with annoying frequency. The British debated moving Nicol's house to a new site but concluded it was not worth the expense. They would sell the existing buildings to Shrubsole and build a new house for Nicol once a site was selected.[17]

In October 1923, Shrubsole wrote to British Resident Commissioner King, enclosing his wife's and daughter's passports and asking King to arrange for visas for them to go to Sydney. He also noted that he had heard that the government wanted to retain the agency at White Sands until June 1924. Shrubsole agreed to this extension of time, despite his concern to establish himself at White Sands as soon as possible. It is not surprising that he was accommodating. Not only did Shrubsole need the government's cooperation for such matters as visas to Australia,

it would have been in his best interests to stay on good terms with the British; they shared a common interest (as did the Presbyterians) in keeping the French out of the southern islands: "The French are endeavouring to get a footing at White Sands," Shrubsole concluded, "and I am determined, if possible, to keep them out. This can only be done by us being established on the spot."[18]

Meanwhile, the British found a new site for Nicol. Burns, Philp and Company of Australia had acquired properties on the west coast of Tanna from disaffected British settlers following the killing of Ross Lewin in 1874. In November 1923, Burns, Philp's agent agreed to lease to the Condominium "five or six acres" of land above Lenakel, at a place called Sangalie (later Isangel). The lease would be for thirty years at a rental of £12 a year.[19]

One irony of the Condominium is that the British and French in the New Hebrides had to create an appearance of cooperation for their superiors in the Pacific and in Europe; but the pretense of cooperation often only thinly disguised that they were doing their best to impede each other's actions. The British could not come right out and oppose a French presence on Tanna, but there was a lot of foot dragging. In the 1924 joint estimate for the Condominium budget, 60,000 francs was allocated for construction of quarters for a government agent on Tanna. These quarters were to have been for the new French agent, for whom the French resident commissioner was pushing strongly. He was therefore reluctant to agree to what his British counterpart regarded as "the more urgent work of providing fresh quarters for the Agent already there [i.e., Nicol]."[20]

British Resident Commissioner King retired on 11 July 1924, the day after his seventieth birthday; he had served seventeen years as British resident commissioner, which would prove to be longer than any of his ten successors in that position. During his tenure, there already had been a succession of eight French resident commissioners. King was a hard act to follow, and the new British resident commissioner, Geoffrey Bingham Whistler Smith-Rewse, seemed uncertain how to proceed. French Resident Commissioner Henri d'Arboussier insisted to the new British resident commissioner that he had reached an agreement with King in August 1923 to post a French Condominium agent to Tanna as a counterpart to Nicol and to build houses for each of them on a new site away from White Sands. Smith-Rewse could find no record of such an agreement.[21] Moreover, he was reluctant to go along with the French resident commissioner's plan for Tanna until the French honored their commitments to the Anglo-French Protocol of 1914. The French resident commissioner, however, insisted that this was a separate matter, irrelevant to the matter of placing a French agent on Tanna.

The protocol provided for the formation of administrative districts. The British view was that the French wanted to appoint agents without dealing sys-

tematically with the administration of the islands. "[T]he French government appears to be disinclined to the formation of administrative districts," wrote Smith-Rewse in August 1924.[22] Ultimately there were four districts: Northern District, based on Santo; Central Districts 1 and 2, headquartered on Vila and Malakula respectively; and Southern District, centered on Tanna. But it took a long time to reach an agreement.[23]

Loath to let the French have administrative space on Tanna, the British strongly favored building a new house for Nicol before dealing with the question of accommodating a second, French, district agent. Smith-Rewse acknowledged, however, that "should they [the French] press the matter it would be difficult to refuse. From articles in the New Caledonian press the French appear at present to attach considerable importance to installing themselves in the Southern Islands."[24]

From White Sands to Isangel

The French resident commissioner agreed, albeit reluctantly, to allow the British to go ahead with the construction of Nicol's house at Isangel near Lenakel. In mid-August 1924, Smith-Rewse wrote Burns, Philp and Company in Sydney to ask them to order a house from Saxton and Company. The order was for "one Ready to Erect 3 roomed Weatherboard cottage according to Plan O, 'Saxton Homes' Catalogue 1924, cost £492." The square footage for this house was later estimated at approximately eighteen hundred square feet (including the verandah) with an additional three hundred square feet for the kitchen. A bathroom extension later provided approximately another hundred square feet.[25] A wood stove, three tanks for catching rainwater from the roof, a bathtub and piping, cement for the pilings on which the house would sit, paint, and shelving were also requested from Saxton. The materials were delivered on the ship *Makambo* on its way from Vila back to Sydney.

Smith-Rewse let Burns, Philp know that a second, identical house probably would be required for Tanna in due course.[26] The French, however, wanted a house for their agent built next door to Nicol's, and they wanted it sooner rather than later. Smith-Rewse wrote to the high commissioner to express his anxiety about his own reputation and his uncertainty about how to proceed. The French resident commissioner seemed to have Smith-Rewse on the defensive: Smith-Rewse reported that the French resident commissioner threatened "if I did not in this case honour Mr. King's signature [approving Condominium expenditures for 1924, including the French agent's Tanna house], how could he feel sure that arrangements made for 1925 would not be similarly dishonoured?" The ever-hesitant

Smith-Rewse continued, "I felt uncertain how to act, especially as the French Resident refused to consider the Estimates for 1925, unless the house for the French Agent on Tanna was built this year." Not surprisingly, Smith-Rewse decided that the right thing to do was to give in on the question of the Tanna house. He obtained in exchange his French colleague's promise to proceed, at some unspecified time, with the establishment of administrative districts.[27] This allowed both sides to save face, but there was no disguising that it was a reversal of Smith-Rewse's earlier position and a tactical victory for the French. The house for the French agent was ordered in October through Burns, Philp, but not confirmed at the Sydney end. An anxious, coded telegram to Burns, Philp in mid-November reads in part: "Essential for political reasons that assurance be given that house will be shipped this trip Fullstop. Very important. Telegraph immediately. Rewse."[28]

By late December, materials for both houses had arrived, but construction was not going well. Burns, Philp's shipment was incomplete, with insufficient flooring, floor joists, verandah posts, and so on. Missionized islanders, "school natives," made matters worse for the carpenter, a Mr. McCoy, by "trying to make a lot of trouble on account of the French house." McCoy was probably Stanley McCoy, one of two brothers from Norfolk Island who arrived in the New Hebrides about the time of World War I. They were direct descendants of the *Bounty* mutineers who had sought refuge on Pitcairn Island before being relocated to Norfolk Island in 1856.[29]

One of the missionized natives even volunteered to shoot the French agent upon arrival, if the others thought that was a good idea. In contrast, the "heathen natives" were being helpful to McCoy, carrying timber from the landing place to the Isangel building site under the leadership of "two of their prisoner boys." McCoy told the British resident commissioner that the prisoners "ought to be liberated for their good conduct." The "boy" who was the aspiring assassin, however, was known for sneaking around while McCoy was at work. The carpenter wrote, "I think he ought to be taken to Vila and be punished for an example to the other natives."[30] The ironic inversions of this colonial project are striking. The convert was marked as sneaky and murderous, the real lawbreaker, and a threat to civil society who ought to be imprisoned. The heathen people, on the other hand, were the good guys: forthright and helpful, in jail but law-abiding, and an aid to the colonial project who ought to be freed.

Local opposition to the French agent's house continued. In January 1925, British Resident Commissioner Smith-Rewse traveled to Tanna to see how the houses were progressing. He was surprised, and annoyed, to find the *chancelier* (assistant to the French resident commissioner), M. Allarouse, already there for the same purpose. Smith-Rewse reported his response to this situation in a self-

serving letter to the high commissioner. He invited the *chancelier* and the resident missionary, Mr. MacMillan, to a meeting with "as many natives as possible." At the meeting the British resident commissioner explained "that there was no such thing as a French or British Government in the New Hebrides, but a Joint Condominium Government; and that it was the duty of all to assist the Government representative regardless of nationality. The position was fully understood."[31] By whom? one wonders, as there is no evidence that the French, British, Presbyterian missionaries, "school natives," or "heathen" accepted the fiction that nationality made no difference in the New Hebrides.

French and British District Agencies

Despite all the delays and difficulties, by 1926 the two houses were finished. They stood side by side on a ridge overlooking the sea to the west. A drawing made for me by a later British district agent, David Dale, shows the placement of the two houses. The office between them, which had a French side and an English side, was built after World War II. Nicol moved into his new house at Isangel in May 1926.[32] He complained to the British resident commissioner that he had received no lining for the verandah (to keep it cooler), no verandah blinds, no furniture for the sitting room, no kitchen table or food safe, and, worst of all, no toilet. There was no separate office at this time, and as late as 1944, just before his accidental death, Nicol complained that he still had to use his sitting room as an office.[33]

The first French district agent took up his post adjacent to Nicol. French District Agent Pinot sailed with his wife and two children from Port Vila on the *Makatea* on 18 September 1926, arriving at Isangel three days later. He was supplied with basic furniture, although less than he wanted, and was encouraged not to buy a horse and saddle for shipment to Tanna, but to procure these locally.

The French district agent was unhappy from the moment he and his family arrived on Tanna. He wrote the French resident commissioner the day after his arrival that it was impossible to find a horse to buy. As travel by horseback was the only practical means of transportation, the French district agent immediately rented a horse for two shillings a day. (English money still was the only currency accepted on Tanna.) Pinot wrote, pointedly, that this could have been avoided if the government had agreed to his request to buy a horse before he departed Port Vila. Further, Pinot proclaimed "Ma maison est inhabitable pour ma famille de quatre personnes." The verandah would have to be enclosed as soon as possible to create adequate space for the family. In addition to the horse and materials to

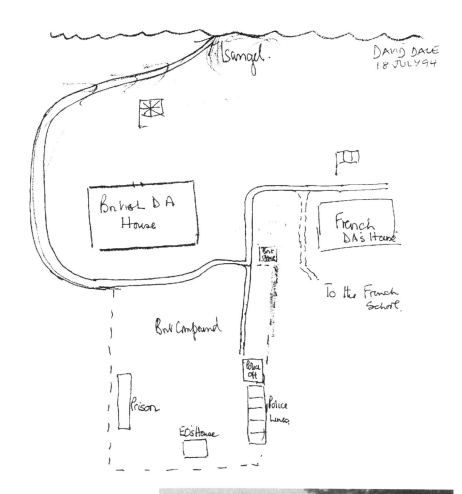

Isangel.

DAVID DALE
18 JULY 94

British D A
House

French
DA's House

Brit
Office

To the French
School.

Brit Compound

Police
Off

Prison

Police
Lines.

EO's House

Figure 44 (above). David Dale's drawing of Tanna BDA/FDA station at Isangel, with permission.

Figure 45 (right). Tanna BDA's house. Photo from George Bristow collection, with permission.

enclose the verandah, Pinot asked, in an unusual gesture of Condominium collegiality, for a typewriter that he could share with Nicol. All were to be sent by the very next boat. (The typewriter sent was, ironically, an English one.)

Pinot and his family lasted less than three months on Tanna before returning to New Caledonia, where he was reintegrated into the Officiers d'Administration des Troupes Coloniales. Although the French resident commissioner wrote optimistically that he expected a replacement for Pinot would soon be found, this did not prove to be the case. The house stood more or less empty for five years. During that time, it was rented for six months to a member of a trader family (N. F. Eedy), and Evelyn Cheesman, a researcher with the Royal Zoological Society, occupied it for a short period in 1930.[34]

In early 1932, the French authorized Dr. Legrosdidier to serve as French district agent on Tanna. He took possession of the French district agent's house, next door to Nicol at Isangel. Although repairs had been made to the French district agent's house before Legrosdidier moved in, the furniture had not received adequate attention. The doctor complained that he and his wife had to share a narrow single bed.

At this time on Tanna, the district agents' biggest problems were with the white settlers. Even Tanna felt the effects of the Great Depression. Nicol wrote British Resident Commissioner Joy describing his difficulties with "impoverished whites" on Tanna. These included the Mr. Shrubsole at White Sands who had once leased his land to the Condominium. Nicol had to respond to a number of complaints about Shrubsole's sexual contact with Tannese boys. In addition, Nicol noted that Shrubsole and others including settlers Suggates and Craig "seem to think they should be given consideration on account of their poverty in their dealings with the natives." There was no market for cattle, the animals had become too numerous, fences were in bad repair, and there was no money to hire labor. Renegade cattle destroying islanders' gardens were "a perpetual source of irritation between them [whites] and the natives who have to pay up in the Native Courts for damage caused by their pigs, horses, or cattle."

Nicol was clearly fed up with his fellow whites, and not the natives at this time, although that would come. He was more than ready for four and a half months of leave, which began about two weeks after he wrote this letter. He went on to list the settlers who were "bumming food and kava from the natives," the ones who had received some money from relatives but would soon be on their "beam ends" once again, and the ones who had a "work is for niggers attitude and we are the elect." He bemoaned the lack of a "self-help spirit" and disliked their "eternal grouch against everyone but themselves." The proximate reason for this tirade was to ask if the natives could have legal recourse so that the poor

whites would have to control their cattle or pay fines. According to an exchange of minuting between the British resident commissioner and the British commandant of the constabulary, E. A. G. Seagoe, there was effectively nothing the natives could do; technically they could "bring a civil action before the British National Court for damages" but this was not a realistic option. Further, Nicol was informed, the district agents had no jurisdiction in the matter.[35]

The John Frum Movement

By 1940, Nicol was much more worried about the islanders' activities than he was about the poor whites. He discovered that for about two years strange things had been happening at Green Point in an isolated area of south Tanna. As men were drinking kava in the evening at a particular dance ground, a stranger would appear. The stranger had light skin, like a mixed European-Melanesian. He wore a jacket with bright buttons and leaned on a glowing cane. A special hut was built for the stranger in which he healed the sick. As his reputation grew, people came from all over Tanna to see him, but the government knew nothing of these appearances until about the time Nicol learned of it in 1940. By then, the stranger was making appearances all over the island. He said his name was John Frum. Like John the Baptist preparing for Jesus, he would prepare the way for the return of Tanna's black god, Karapanemum, and like a broom he would clean the place first. Karapanemum was the god "whom all the missionaries had labeled as their personal enemy and the incarnation of the devil."[36] To ensure his return, the Tannese had to rid the island of European money and of all non-Tannese people, including whites. They had to resume traditional activities that the Presbyterians had banned, such as dancing and kava drinking.

In November 1940, Nicol grew frustrated with the seeming inability of his native assistants to bring back any news from Green Point. He began personally to investigate the movement, which became known as the John Frum cult. He led twenty armed policemen to Green Point, where they arrested eleven people and burned John Frum's hut. By April 1941, the movement had gone public as islanders spent huge amounts of cash in local stores—as much as a thousand pounds sterling in a single day. They stopped working for whites and stopped going to church. "It was as if the Christian people of Tanna, a vast majority until then, had vanished entirely."[37] Even Christianized space reverted to old forms:

Nearly all Presbyterian model villages—carefully laid out around a central lawn where church, school, and bell were in proximity—became empty. More than

any discourse or deliberate stand, the spatial redistribution of the population that followed meant the end of the missionary era. So far as they were able, the Tannese went back to their original territories and waited for John's return.[38]

Nicol was effectively alone in trying to quell the John Frum movement because the part-time French district agent, Dr. Legrosdidier, remained adamantly unpolitical. Nicol called for extra police, repeatedly levied stiff fines, and took prisoners, sending many of them to Port Vila. Although there was by this time a jail on Tanna, it was a grass hut rather than the more secure but more expensive building discussed in archival correspondence. Bonnemaison describes Nicol's responses as ruthless and brutal, but ultimately futile: "What could the district agent do against a revolution of minds that was not attacking him directly but was developing as if he did not exist? Unless he imposed a totalitarian regime . . . and tried to subdue minds, which he was unable to do, Nicol was reduced to watching things slip from his grasp."[39]

As World War II entered the Pacific, Tannese in Port Vila reported that they had learned John Frum's identity. He was American, and the American presence in the New Hebrides beginning in 1942 signaled the millennium for his Tannese followers. The fact that many of the American soldiers were black confirmed the Tannese expectation that they would be part of a new age. The U.S. dollar became the currency of choice on Tanna. Red crosses were erected as symbols of the movement. American flags were flown, as they still are today in some parts of Tanna.

By 1943, John Frum had appeared to a man from north Tanna in a dream. Upon awakening, the man claimed that he had established an alliance with President Roosevelt and that the American arrival was imminent. He organized "police" to clear an airstrip for the American planes, and every night there was dancing in anticipation of this millennial event. The Tannese had resented Nicol's strong stance, but they had not challenged his authority until he sent a patrol to confront the John Frum "police." Nicol telegraphed Port Vila: "I am losing my grip on the situation. Practically the whole of Tanna is siding with [John Frum] supporters. Send one hundred men as soon as possible."[40]

From this point onward, Nicol seemed to question the effectiveness of a policy of repression. The strain of responding to the John Frum movement, coupled with the war and the death of Nicol's wife in 1943, all may have contributed to the accident that ended his life. Or perhaps they had nothing to do with it. His death received the following endnote from Bonnemaison: "James Nicol died alone in December 1944, run over by his jeep on an island trail: the vehicle had started moving by itself while he was closing a cattle fence on a steep hill [crushing him

against the gate]. The Islanders remember Nicol as a controversial figure. Yet they do show some respect for him, to the extent of calling him a 'strong man.'"[41]

Unbearable Verandahs and Other Problems

After Nicol's death, the first full-time French district agent joined a new British district agent on Tanna. The French district agent, Jules Jocteur, was the son of a French settler and had been born at Mele, near Port Vila. His wife, Melvina McCoy, known as Vina, was the daughter of Stanley McCoy, the builder of the district agents' houses on Tanna. They moved into the French district agent's house adjacent to the British district agent's house at Isangel. The new British district agent was Gordon White, who had settled on Tanna earlier and would soon go mad there. Both district agents continued to use the force they felt was necessary to deal with the John Frum movement, to little effect.

The French resident commissioner visited both district agents in June 1945. He reported to the British resident commissioner, Blandy, that the French district agent needed some repairs to his roof and that White wanted his verandah enclosed to a height of several feet to keep out the rain. White wanted a private room for his radio apparatus. The most urgent need, the French district agent felt, was for a ceiling or lining to both verandahs: "generalement, l'apres midi, elles sont pratiquement intenables" (typed on an English typewriter without accents).[42] A typed response from Blandy at the end of his colleague's letter reads: "In entire agreement. I am in favour of a very liberal treatment of isolated officers in the matter of houses and furniture." Despite this sentiment, apparently nothing was done. By January 1946, Blandy blamed the state of disrepair at the Tanna agency on White's "not taking sufficient initiative."[43] At the same time, White complained:

> The heat on the front verandah [facing west] from midday onwards is almost unbearable on account of the unlined galvanised ceiling. For an office I use the front verandah in the mornings but am driven into the sitting room (practically the only other room besides the bedroom) in the afternoons. My Court is a tent which . . . I brought from Sydney.[44]

He called for an inspection and report on housing conditions on Tanna; this time a British official should be sent, White wrote, as the French official who made the previous inspection seemed to have helped only the French district agent. (A seemingly unfair allegation; if anyone dropped the ball, it was more likely Blandy.) White later filed a long list of furniture he felt was essential. When White and his

wife departed to Sydney for leave in July 1946, he suggested they might look for furniture in Australia, but the British resident commissioner did nothing to encourage this idea.

In White's absence, George R. Johnson was posted to Tanna. He had gone to the New Hebrides as a correspondence clerk in 1940. The temporary assignment to Tanna was his first, and probably his only, posting outside Port Vila. He was unhappy about the office that White had made out of the southeast corner of the verandah, the office in which the next regular British district agent, Neven-Spence, would kill himself. White had used "fibrous plaster" for the exterior walls of the office, which Johnson said was completely unsuitable. In any case, Johnson wanted an office that was detached from the house.

Johnson's concern with boundaries between domestic and business affairs seems, from the following, to reflect his anxiety about contamination from Melanesians, which he presented as especially threatening to his wife and baby: "The office is not only an eyesore but an inconvenience as at present my front verandah often has to accommodate a large number of natives in all stages of uncleanliness and disease. I am therefore most desirous of having an office building completed before the arrival of my wife and baby in a few months time."[45] Those few months had passed when Johnson wrote a plaintive letter to Acting British Resident Commissioner Bernard Blackwell, headed "Personal":

> The house, furniture, office etc. are all pretty bad—I hope it won't be too long before the new stuff comes to light. If I am to stay here I should like to apply for new quarters—this place is really hardly worth much attention—facing due west the unceilinged unlouvred front verandah is unbearably hot in the afternoons, and there is no alternative place to disport oneself. However, if the verandah ceiling and louvres are provided (as ordered by White) the place will take on a new aspect. In the meantime I should be grateful if you would give me an indication whether the provision of a new house within the next couple of years would be considered. If so I would go carefully into the matter of site, etc, and put up a suggested plan. I don't know whether you know this house or not but it really only consists of a dining-sitting room combined and a bedroom, plus of course bathroom, kitchen, etc. White made small alterations which improved the place a bit, but it's really too small and poky to do much with. FDA is getting a new place and his house in its present condition is better than mine. However, I don't wish to groan as I like the work here too much to worry about the quarters question.[46]

Will Stober, also an ex–Tanna British district agent, wrote in the margins of Johnson's archived letter, "It will have done him no harm to experience conditions

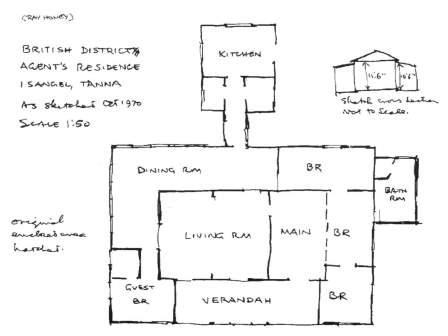

Figure 46. Floor plan of Tanna BDA's house in 1970. Drawn by Ray Honey, 1995, with permission.

familiar to the DAs." However normal the conditions on Tanna might have been to some, as far as Johnson was concerned, the accommodations were horrid.

Johnson's appeal for better housing, even on grounds of keeping up with the French, fell on deaf ears in Port Vila. A separate office was, however, a possibility. Blackwell sent Johnson a telegram asking him to estimate the cost of building one from local stone and lime, with a thatched roof, such as British District Agent Adam was constructing in the Northern District. Having made this estimate (cost: £30), Johnson departed Tanna before Christmas 1946.

From early 1947 until November of the same year, Peter Colley acted as British district agent on Tanna.[47] Colley was a flamboyant Australian who had served in Fiji and the Solomon Islands before being posted to the New Hebrides in 1942. He spent most of his time in Port Vila as commandant of police but was dispatched for short tours as the need arose.

By April 1947, the threat posed by natives on the front verandah was presented as even more dire and sexualized; Acting British Resident Commissioner Blackwell wrote the French resident commissioner that the office in the corner of the verandah was unsuitable because it entailed "having numbers of native visitors

right at the entrance to the only bedroom in the house." This would seem to be the antithesis of McClintock's comment in *Imperial Leather* that "as domestic space became racialized, colonial space became domesticated."[48] Here we find tension between domesticated colonial space (an office on the verandah) and racialized domestic space (natives too near the bedroom) that leads to the relocation of the official colonial space to a separate structure at a "safe distance" from the house.

The detached office of native materials was built under Colley's supervision. He was unable to find any native who was willing to construct the building out of lime as originally planned. Instead, Colley settled for a simpler construction method, one that did not use cement or lime. The cost was between £15 and £20 instead of the estimated £30. Acting British Resident Commissioner Blackwell considered this "a suitable type of construction in view of the advanced state of disrepair of the house itself." In other words, if a European-style house was run-down enough, it could be paired appropriately with native-style accommodations. In addition to the office, Colley was to arrange for a similar house to be built for the native clerk, Oscar Toa Ling. Native-style houses were always deemed suitable for native peoples.[49]

Blood on the Floor

Basil St. Clair Neven-Spence departed Port Vila reluctantly in December 1947 to take up his new post as British district agent on Tanna. He had only recently arrived in the New Hebrides. He had served in the Second World War, and, later, in the Solomon Islands, but was still in the early stages of his career in the Colonial Service, a career for which his father, Sir Basil, had high hopes.

Some background about his father may help to put the story in perspective. Sir Basil Hamilton Hebden Neven-Spence (1888–1974) led a long and distinguished life, much of it overseas. He came from a prominent landowning family in the Shetland Islands. Educated at Edinburgh University, he was seconded to the Egyptian Army during World War I, receiving the Order of the Nile for his service in the Darfur Expedition. After the war, Neven-Spence père organized a campaign, not military but medical this time, against sleeping sickness in the Sudan. With this experience under his belt, he returned to Edinburgh University for an M.D. degree. Later, Neven-Spence had a successful political career, holding his seat as Conservative Member of Parliament for Orkney and Shetland from 1935 to 1950. He married Margaret Mackenzie in 1917. They had two daughters and a son, his namesake, the ill-fated Basil St. Clair Neven-Spence.[49]

On 6 May 1948, the British Residency in Port Vila received word that the young British district agent on Tanna had shot and killed himself in the early

12 May 1948

Dear Mr. Blandy

My wife and I got a most terrible shock when we heard of our son's death, particularly the cause of it. Having survived the war and got into the service he had set his heart on whilst still a boy at Winchester, he seemed to have as bright a future as any youngster of his age could look forward to. He was completely happy in his family life, was heir to the family property in Shetland, and was due to inherit a fortune which would have made him entirely independent and free to enter politics as he hoped to do eventually.

   The last letter we got before we received this grievous news was as cheerful as all his letters have been since the day he arrived in the Western Pacific. There has never been the slightest indication of trouble or worry of any kind. It may be that one or two letters still to come will reveal some recent cause of depression, though I have never known anybody less subject to that affliction.

   To set my mind at rest I hope you will tell me quite frankly about anything that comes to light because we are so completely in the dark at present. I am a member of the medical profession so I can use my discretion in revealing to the family anything you may wish to tell me.

Figure 47. Sir Basil's first letter to BRC Blandy. 12 May 1948, NHBS 4/1/18 1948.

hours of the morning. He had been drinking heavily. His body was found in the enclosed portion of the verandah used previously as the agency office. The blood-stains allegedly could not be removed from the floorboards.

   Upon receiving news of his son's death, Sir Basil wrote to British Resident Commissioner Richard Blandy. A portion of his letter is reproduced in figure 47. The letter goes on to discuss Colonial Office procedure for the Crown Colonies regarding deaths of officers overseas, which Sir Basil thought, incorrectly as it later turned out, did not prevail in the New Hebrides. Only the deceased's papers, photographs, some small china ornaments, binoculars, and a set of table silver marked "M" were to be sent home. Sir Basil expressed concern about a yacht that his son had bought in Sydney for £450 just before "the possibility arose (in November) of his transfer to the New Hebrides." As soon as the young British district agent reached Tanna he could see that the yacht was unsuited for Tanna with its rocky coastline, lack of good harbors near Lenakel, and high seas offshore, unbroken by other islands. He wrote his father that he planned to arrange for the yacht to be sold rather than shipped out to him from Sydney, but Sir Basil was unsure whether the sale had gone through.

   The question of the yacht points to the unusual wealth of young Neven-Spence, and of his family. The cost of the yacht was about two-thirds of the British district agent's annual salary.[50] The purchase also suggests that Neven-Spence expected to have adequate leisure time while in the Colonial Service to spend enjoyable hours on the water. Other district agents sailed small craft, and the low-key Port Vila Yacht Club was an important recreational alternative to the British Ex-

Servicemen's Association. Nevertheless, an expensive yacht suggested a certain life-style and expectations that the realities of Tanna could hardly fail to disappoint.

The night that the news of Neven-Spence's death reached the Residency, the commandant of British police, Peter Colley, sailed for Tanna on the *Concorde*. Having recently served as British district agent on Tanna himself, Colley was fa-miliar with the place, and with the unpleasantness of the sea voyage to reach the southern island. The outbound journey took thirty-six hours because of bad weather and engine breakdowns. The passage home, carrying seventeen cases of the deceased British district agent's belongings, was even worse. The ship left Tanna before midnight, Sunday, 9 May, and finally reached Port Vila at 10:30 A.M. on Tuesday. Colley reported that it was "an appaling trip—a combination of bad weather, mechanical breakdowns, and bad steering by the native crew."

Arriving on the morning of 8 May 1948, Colley went up to the British district agent's house and inspected the situation. He gave orders for Neven-Spence's things to be packed for shipment to Vila, then searched the house for private pa-pers or letters. The native clerk, Oscar Toa Ling, had locked the separate office building. Colley commended him for his "excellent showing . . . in the difficult time following the discovery of the deceased" (actually made by Corporal Jack) as well as in packing up. Colley got the key from Toa Ling and searched the office for "anything that might have a bearing, direct or indirect, on the death of Mr. Neven Spence." He reported finding "some private letters but nothing to aid me in my official enquiry into the death." Perhaps, as we shall see, the private ones would have been the most important. Colley then locked up all the files and the Government Telegraphic Code Book and locked the office. He proceeded to hold his enquiry in the afternoon, hand-delivering his findings to the British resident commissioner upon returning to Vila rather than mentioning them in his official report.

Colley did write that during the afternoon following Neven-Spence's death, the mentally disturbed ex–British District Agent White had

> appeared at the French Agency and ordered the French District Agent to hand over to him the Government Telegraphic Code to prevent it falling into "enemy" hands. M. Jocteur refused to do this as the Book was still in the hands of the Native Clerk locked up in the Agency Office. M. Jocteur sent for Dr. Armstrong, who supported him in his refusal to hand over the book; Mr. White based his claims on the fact that he was an ex–District Agent.

A handwritten minute from British Resident Commissioner Blandy at the bottom of Colley's report says simply, "White is mad." Blandy notes that he will write Jocteur and Armstrong to thank them for dealing with White, as well as with the

funeral for Neven-Spence, which was held at noon on 7 May at Lenakel. Dr. Armstrong, the Presbyterian minister, conducted the ceremony, and "all available Europeans were present."[51] There can't have been many. Jocteur built the coffin. His wife, Vina, prepared the body for burial.

George Bristow, who served as British district agent on Tanna from June 1951 to 1953, wrote to Will Stober that Neven-Spence "left no trace in the New Hebrides or in the Solomon Islands save for the irremovable blood stain on the floor of the District Agency and the pathetic, small, wooden cross in the Mission compound where Bill Armstrong buried him." Saddest of all, Bristow wrote, " I never heard his name mentioned spontaneously." But Vina Jocteur did not forget him. She "had a soft spot for his memory. She spoke to me [Bristow] of his end and it was she who told me how desperate he was at being made to leave Vila, of how he had pleaded with Blandy not to send him to Tanna. He was of course drinking heavily."[52] Corporal Jack, an islander from Santo who had married a Tannese woman, was the one who found the body. He spoke of Neven-Spence's attempts to get him to join in drinking sessions, but Corporal Jack declined, being a staunch Seventh Day Adventist.

Sexual and racial overtones enhanced the mysteriousness of his death for the colonial officers I interviewed, but class and war experiences helped to explain to Sir Basil why his son killed himself. Sir Basil wrote Blandy again on 16 June 1948. He explained that he was answering a sympathy note of Blandy's because his wife was still in shock and unable to deal with correspondence. Completely baffled about the cause of his son's death, and finding that the results of Peter Colley's inquest shed no light on the subject, Sir Basil tried to explain the suicide to himself in medical terms. Perhaps his son's fatal shooting was a response to depression resulting from "damage to his subconscious mind caused by his [World War II] experiences including the death of many friends." As a doctor, Sir Basil had seen similar cases resulting from World War I. To deal with the death of his only son, he turned him into a case. But Sir Basil also blamed himself, and by unspoken implication Blandy, "for not having considered this possibility and settled him where he would have had less chance to brood." After all, Blandy, not Sir Basil, had insisted on the Tanna posting. Yet Sir Basil had counted on the aristocratic blood in his son's veins to give him the sense of superiority that was deemed necessary to carry him through: "I always regarded him as physically and mentally tough enough to rise superior to any circumstances in which he was likely to find himself."[53]

Sir Basil's explanation was conjecture. So was Blandy's, which followed a month later. It is worth noting that Richard Blandy had served in the Indian police from 1911 to 1924 and had been chief of the Tangier International Police before going to the New Hebrides as assistant resident commissioner in 1929. His experience in India may have led him to the conjecture he expressed in his delayed reply

to Sir Basil Neven-Spence's request, in May, for further, frank details about his son's death. After all, as Sir Basil had put it, being a medical doctor, he could take whatever that news might be and he could be trusted to convey it diplomatically to his family in England. So Blandy wrote on 13 July 1948 that the suicide "was, and is, a very sad business and I have been unable to find any explanation which would exactly fit." He continued, nevertheless, offering two tried-and-true explanations for problems in the Colonial Service—drink and a woman:

> However, as you wish me to be quite frank, I fear I must tell you that I have evidence that your son had, for some time, been given to bouts of heavy drinking of hard liquor, both in the Solomons and here. I did not discover this during our very brief acquaintance until his death was being investigated. Whether from this cause or another, I (and other officers) found him somewhat irritable and moody. A possible contributory element was that, shortly before he left for Tanna he fell violently in love with a young Frenchwoman.

So it becomes clear why Neven-Spence might have been, as Vina Jocteur put it, so desperately opposed to Blandy's orders for him to leave Vila. In the short time that Neven-Spence was in Port Vila, awaiting posting to Tanna, he fell "violently in love with a young Frenchwoman" whom Blandy went on to describe in the letter to Sir Basil as parenthetically "(quite bright and attractive but without any particular culture or background)." What did it mean to lack culture or background? Not that she was without culture; her lack was rather one of refinement. She was uncultured. Or did she perhaps partake of another culture, a "particular" one that could not be spoken of? To be without culture or background denied the nameless "young Frenchwoman" a family history, a past, values, taste. It made her if not worthless, at least worth less than the kind of match Neven-Spence would have been expected to make. To make matters worse, Blandy then revealed that when Neven-Spence had met her, the Frenchwoman had been in the process of divorcing her husband. The woman is thus given agency. She is no victim; she is not being divorced, she is divorcing, and this is the kind of action that could lead her to be predatory. Then, in Blandy's letter came the clincher: "This girl and her family are probably not without an admixture of dark blood, and it is possible that your son discovered this after he had asked her to marry him." Blandy went on to say that this was only speculation.

Blandy and Sir Basil agreed that they knew little about what had driven Neven-Spence to commit suicide, but they offered explanations anyway. His death also fascinated the people I interviewed more than forty-five years later. The archival material intersects with memories, and all of these speculations reveal aspects of

the pressures to which district agents were subject, as well as the ways in which race, culture, and sexuality were constructed in different times and places. Stober saw a strong connection between Neven-Spence's suicide and the tragic story of Martin Sharp, a nexus of cultural, racial, gender, and class angst. He copied this story from Anton Gill's book *Ruling Passions* to George Bristow, positing that Martin Sharp and Neven-Spence were cut from the same cloth and made similarly unfortunate romantic choices. The story of Martin Sharp, which Will Stober gave Bristow and me, begins with the arrival of the twenty-four-year-old Englishman in Bombay in 1924. He lived as a boarder in a private home where he fell in love with one of the daughters of the household, a seventeen-year-old named Pauline. The red-haired girl had been born in India, which put her at a social disadvantage, and Martin knew little about her background. They became engaged, but Martin grew suspicious about her motive for agreeing to marry him. Finally, he concluded that she was of part Eurasian blood and that she wanted to marry him to elevate herself to European status. He confronted her father: " 'First of all is there any Eurasian blood in you?' There was a pause of several seconds and therefore I knew they were Eurasian, for if you put that question to an Englishman he would knock you down." (English is equated implicitly with white here.) Her stunned father did then "flare into a rage" and throw Martin out of the house. The father was, after all, part English. But for Martin the jig was up. He returned to England, where he married someone else, and the secret of his relationship with Pauline never came out until Martin's daughters looked through his letters and diaries after his death in 1987.[54]

Bristow was skeptical about the link that Stober made between Martin Sharp in India and the 1948 suicide in the Tanna house. He questioned whether the French woman had any "dark blood" in her; indeed this question also remains regarding Pauline in the Indian story. Bristow's suggestion that Blandy may have had experience in India, which indeed he had, and that this, rather than any information from Port Vila, might have shaped his speculations about the Frenchwoman, certainly seems plausible. Finally, even if the French woman had been of mixed ancestry, Bristow was doubtful that this would have made any difference to Neven-Spence, so madly in love was he with the woman. Bristow and Stober understood Neven-Spence's weakness for the bottle all too well; Bristow felt that depression induced by excessive drinking was the main cause of Neven-Spence's death. This was certainly an occupational hazard, and the isolation of Tanna probably made it worse.

The trader Bob Paul had a different view of Neven-Spence's death. When I queried Bob Paul, through his biographer, Marnie Dunn, about Paul's views on Neven-Spence's death, the reply was that Neven-Spence's death was not suicide.

It was purely accidental. Bob and Kath Paul remembered the young British district agent as "a happy-go-lucky young fellow who loved a party and would never have taken his own life."[55] The Pauls were well aware that Neven-Spence had been "bowled over" by a "very beautiful girlfriend" in Port Vila, but they did not think he would kill himself over the separation from her, as there was some possibility of resuming the relationship once he had served his time on Tanna. Nor did the Pauls find the theory of post–World War II depression convincing. The idiosyncracies of the weapon—an American carbine—that killed Neven-Spence were sufficient explanation for Bob Paul. These guns "were known for their hair-trigger mechanism. If there were bullets in the magazine and Neven-Spence, for example, bumped the gun on the floor, it could have self-loaded and gone off." What's more, neither Bob nor Kath Paul could recall a bloodstain on the agency floor, and they knew the place very well.

House Repairs and "Tonks"

A brief interregnum followed Neven-Spence's death in which Len Barrow (like Will Stober, a Magdalen College, Cambridge, graduate) was acting British district agent on Tanna. Neven-Spence apparently had received £20 to pay for the construction of an appropriately native-style house for his native clerk, Oscar Toa Ling, but the house had not been built, nor had the money been found in Colley's search of the agency following Neven-Spence's death. Barrow organized the construction of this house, as well as repairs to the agency and the relocation of the prison from a site "about a quarter of a mile away down the hill from the Agency proper. It is of course impractical to keep the prisoners there by themselves and they are at present housed in the building which is properly speaking the quarters of the District Agent's servants." Barrow suggested that a new prison be built entirely of native materials—the existing one had cement walls and an iron roof—in the corner of the station near the police barracks. To improve security a barbed wire fenced enclosure was added—quite a change for the prisoners, one imagines, from life in the servants' quarters.[56]

Mrs. Barrow apparently found the Tanna house unbearable and left very shortly. The famously hot verandah still lacked louvers. Barrow asked that glass and metal Cooper louvers be ordered. A thatched extension had been added in an attempt to reduce the solar gain, producing a hybrid European–native-style house. The house also needed water tanks repaired, and it needed painting. Cream-colored paint was ordered for the walls with white for the trim and red oxide for the iron roof. Electricity was being installed, or planned for, in all agencies

that requested it, so Tanna got on the list. The Condominium paid for the wiring and bulbs, but the national governments had to provide generators. In fact, differences between French and English wiring and plumbing were a recurring nightmare in the Condominium.[57]

Barrow was promised a "Tonk" worker, but none could be found in Vila who was willing to go to Tanna. He would have to wait for a Tonkinese named Hoa, who was working on the French district agent's house on Malakula. Hoa would be sent to Tanna to carry out the repairs in early 1949. When Jocteur heard that Barrow's requests for repairs and for a carpenter were quickly granted, he was furious. He had been asking for repairs to the French District Agency on Tanna for years. The house had been in a state of complete abandon when Jocteur took it over, and it had never received the repairs that were urgently required to return it to habitable condition. Jocteur felt that he had been slighted on the basis of nationality. Public Works had repeatedly promised him a carpenter but, Jocteur felt, had never made even a halfhearted effort to make good on that promise. He observed that suddenly, when his British colleague made a request for repairs, Barrow got what he wanted, including a Tonkinese carpenter from Public Works, while such a worker seemed to be impossible to find on behalf of the French agent.

Jocteur noted that he did not especially want a Tonkinese anyway, preferring to hire a particular Melanesian (a Tongoan living on Aniwa) he had in mind. His objection indicated prejudice against all Tonkinese as well as the belief that this particular Mr. Hoa made a practice of illegally selling alcohol to islanders: "Je préfère avoir cet indigene à mon service qu'un tonkinois, qu'il faudra toujours surveiller à cause des histories avec les indigenes, surtout s'il fait comme Hao, vendre de l'alcool aux indigènes."[58] Ironically, Jocteur himself was suspected of selling alcohol to the natives, so his objection to Hoa may have reflected a concern with competition rather than legality. In any case, as no Tonkinese worker in Vila was willing to go to Tanna anyway, it was just as well that Jocteur preferred to hire a Melanesian.

Jocteur left his job as French district agent soon after, running his business as a trader on Tanna and living with his family in a native-style house near Lenakel. He left Tanna in 1951, deciding to go into business full time. He purchased a store from Georges Forestier as well as a plantation at Blacksands outside Port Vila. Presumably some of the many Tannese who make up a large share of Blacksands' population nearly fifty years later came from their home island to work on Jocteur's plantation. Jocteur's replacement, Raymond Demarbre, quickly cut his losses with the derelict French district agent house, arranged for a branch of Public Works to be established on Tanna, and had a new house built for himself and his wife.[59] Demarbre favored a continuation of the policy of repressing the John Frum movement. He soon became well known among the Tannese as a particularly harsh man.

Demons and Gods

George Bristow took over Len Barrow's post as British district agent in June of 1951, the year that Jocteur left. Looking back on his time in Tanna from the viewpoint of retirement in Lincolnshire, Bristow was reluctant in 1995 to provide a written submission for Stober and Woodward's proposed history of British district agents in the New Hebrides. His concerns about the fallibility and selectivity of memory were expressed by others with whom I spoke, as was the conviction that memoirs had to form a coherent whole. Bristow's difficulty with the idea of drawing a circle around his life in the New Hebrides and reproducing it as a narrative is one that many reflective people share, especially given increasing interest in the fragmentary, created, and imaginary qualities of late-twentieth-century selves. The task seemed too daunting. He wrote to Stober:

> There seems to be a mental prohibition to my thought processes which prevents me standing back and considering my years in the Pacific as a self-bounded period in my life, as something to be isolated and syncretized. I couldn't write to any extent unless there was some unity to the whole and I just do not know what the unifying factors would be. Or perhaps I do. My abiding recollection of my time in the Pacific is one of futility—personal and imposed—and that is not a basis for one's memoirs.[60]

Tanna seemed to Bristow an especially futile posting, yet to at least one Tannese he symbolized the hoped for second coming of their god. The unity in British District Agent Bristow's work on Tanna was obvious; he was the son of Noah or John Frum's hidden son and his purpose was nothing short of millennial. In contrast, the Tannese predicted that French District Agent Demarbre would become ill and die, as indeed he did, on Tanna in 1952. Demarbre and Bristow rapidly came to dislike each other. They had entirely different approaches to dealing with the Tannese. The islanders, according to Bonnemaison, "relished any opportunity to exacerbate their ongoing dispute." Demarbre had organized corvée labor to build a road from Lenakel to White Sands. Each subaltern native assessor had to recruit a certain number of Tannese to work on the road. This was a revival of a practice initiated much earlier by the Presbyterians, and the Tannese greatly resented it. Bristow emerged as "a champion of liberalism" when he made Demarbre stop using forced labor.

Meanwhile, John Frum activity was heating up. People began wearing traditional *nesei* leaves on their arms, as for a *kastom* dance. "Jack Navy," the image of a blond English sailor on the Players cigarette box, became an icon of John

Figure 48. Kathleen Bristow playing tennis with B. F. Black-well. Photo from George Bristow collection, with permission.

Frum. Demarbre was very agitated by these happenings but complained that "Mr. Bristow thinks the situation is normal, nothing seems to worry him."[61] Unilaterally, Demarbre began arresting and trying Tannese. Bristow eventually assisted in this attempted suppression of the John Frum movement, but his heart was not in it.

Will Stober and I interviewed George Bristow in his small, modern house in Frampton, a village in the flat, fen lands of Lincolnshire, in April 1995. His old dog, William, was on his last legs, and George said he felt similar. He explained to me why he felt his job on Tanna had been futile. It seemed to him now, and perhaps then as well, that there was nothing he could have done to control the John Frum movement. It was an exercise in futility to try to suppress it; it was equally futile to expect to wait it out. All that Bristow felt he could aspire to was to maintain the status quo and to contain Demarbre's actions, which Bristow felt were based on his French colleague's "loathing" for the Tannese people.

The Phyllida Problem

When the John Frum movement was in an active phase, the Tannese stopped cutting coconuts and making copra (dried coconut for sale).[62] Without cash crops to collect, ships stopped coming to Tanna. Without ships, people on Tanna, such as the British district agent, had to make do without supplies from Vila. Without

supplies from Port Vila, it was very hard to entertain guests. Kathleen Bristow was the first wife of a British district agent to spend most of her husband's tour with him in Tanna, from 1951 to 1953. Apparently Mrs. Nicol had rarely lived on Tanna. There was no Mrs. White. Mrs. Barrow had left quickly. Colley had been only temporarily on Tanna. So Kathleen Bristow, deceased by the time of my research, was, according to her husband, the first wife on Tanna to try to make the British district agent's house a home suitable for entertaining. It was a struggle given the attractiveness of Tanna, particularly the volcano, as a tourist site, on the one hand, and the periodic lack of provisions from Port Vila on the other.

For example, when the British high commissioner, Lord Stanley, came to visit with Lady Stanley and their teenaged daughter, Phyllida, Kathleen wondered how she would ever feed them in the expected style. Even with the friendly assistance of Vina Jocteur, it was a challenge. At the time, the house had no electricity, only cold water from the rainwater cisterns, and an outdoor privy, no toilet. Kathleen filled the little kerosene refrigerator with local fruits and vegetables. One of the good qualities of Tanna, which all the district agents I spoke with remembered, was that because of Tanna's rich volcanic soil and cooler climate, all sorts of vegetables that would grow nowhere else in the New Hebrides—such as asparagus—would grow there.

Phyllida apparently regarded her father's contentment as her main mission on this trip, and, in trying to ensure it, managed to alienate almost everyone she came in contact with. She annoyed Kathleen by immediately demanding that the refrigerator be emptied sufficiently to make room for "Daddy's beer" in anticipation of the midday meal. Daddy fell down the volcano. Mummy had to lick her own cigarettes, rolled for her by a local trader. Remarkably, everyone, of the visitors at least, had a fine time.

A Heavy Place

For the Bristows, however, Tanna was a "heavy place." The district agent's house was physically uncomfortable and spiritually ghost-ridden. Corporal Jack, who had to look after the house during the interregnum, refused to sleep there, or even to check on the place after dark. Later district agents told me that they were unable to get house girls to babysit their children at night in the house. But it was not just the house that had an oppressive atmosphere, as far as the Bristows were concerned. Figure 49 is an excerpt from our 1995 interview.

Bristow suspected that his successors in the Tanna house, Mike and Nan Townsend, also found it initially oppressive; but in my interview with them they

BRISTOW: Tanna was a heavy place, there was something terribly ominous about the place. I don't know what it was. I think among other things it was the fact that you knew there were a lot of people there. . . . On most islands in the New Hebrides, . . . you go outside the village . . . into the bush, and you know that there's no one there, because everyone lives in little coastal villages. . . . Tanna was different. There were seven or eight thousand people living on Tanna, and they were scattered all over the island. There were villages, little settlements all over the island, and . . . it was an eerie feeling, say if I'd spent all day on the other side of the island at White Sands and I was coming back in the evening. . . . You'd come back at nighttime, five or six o'clock as night was falling, . . . and it would be absolutely silent. There would be nothing, and yet you'd know that there were hundreds—there were many, many people living through where you were walking. It was an eerie sort of closeness, pressing in on you.

STOBER: Did Kathleen feel it, did you talk about it?

BRISTOW: . . . No, because Kathleen wasn't terribly happy there and I wouldn't have wanted to sort of make it real. . . . One time we were coming down across the island and we went through . . . a *na gamal* [dance ground where men drink kava], because the main track across the island happened to go right through the *na gamal*. There was a great geffufel because the old men were sitting in one corner drinking their kava, and they suddenly saw the car go through with Kathleen sitting there, and of course a woman must never . . . intrude upon this solemn rite of the kava drink, and there was a lot of scurrying and . . . passing into the bush. . . .

RODMAN: I wonder how much this was . . . specific to this island, and how much was because you were government people, and thus somewhat on the periphery of life there.

BRISTOW: Well, I would have said it was Tanna. I mean, I never felt it, say, on Aoba, where I spent some several weeks altogether living on my own. I'd wander off in the evening . . . along the coast, just a mile or two through the bush and . . . perhaps I might see a late person wandering along the road, but generally I wouldn't expect to see anyone, because they'd all be back in their villages. I'd never feel this oppressiveness that I did on Tanna. It was a gloomy place altogether, it was a sad place.

Figure 49. Tanna as a heavy place. Interview with George Bristow, April 1995.

spoke fondly of their time on Tanna. Compared to the atolls of the Gilbert Islands, their previous post, Tanna's variety of crops and its lush environment seemed idyllic.

The Townsends' happy memories of Tanna contrast with the fact that Mike was the first British district agent to ask for a rent reduction because of the inadequacy of his housing. The selectivity of memory was apparent to Townsend in the fact that he did not remember asking for a rent reduction for the Tanna house. When shown a document that Will Stober and I had found in the archives, he laughingly said, yes, it must have been him. He remembered requesting rent reductions for their very simple thatched housing in the Gilberts, but not for the Tanna house. Apparently, rent reductions were an accepted practice for inadequate housing in the Solomons and Gilberts, but they had not been introduced to the New Hebrides. British Resident Commissioner Flaxman endorsed Townsend's request for a reduction of rent from 10 percent to 7 percent of his

salary; in fact, he went further, arguing that "in view of the discomfort and inconvenience caused particularly to a married officer with a young child, I would recommend a reduction to 5%." Flaxman added that only the British district agents had rent deducted from their salaries despite living in a house that was owned by the Condominium, not the British government. The French district agents did not have rent deducted from their salaries. Not surprisingly, this was a source of considerable resentment among British district agents.

The assistant financial secretary for the High Commission was unsympathetic, minuting his superior that Flaxman's argument "that payment of rent is a source of dissatisfaction is invalid in that salaries of British Service officers were specifically raised in 1947 by ten percent to cover an element of rental and no demur was made at the time for the increase; it is therefore illogical to object to a rental payment now." The high commissioner noted that "the Tanna house is neither very commodious nor well finished but it is not much if at all inferior to e.g. the D.C.'s [district commissioner's] house at Kirakira (which also has outside 'sanitation') or at Auki [in the Solomons]." He did, however, recommend that Flaxman give Townsend a reduction to 7.5 percent and that future requests for rent reductions in the New Hebrides be evaluated on a case-by-case basis.[63]

The Townsends remarked on the bloodstained office floor but did not feel that the house was haunted. Mike Townsend used the office on the verandah in which Neven-Spence had killed himself. Nan remembered hiding in her pajamas in the adjacent bedroom when the police would arrive early on a Friday morning to collect their pay. The office in the house was used because the free-standing native-style hut built as an office in 1947 had burned down in Bristow's time.

In 1995, Bristow was unable to locate for me the photo of the office on fire that Demarbre had taken in 1952. Demarbre was a good photographer, Bristow acknowledged grudgingly. The office hut had also served as a storage shed for benzine (petrol or gasoline) for the generator. The archival account of the fire provides a rare opportunity to hear different voices, including those of New Hebrideans. On 24 February 1952, Bristow and Corporal Jack had spent the whole day working on the charging motor. They finally got it going in the early evening. Bristow told Private Kaluran of the police to go into the office and get fuel to refill the generator's tank when it ran dry. Kaluran later gave this statement to Bristow:

> At about seven o'clock the engine stopped and I took a bottle into the [office] hut to fill it up from the four gallon drum that was there. I was carrying the hurricane lamp. I must have put it too near the four gallon drum, for suddenly a gust of wind blew the flame towards the drum out of which I was syphoning benzine into the bottle. The petrol caught alight and the fire caught the walls of the

house. I called for help from the other Police but, by the time they came the hut was burning strongly.[64]

Private Charlie reported that "I heard Private Kaluran call out that the hut had caught alight. I ran to the fire and with the help of a long stick pulled the burning four gallon drum of benzine from the hut. At this moment the roof caught alight and there was nothing further to be done."

Bristow himself "heard the noise from outside the house and ran out. The hut was burning about twenty yards from the house. As I arrived, Private Charlie was pulling out the drum of benzine. Any further attempts to save the building were useless as the roof had caught alight. I organized all available manpower with water containers in case there was any possibility of the fire spreading, but there was no further damage." The losses were reported as four gallons of benzine, a typewriter, and spare equipment, although Bristow told me and Will that many files also were destroyed in the blaze. Unlike other accounts of fires—for example, the boat house at the British Residency and the superintendent of works' house—New Hebrideans are not blamed for negligence or clumsiness here, although Private Kaluran accidentally started the fire.

Southwest Pacific Corrugated Edwardian

By the time John Leaney was posted to Tanna in 1963, the British district agent's house was a story in built form of the housing needs and preferences of its many inhabitants over the years. "Southwest Pacific corrugated Edwardian" was how Leaney described the older housing in the region when I interviewed him at his home in Wales in 1994:

> Isangel is an excellent example. That is, an internal box with a verandah, modified endlessly in response to contemporary occupation, and that's what happened, because this was the typical Queensland squatter's house, which was a simple verandah, with a sitting room, a bathroom, and a sleeping room. Then thereafter somebody moved in who'd got—I mean, originally you had a single district agent, then you had one with a wife, that was all right, then they had a child, so then they cut that bit off the verandah to make a nursery, and then they had another child, so they cut a bit more off it. Then they went away, and somebody else came who was unmarried, but he turned that into a darkroom, and he kept a visitor's room, and so you went on.

Leaney enjoyed the Tanna house. Of course it was haunted, he told me; virtually

Figure 50. David and Hannah Dale in their Somerset garden with the author (left). Photo by Will Stober, with permission.

all such houses were: "It was fun, they were nice sort of houses to live in. They had a bit of character by virtue of all the things that had happened to them. You felt the woodwork was a bit steeped in tradition, bloodstains and bullets, et cetera."

John Leaney drew a very useful sketch of the layout of the Tanna house for me. So did David Dale, who lived in the Tanna house later in the 1960s with his wife, Hannah, and their young son, Peter. Both Leaney and Dale had excellent recall for the house, with one notable, shared exception. Neither man could remember where the kitchen had been, which suggested to me that the kitchen was a relatively unimportant space to them and one with which they had little contact. The kitchen was a gendered space, as well as a racialized one. It was for white women and natives, male or female. Hannah remembered the kitchen of the Tanna house all too clearly. In particular, she remembered the kerosene refrigerator: "I used to spend one afternoon a week lying underneath the wretched thing, because you had to do the wick, shave it off just right. Because if you didn't, if it was uneven, it smoked. They [the servants] used to say 'Oh, Madam is very cross, she's got to do the fridge today.'"

David Dale also drew me a sketch of the layout of the entire British District Agency at Isangel, which appears earlier in this chapter. It is a lesson in Condominium politics of space. The British and French flags, which are drawn on Dale's sketch, flew at the same height ("no cheating," he said). "They had some chaos in the morning when they raised the flags," according to David, "because the trumpeters blew both the British calls and the French calls at the same time!" Although the French and British agents lived side by side, each used a different road to

approach his premises. Dale wasn't even sure which "back road" his French counterpart used; the British access road, however, is clearly drawn on his sketch. The little building he labeled the British office was in fact a new structure, built after Bristow's fire for British District Agent Darvall Wilkins and French District Agent Duc-Dufayard. The British offices were on the side closest to the British house and the French offices were on the other side. By the mid-1960s, there was a full-fledged "British Paddock" at Isangel. The twofold emphasis on education and law enforcement are evident in the organization of space. David described the sketch he drew:

> Behind the house was the Paddock, the British compound. There was the prison, there was the education officer's bungalow, there were the police lines, and the police office. The British district agent's office was just there. . . . This was a lovely garden, a beautiful garden, vegetable gardens down here. Lovely trees, beautiful banyan trees, a most attractive place.

The Pleasures of Backwardness

The Dales' recollections of Tanna were very positive, partly because of the contrast with Port Vila, where David was posted for much of his eight years in the New Hebrides. Hannah, who is of Polish origin, did not regard herself as having much in common with the British wives in Port Vila who wanted to live near one another in comfortable houses in an area of Port Vila she labeled Shepherd's Bush by-the-Sea. "I'm very unconventional," she told me. "I'd rather live in a very small place, or in a so-called backward place, away from civilization." She and David construed the Tannese as romantic in their "backwardness." Collapsing time and space, they said they found the Kenyans most satisfying in this regard, but that the New Hebrideans of the southern islands compared quite well. Anthropologists have been criticized for conflating time and space, speaking of the people they study as if they lived long ago—for example, in the Stone Age—rather than sharing the same present moment as the researcher.[65] Not only unwary, or unrepentant, anthropologists still use the ethnographic present while describing people as living in the past; so do many in the general public. David and Hannah Dale saw no problem in this, and it would be easy to fall into the same trap by saying that they are living in the past, that their voices represent another age, a time when people savored the last taste of empire. But there we all were in 1994—me and Will Stober and David and Hannah Dale—and what we were savoring was homemade elderberry wine on a bright summer's day in a walled English garden filled with roses. Were the Tannese living in the past? Or were we?

DAVID DALE: They were lovely islands. You could walk across the islands, talk to the people. Futuna [south of Tanna] was particularly nice because they were a very backward people, very secretive. They had the John Frum movement, and all that sort of thing.

WILL STOBER: Are you saying that you liked them because they were backward?

DAVID DALE: Yes, yes. Put it this way, they were not in the twentieth century. They had their own customs and all the rest of it.

HANNAH DALE: They were not overcivilized by our civilization. They had their own civilization. They were backward in our view, but they had very strict rules.

DAVID DALE: Basically, I enjoyed it enormously.

Figure 51. The Charms of Backwardness.

The exchange in figure 51 also brings to mind the idea of the "good Parsi" who could be dressed in English clothes and speak the English language but could never really be an Englishman. Much literature on colonialism and hybridity points to the colonial fascination with incomplete conversion, the travesty of "natives" in Western clothes, for example, using knives and forks, sitting at table in European-style houses.

Hannah and David loved the Tanna house, as well as the Tannese, and for some of the same reasons: it was primitive, romantic, a little scary, but basically friendly. Hannah described the house for me:

The Tanna house was a large one. It had a very high roof, and when the wind blew, which blew quite often in Tanna, you had a sort of odd moaning noise in the rafters, which a lot of Tannese said was "spooky." Peter [Hannah and David's son] was then six or seven, and if we wanted to go out, very seldom would they come and baby-sit. They'd rather not. So we used to bundle Peter, put him in the car we had, and take him with us. But they would not stay in that house after dark. The first thing when we arrived, I was shown into the room which was sort of leading off our bedroom and shown an enormous stain, which could have been anything, really, and was told that this is where the chap had shot himself, and this is the bloodstain which would not come out. But as far as I was concerned, there were good vibes. You know when you walk into a house, and you have bad vibes and good vibes. I walked into the Tanna, and I had good vibes. But, I remember there was a big central sitting room. Everything went off. So, if you went to the bathroom, you had to go through endless rooms. There wasn't a corridor, as such. It was all added on to. Lovely wooden floors, very uneven. And lovely painted wooden walls, and, as I said, this enormous ceiling, which moaned and groaned in the wind. There was a lot of unpleasantness

because as you know, somebody killed himself. Then, Susan, who died there after we left.

Gone with the Wind

Will Stober thought it would be "too painful" for Guy Wallington if we were to interview him, so we didn't.[66] Although Wallington was in the New Hebrides from 1958 until 1977, the death of his wife in the bath of the Tanna house in 1970, Will felt, would color all his memories. Initial reports from Tanna in October 1970 led some alarmists in Port Vila to conclude that the Tannese had risen up and attacked the British district agent's house. I interviewed Ray and Margaret Honey in Herefordshire in 1995. Ray, an architect and expert on building standards, arrived in the New Hebrides when, as he put it,[67]

> the Colonial Service was really running out of puff. Whereas, you see, when I joined in 1950, one had expectations of a full career, and there was a tremendous range of places you could go to. Twenty years later, of course, it was a very, very different scene. And it had come down to a very small number of places. . . . [For example, my] branch was called CAMPS—Central Africa, Mediterranean, and Pacific.

Moreover, those small number of places were hothouses in which the British socialized too little with local people and gossip traveled too fast. Ray remembered receiving the news of Sue Wallington's death:

> Interesting, really, how in a setup like that, news gets around. I was in my office down above the pâtisserie, which I shared with Alan Collins, who was financial secretary. And we shared a phone. The phone went, and Alan said, in effect, they'd found Sue dead. Guy had gone to find her in the morning and slipped and cracked his head. He was concussed. And the interpretation of that first message was that the Tannese were revolting and they'd got at the BDA's house.

Investigation showed that Susan Wallington had died from asphyxiation. The gas heater in the bathroom apparently consumed all the available oxygen, causing her death. Why this happened remains a mystery. Possibly, Ray Honey suggested in our interview, the wind had jammed the fresh air vent shut. The Tanna house, with its moaning ceilings, was indeed a windy place.

A different explanation emphasizing race and space was offered by another

British retiree: Susan had shut the window tightly because she was afraid of unseen New Hebrideans hiding in the darkness outside the house and peering at her in the bath. So much for the power of the "colonial gaze." Power also lay in the threat of looking back. In this sense, the rumor that the Tannese had killed her was partly true, but with a twist. If anything, her fear of the Tannese had killed her. This is an accepted form of self-sorcery in the northern New Hebridean island of Ambae. Bill Rodman and I once wrote a paper about the death of a young islander we called Sara Mata, whose lustful thoughts people said bounced back and killed her. Fears, too, can reflect back on the fearful.

British Resident Commissioner Colin Allan, who had once courted Susan Wallington, sent Ray Honey to report on the Tanna house after the tragedy in 1970. Susan Wallington was very familiar with life in the Southwest Pacific. Her father was the last resident commissioner for the British Solomon Islands Protectorate,[68] so it seemed unlikely that the living conditions of the Tanna house, substandard though they may have been, played a role in her state of mind. Her death seemed clearly accidental. The house itself, however, might have been to blame.

Honey felt that Colin Allan sent him down to Tanna to condemn the house because of its history of tragedy, so that the British resident commissioner could order it destroyed. In the event, Honey refused to condemn it: "I said in effect that the core of the house is perfectly sound, but all of the additions, the kitchen, enclosing the verandahs and the bathrooms were of very poor construction." He wrote in his report: "The shapes, sizes and dispositions of individual rooms are such as to make the house less convenient than many much smaller houses, particularly in respect of the family bedroom arrangements." The hardwood timber and concrete piles were in excellent shape. The house was "competently built and well braced." The hardwood floor was "very well fitting" and "well maintained." In short, the only problems arose from the *bricolage* engaged in by the various occupants over the years as they enclosed the verandah and added extensions. Honey concluded that "restoration of the house to its original plan could provide a sound, comfortable, attractive building," but one much too small for a district agent's house.

He outlined three possibilities: tear down the old building and replace it with a new one on the same site; incorporate the old core into a new, larger residence; or preserve the core as a separate building for reception or guest accommodation and build an adjacent new house. In refusing to recommend one option over the others, Honey gave the old house a reprieve. It stood for two more years until the notorious Tanna wind swept its roof away in a cyclone, over the heads of its occupants, British District Agent John Wilson and his family.

ON ISLANDS OFF ISLANDS

A n islet, a bathtub, and a front door were what I wanted most to see during the two weeks I spent in 1995 on Santo. The bathtub and the front door were all that remained of the British District Agency at Venui (pronounced *Ve'new wee*).[1] From 1938 until the early 1950s, the British district agent lived on Venui, a round, heavily wooded, fifteen-acre island a few hundred yards off the south coast of Santo. The house was prefabricated, a kit ordered from Sydney and assembled on the island. It was by all accounts a fine-looking bungalow on concrete piers with wide verandahs. Nothing was left of the house now, or so I was told, but I wanted to see for myself. The remains of the concrete house posts would mark the site like tombstones in an overgrown cemetery. A site visit might give me a sense of the place in its heyday and of the decline of the British presence, not only in South Santo, but throughout the islands.

Visiting Venui might seem easy, but the number of people who had to be consulted indicates the climate of caution, as well as the difficulties of transportation, in the islands. Venui was only about half an hour's drive from town along twenty kilometers of broad, dusty road. The drive wasn't the problem, thanks to the kindness of friends' friends. (This willingness to help out coexisted, ironically, with suspicion of virtually everyone's motives.) In Vila, I had been given two people to contact in Santo who, I was assured, would drive me wherever I

Thomas F. Salisbury	Condominium Agent	1913–1914, 1920–1922
	British District Agent	1922–1935
Alan J. K. Thomas	BDA Hog Harbour	1935–1940
G. Reginald Johnson	BDA Venui	1940–1947
Joseph Maxwell	BDA Venui	1947–1951
Douglas Freegard	BDA Venui	1952–1953
George Bristow	BDA Venui	1953–1953
J. R. Wrightson	BDA Venui	1953–1954
George Bristow	BDA Venui	1954–1957
John Field	BDA Luganville	1957–1961
Richard Hutchinson	BDA Luganville	1961–1967
John Field	BDA Luganville	1967–1970
Christopher Turner	BDA Luganville	1970–1973
F. E. Baker	BDA Luganville	1973–1978
Colin Redston	BDA Luganville	1978–1978
David Browning	BDA Luganville	1978–1980

This list is partial as it includes only some of those who served as relief appointments for district agents on leave.

Figure 52. British district agents on Santo.

needed to go. This proved to be true. One was David Wanamay, a Santo man married to an Ambae woman, who drove a huge white truck for Speedy Gas. The other was Peter Bouchard, owner of a blue pickup truck, son of a French naval officer, and, on his mother's side, a descendant of *Bounty* mutineers. Peter grew up in Tasmania and worked in Papua New Guinea before moving to Vanuatu, where his wide-ranging business experience included owning a lumber company and running Pinnochio's Restaurant with his wife, Yvonne.

The boat to Venui was the stumbling block. To get a ride in a launch from the main island to Venui, I needed the cooperation of two more people: the current leaseholder of the mainland property and the leaseholder of the island itself. The former was Piero Bianchessi, an Italian grower of fine vanilla, beekeeper, and gardener who supplied his American wife with fresh salad greens for her café

Figure 53. Aerial photo of Venui Island (circa 1950). From George Bristow collection, with permission.

in Luganville, Santo's only town. Piero had a rowboat with an outboard that could take me out to Venui Island. The island's leaseholder was Peter Morris, a legend in his own time, who cheerfully cooperated with my colonial research while insisting that he was "a hundred percent anti–British government." When Will Stober, my erstwhile English research coordinator, was a British Lands officer, Morris once threatened to shoot at Stober if he tried to enter Morris' South Santo property. I did not want to annoy him. As soon as I had Peter Morris' blessing, Piero made the time to take me to the island in his boat.

Peter Bouchard drove me in his blue pickup truck to Piero's place at 8:30 on a Saturday morning. All the way from town down the South Santo coast it threatened to rain, and I thought maybe this trip was a big mistake. The difficulties of

arranging the visit to Venui, plus the imposition on Peter, who wanted to play golf before it rained, added to my anxiety.

I need not have worried. Piero greeted us warmly, although he and Peter barely knew each other. Piero was a wiry, gray-bearded fellow with twinkling eyes and a seemingly affable nature, although no one who lives amidst the politics of land in South Santo is a pushover. The residents of Tanovoli, a nearby village whose name means "purchased ground," bought the land from a settler family.[2] The people of Tanovoli frequently contested the settlers' rights to occupy land such as Venui, although various settlers had leased it from the commercial firm of Burns, Philp for a century, and, since independence, it had been leased from the indigenous owners. Young men from Tanovoli attacked Piero one night as he closed his cattle gate behind Peter Morris, who had come for dinner.

South Santo and Violence

South Santo earned its reputation in the nineteenth century as a place of violent encounters between islanders and whites. On a single South Santo site, islanders killed one settler, Peter Sawers, and his laborer in 1891 and three members of another family, the Greigs, in 1908. Settlers often explained native murders of whites in terms of "cargo" beliefs. Some say that the Greigs and the settler before them were blocking the path that "cargo," or Western-style wealth, must follow to reach the islanders. Greig's murderer, however, said that he was owed back wages, which Greig had refused to pay. The incident is described in figure 54.[3]

White murders of natives were often explained, by whites, as "punishment." Sawers' murderer was never apprehended, despite eight punitive expeditions

PETER C. GREIG, a Scotsman, settled with his family on South Santo in 1902. Three years later Ada Methven Greig died of malaria, leaving her husband with five children. The two youngest were sent to Australia, while teenagers Joyce, Marion, and their younger brother, Alex, stayed on to help their father work the plantation, called Makiri.

On 7 October 1908, Greig was attacked and killed by islanders, who hid his body in the corn crib and covered it with corn husks. Joyce and Marion were attacked coming home from the vegetable garden. Alex, aged about 14, came home from a different direction having milked the goats. When he found his father's body in the corn crib, he raced to look for his sisters. He found their bodies at dusk, so he climbed to the roof of the family home where he hid for the night. At dawn, Alex crept along the foreshore, avoiding the usual trails, where he feared he too might be attacked. He made his way to the Reverend Annand at the Presbyterian mission on Tangoa Island.

About ten years later, Alex died of pneumonia in Scotland. The little sisters who were in Australia at the time of the attack have descendants now living in Queensland.

Figure 54. The Greig murders, 1908.

174 ■   CHAPTER 7

into the Santo bush. Three such expeditions led to the arrest of the Greig murderers. The first expedition resulted in three hostages from the wrong village. The
second yielded more hostages, and salvos fired into the bush caused the deaths of
five or six women and a little girl. The alleged murderer, along with seven others
deemed to have been accomplices, was apprehended on the third expedition.

The severity of these punitive expeditions was debated in the British House
of Lords.[4] The Presbyterian missionary in South Santo, Joseph Annand, wrote,
"The slaughter of their women, painful though it may appear to many, had a very
good effect upon the bushmen generally. . . . This has been a severe but much
needed lesson to man Santo."[5] It is unlikely that the islanders were learning the
lesson that Annand had in mind. Although nowadays deaths are very rare, islanders continue to resist white occupation, and settlers persist in defending their as-
sets, as the relationship between the Tanovoli people, Piero, and Peter Morris
suggests. Yet the line between white and islander is by no means clear. Most of the
old settler families have been in the islands for more than a century. Today's
generation of these families is often as Melanesian as it is white, not "really" ni-
Vanuatu in Vanuatu, not "really" white in Australia.[6] Their houses far from home
may be in Australia or France, and if they still have a home in the islands it may
be an uneasy one.

On Islands off Islands

In the early days, whites preferred to settle on small islands near the coasts of big
islands. Small islands offered a sense of protection from attack. It was, as Peter
Morris told me, a false sense of security, but at least the settlers could see the
canoes coming. The symbolism also is obvious, evoking the peripheral position
of settlers, both to the Condominium government whose reach barely extended
outside Vila for many years and to the native peoples who held the "mainland."
Even today, settlers' descendants are on the edge of a society dominated by ni-
Vanuatu. Sometimes they play key political roles.[7] They are edgy as well. Their
shifting mixed-race identity and an awareness of the sins of their ancestors, especially regarding land acquisition and the abuses of their parents against plantation laborers, provide some opportunities and more than a few liabilities.

Ned Hooker's descendants still live on family property in the New Hebrides.
Hooker was living on Malo Island in 1910 when Burns, Philp and Company
asked him to take over the late Mr. Greig's lease of five hundred acres of Commonwealth land. In 1901 the Australian government had awarded Burns, Philp
and Company a postal contract that made the company the sole carrier of mail

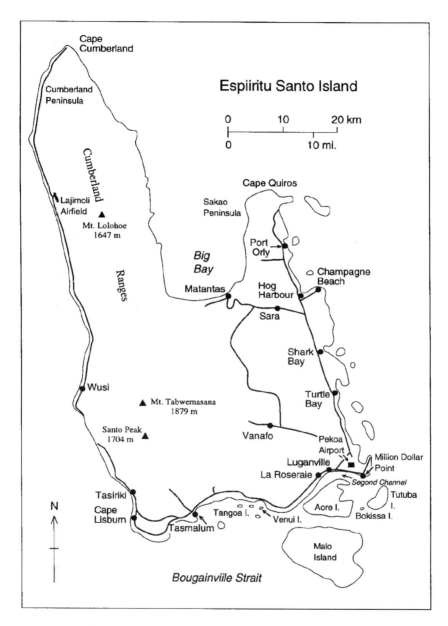

Figure 55. Map of Santo. Carol Randall, Cartographic Office, Department of Geography, York University.

from Lord Howe Island to the Santa Cruz group. Burns, Philp could even issue its own stamps and currency. In return, Burns, Philp, to encourage Australian settlement and thus strengthen the British position in the New Hebrides, had given a hundred thousand acres of land, mostly on South Santo, to the Commonwealth of Australia. The company would act as the Commonwealth's leasing agent. Settlers, known as Burns, Philp Pilgrims, leased five hundred–acre blocks of land.[8]

Ned Hooker agreed to take over Greig's lease but only if he could lease Tangis Islet, separated by a narrow, calm channel from the main island just across from Greig's property. He was allowed to do so for a shilling a year. He and his family would live on Tangis.[9] "I don't want my family to be the third one to be wiped out here!" he allegedly said.

Whole islands have a history of moving around in Vanuatu. In 1985, when I conducted research on fishing in Port Olry on the northeast coast of Santo, people told me the story of Araki Island, which used to be just offshore. One day long ago, the island cut loose, magically, and sailed away to South Santo, where it is today. The floating island carried with it many men and women who were already married to other people in Port Olry, leaving the abandoned husbands and wives to wade out into the sea, helplessly protesting.[10] Stones on Tanna move, as do rocks on Ambae. Not surprisingly, and less mystically, houses move, too. Like the Anglican missionaries' peripatetic house mentioned in chapter 1, settlers' houses often have a history of relocation, as do islanders'.[11] Ned Hooker simply dismantled the family home on Malo, transported it to Tangis, and re-erected it. He and his daughters, Jane and Nellie, slept with guns under their pillows. Descendants remember "Granny Jane" telling of the fear she had felt as she lay awake listening to "the natives calling and calling." The natives said they wanted to come to the Hookers' store on Tangis, and maybe they did, but the "Hooker girls," as they were known all their lives, thought otherwise.[12]

French or British, settler or missionary, all preferred small islands for the same reason: safety. The British government, too, seems to have preferred to locate its offices on small islands, although less for safety reasons than to make symbolic statements—to see and to be seen.[13] The British Residency on Iririki Island in Port Vila harbor discussed in chapter 3 is only one of many examples. So it should come as no surprise that the government looked for a small island when the decision was made to relocate the original British District Agency, built in 1912 at Hog Harbour on Santo's east coast.

The decision seems to come out of the blue in the archival correspondence. In his twelfth year as resident commissioner, G. A. Joy finally felt that financially and politically the time was right to carry out a change he had wanted to make

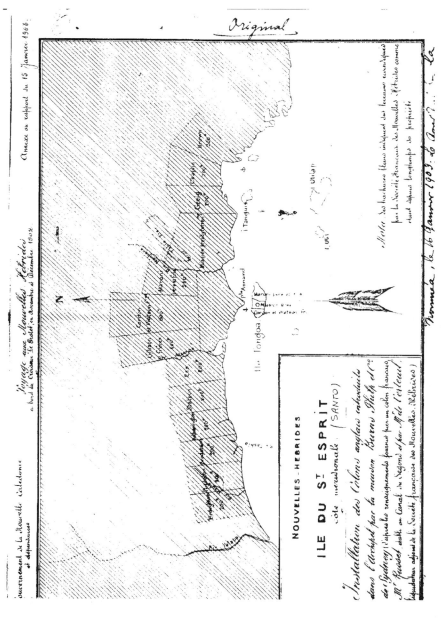

Figure 56. Map of South Santo showing British settlers' properties, 1902. Gouvernement de la Nouvelle Caledonie, 1903. From Reece Discombe collection, with permission.

for a long time. He wrote the British district agent, Alan Thomas, that he wanted to move the agency from Hog Harbour to a site to be selected in South Santo.

Why South Santo? First, because the area was Commonwealth government land and "the title is good." (Actually the title was never registered, but Joy did not seem to know that.) Burns, Philp as agent for the Commonwealth would sign leases only with settlers who were British *ressortissants*. Joy's other priorities were that the agency be on "a small island of its own." It should be "as healthy as possible and have an anchorage. Also, a pleasant aspect." The British resident commissioner suggested five small islands, including Venui and "even Urelapa on which the Stephens are located at present."[14]

Alan Thomas had been British district agent at Santo since 1935. He replaced Thomas Salisbury, a bachelor who lived at Hog Harbour for many years, first as the Condominium agent before and after his service in World War I, then, after 1922, as British district agent. Salisbury lived comfortably enough at Hog Harbour, where he even had a pool table, but he suffered from recurrent malaria, old war injuries, and a bad foot. These health problems, plus the isolation, made him something of "a 'crank' and a hermit," albeit "a man of sterling qualities." He was evaluated as "an officer who has tact and discretion and understands the native but lacks the quality of initiative and energy."[15]

The land on which the agency was situated at Hog Harbour was leased from Graham Kerr and Jean My. By lucky coincidence, just a month after Joy's sudden decision to move the agency, Kerr notified the British government that the lease would not be renewed. Relations between Kerr and the government clearly were strained, and both Joy and Thomas expressed pleasure at being able to abandon the Hog Harbour site. The district agent's house itself was sold to M. Harbulot, who relocated it to his plantation up the coast. I hesitate to report because it sounds ridiculously romantic, but it is true that when I went looking for the remains of the Hog Harbour District Agency in 1995 I found only clouds of blue butterflies.

Thomas was happy to leave Hog Harbour. Recent troubles with South Santo natives and the implementation of a new "native policy" had required him to have frequent contact with his French counterpart. The French district agent was in the more heavily settled area known as the Segond Channel or the "Canal" (meaning "channel" in French, but sounding as if it were a "canal" in English). Because Thomas was inconveniently located at Hog Harbour, they had to deal with these matters by correspondence. "How much easier it would have been if [French District Agent] M. Laïné and Mr. Thomas had been able to make frequent contact with one another and discuss their business over a glass of wine." Indeed, perhaps the whole political history of Santo would have been different had the British district agent relocated to within toasting distance of the French district agent, but

the Canal was too French for the British. Until the Americans vacated the PT boat base there after World War II, it would have been hard for the British to find a "suitable site." Meanwhile, Burns, Philp land was securely British.

Thomas agreed that an island would be a good idea. "The mainland is unhealthy and infested with mosquitoes besides being painfully hot." The island should be close enough to the mainland so that "bush natives may be able to visit the Government Agency." Thomas' choice was Tangis Island, where the Hooker family had settled precisely to put some distance between themselves and the natives. Ned Hooker had passed away in 1934, and although Mrs. Hooker planned to retire to Norfolk Island, she declined to sell Tangis to the British government. Instead she left the property to her "adopted son, George" (actually the natural child of her stepdaughter Jane), allowing Jane and Nellie to stay there as long as they wanted.

The British district agent then turned to Venui, which both he and the British resident commissioner had regarded as a good choice, although a bit small with more difficult access and poorer anchorage. The leaseholder, S. E. Wells, agreed to let them rent the land for £15 per annum.[16] When the District Agency relocated to the Canal in the 1950s, the island reverted to Fred Jones, who had bought the lease on the property when Wells died in 1948.

Venui Island was an acceptable second best, and so were the plans for the house constructed on it. Plans were considered for a ready-cut house available through Burns, Philp from Saxton's or Hudson's companies in Sydney. Saxton's design was adapted to tropical conditions, with the rooms built on a straight-line principle, each opening onto a verandah on two sides for cross ventilation. It was, however, deemed too expensive, and the decision was made to go with a four-square design from the more affordable Hudson's, although the house would be hotter.[17] Venui was a compromise in a third way, not only as the second-best island and the second-best house. The chief surveyor also warned that the site selected for the agency was too small to have a parade ground.

The district agent's house on Venui was delivered in November 1938, ready for assembly within nine weeks by a skilled Seventh Day Adventist mission carpenter, Mr. Rose. Thomas commented that the island suddenly looked like Hudson's timber yard. He and Mr. Rose stayed in one of the Stephens' houses on the mainland while the construction went ahead and the furniture was moved by ship from Hog Harbour.

The house was sufficiently sound and well built that when the government left and Fred Jones took possession of it, he decided to move the building to his property on the mainland. The house was to be reassembled as a wedding gift to Jones' daughter, Margaret, when she married Jane Hooker's son, David. Through

bad luck and bad planning, the house was still on a raft tied to the mainland when a fierce storm blew it to bits. All that survived in reusable condition from the British district agent's house were the doors and the bathtub. I wanted to see them.

Visiting Venui

I was wearing a skirt, my usual fieldwork uniform in Vanuatu. This one was below the knee, denim, the sort of skirt that gets very heavy when wet. The blessings of a long, thick skirt have been written about, but I had my doubts as I looked down at the thick, green slime covering the thwarts of Piero's boat.[18] The tide was out, way out. The little boat was practically aground, a meter and a half below the dock.

Piero climbed aboard and fooled with the engine for quite a while. Peter muttered, good-naturedly, that we could have rowed to the island by now, and he was right. Eventually, that is just what we did. I jumped in; my skirt was instantly wet and slimy, but it took only about five or ten minutes for Piero to row across the channel. The usual approach for the British district agent used to be even closer. He went to and from a place with the odd name of Beer, the next beach to the east. I was told that it marked the site of the first beer imported to Santo. Apparently the name stuck when Mr. Fox, a planter, proposed a toast "To Beer" at a picnic held near what later became the British district agent's landing.[19] As Piero rowed us out I looked at the bay and tried to imagine Venui as a busy place in the midst of a community of British settlers. All I saw were green growing things and blue-green sea.

We landed on a steep coral shore at Venui, perhaps twenty meters to the right of the remains of the old wharf. Piero anchored the stern of the boat and tied the bow to a chunk of coral. The current and chop were surprisingly strong as we crossed. Piero said that the only island from which you could always find a calm crossing was Tangis. Above Venui, large numbers of the fruit bats known as "flying fox" were wheeling and crying. Peter Morris had tried to make this a reserve for flying fox and coconut crabs, but there were constant problems with intruders. Apparently someone was on the island as we approached. Later we could see a ni-Vanuatu man paddling away from the far side. We found our way through the scrub, clearly secondary growth but quite dense. We saw the foundations of what had been the office for the British district agent; only stones were left. We crossed a clearing where Gabrielle, Peter Morris' partner, had recently planted a garden—mostly manioc and bananas. I remembered that when the British district agent installed himself on Venui, he had to compensate Ruby

Stephens (stepmother of the rebel leader Jimmy Stephens) for the gardens she had planted on the island. Beyond Gabrielle's garden, through more scrub, were the remains of the British district agent's house. There were the concrete "pilotis" or pylons I had hoped for, marking the footprint the house had once made.

There were traces of the coral that surrounded the house and covered the paths down to the water. There was also an old oven, metal encased in concrete, on the western side of the house, and two water tanks behind. Piero led us through the bush to the left to try to find the old prison, but we got lost and gave up.

Piero couldn't see his boat at first and was afraid someone had cut it loose. Life in South Santo seems fraught with threats of intrusions and violence. All was well, however, and in fact this time the old Suzuki outboard caught and we were able to motor along the coast of the island counterclockwise for a while, until the motor overheated and died. The water close to the shore of the island was bright azure, and some coral was beginning to grow there. Both Piero and Peter Morris had stopped fishing in the bay to give the environment a chance to recover, so Piero was pleased to see the coral.

Back on shore, Piero genially invited us in for a coffee. Peter wanted to be back in town for golf by 11:00 A.M., but it was just after 10:00 A.M. and he accepted the invitation. He knew, he told me later, that he would get an excellent cup of espresso coffee. He was right. Piero brewed the coffee and served it in elegant small stainless steel cups. Meanwhile, he let me photograph the bathtub, which came from Venui, and the glass-paneled front doors, which also came from the British District Agency.

Piero and Leslie's house looked very simple: an enclosed verandah on a concrete slab running the length of a bungalow that was two steps higher, on the inland side of the verandah. What was distinctive was how comfortable it looked. There was an open kitchen at the far end, with an excellent gas stove and a gas refrigerator. The central area of the verandah was a sitting area with comfortable couch and chairs, and a friendly cat. The far end was a very appealing reading area with two hammocks, each with a reading light, a wall of books, and a stereo system. It looked as comfortable as our house in Longana, with modern conveniences. I was ready to move in.

Champagne in the Sea

In its day, Venui looked just as appealing to visitors as Piero and Leslie's place did to me in 1995. Angela Eaton was seventeen when she arrived on Venui in 1947 with her mother and her stepfather, Joe Maxwell, the new British district agent for

Figure 57. Venui District Agency doors. Author's photo.

Figure 58. Venui District Agency bathtub. Author's photo.

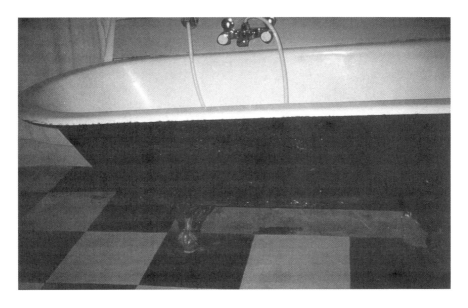

the Northern District. In a lightly fictionalized account of her experiences, she wrote about first seeing the island: "And there it was— . . . clean, efficient and terribly British. The beach, hiding under its overhanging fringe of trees, looked as if it had been swept and there was a neat jetty of stones—whitewashed. Only the path had stepped out of line—curving and weaving up to the small plateau where the house stood on a bed of coral chippings."[20] The image of an outpost of empire that impressed this teenager was also clear in George Bristow's reminiscences about the pleasures of life on Venui. George Bristow came to Venui from Tanna to serve as British district agent for the Northern District in April 1953. His account evokes a sense of being lord of a manor seldom visited, but lovely nonetheless.

> You went across in a little boat, in your own little boat, from the landing, which was a place called Beer. A little stream came down, and just at the entrance to the stream [was the landing]. . . . The thing to do when you got to Beer was to go up onto the point and yell out, make a noise. Your policeman would hear it, and then he [wearing a green cap with red pompons] used to row across to you, and you'd get in the boat and he would row you back. It was a beautiful, idyllic place to live, I thought.
>
> There was a little shack of an office halfway up the hill between the landing spot and the house. You kept your files there and the safe was in there, but you really didn't do very much, didn't spend very much time in the office. No one came to the office, you know, no one could just sort of just drop in the office. If anyone was coming to see you, which was rare, you knew they were coming because you'd hear their boat, and you'd go down to meet them or they'd come up to the house, and so you didn't spend much time in the office itself.

The house itself was a prefabricated bungalow, of a type found on many sheep stations in Australia, but commodious by the standards of South Santo. There was a small generator for emergencies, but Coleman lights were the norm; rainwater was piped from catchment tanks for washing and cooking, but there were no flush toilets. The house was solid, if somewhat hot, with hurricane shutters all around, and well sited, commanding a view of South Santo second to none.

Those Eyes

British District Agent Joe Maxwell had a ringside seat when a settler, John Stephens, sailed out in the *Eveline* one night in the late 1940s. Bristow recounted to me and Will this striking example of the colonial gaze: "There was Joe sitting

Figure 59. Raising the flag at Venui. From George Bristow collection, with permission.

between the flags having his evening gin, and out from Johnny's creek just a mile and a half across the water came Johnny's boat, and it chugged out into the middle of channel, then went google-google-google and went down." John Stephens scuttled the ship, escaping with his two local employees in a rowboat. The idea was to collect on the insurance. John had tried to buy his "boys'" silence with $2 each, not nearly enough to make them impervious to the British district agent's questioning.

John Stephens soon found himself in Vila serving time for the crime of barratry and practicing his other trade, carpentry. Instead of actually being imprisoned, John was allowed to live in the house in the British Paddock that he was sentenced to build.[21] According to Bristow,

> John lived an excellent life. He had about four or five native prisoners, colleagues, under his command, and he used them as his personal servants, so he lived very well. He used to come around and play chess with my wife [Kathleen Bristow] in the evening, I remember that. In fact, he'd come around and had two or three evenings with us playing chess with my wife who loved the game, before we learned that in fact he was a prisoner.

John Stephens had earlier served time in Fiji for raping a native woman with a piece of wood. Yet when he was sent to Vila for sinking his own ship under the gaze of the British district agent he was given greater freedom than the considerable liberty allowed to native prisoners, who cut the grass on the British Paddock and sometime took advantage of "weekend passes" no one knew they had.[22] As seems generally to have been the case, those who committed even the most horrifying crimes against native women were believed to pose no danger to whites.

Only one thing really frightened Angela Eaton, Maxwell's stepdaughter (now known as Angela Sewell). Her fear had to do with the colonial gaze in a way quite different from her stepfather's arrest of Johnny Stephens. Her comments put an unusual twist on colonial "Heart of Darkness" imagery. They suggest that she was dramatically aware of boundaries between nature and culture (construed as native and white), of the nearness of "hell" to her particular heaven, and of the gaze turning back at her. When she told me this story I thought the punch line was going to be that the eyes were those of the natives, peering at her from the perimeter.

> The house stood on a bed of coral chippings. . . . As dusk fell—and twilight in the islands never lasts very long, [it's] very quick—you would hear "chink, chink, chink, chink, chink," and then you would get the smell, a terrible smell,

and I would go out on the verandah, and the light had [gone]. It was dark all around the perimeter of the coral chips. On the rim of the chips would be these eyes, these terrible glinting red eyes, and then you would see them moving in the coconut husks, because we had coconuts on the island, and they were all the coconut crabs that had come up to start opening the coconuts up, and they were as big as that, and the smell of them was dreadful. And I used to lean over the verandah, and I'd be terrified of these things. They wouldn't come over the coral, you see they didn't like sliding over the coral, so Joe had coral spread all around the edge of the whole house and kitchen area. And beyond that was a fence, and then there were the coconut trees, and all the fallen coconuts. And these devils would come up, and they would start opening these coconuts with these huge [claws]. And the smell was dreadful, and their eyes, oh!

I asked if they ate the crabs, which became a delicacy in Vila restaurants. Her answer slides from crabs to her fears of what she regarded as the unknown, wild, and heathen in native people. "Hell" might be full of witch doctors or coconut crabs—or both.

> ANGELA EATON: The natives did, we didn't. We went to a village once, because I used to go around with Mommy and Joe. Joe had a lot of visits to make to villages, and so on.
> WILL STOBER: You went on tour with—your mother and you went on tour when he was—
> EATON: Oh yes, in [the British district agent's boat] the *Honey*. We went up to Big Bay when he captured the two witch doctors. We were there in the boat. That is in my—that was an incredible experience. I hated these crabs, but every night we'd hear this chinking, and this dreadful smell. And I always thought that hell was full of these crabs.

It is ironic that the crabs now have the run of the island, which has become a nature preserve, and that native people's access is now restricted not because of the presence of government, but in the name of conservation.

The Social Ladder

Angela Eaton learned to drink and smoke in the islands. To hear her tell it, life on Venui was a continuous party, but then she was a teenager on holiday, not the government officer. Even she said they had to make their own fun, that South

Santo was not in itself a "fun place." She found the frequent earthquakes discon-
certing although they did little to ruin the party. The house was built on the concrete pylons that are now all that remains of the place. They amplified the
movement of earthquakes. When the lamps began to swing, Angela told us, they
would gather up the gin and escape from the house, relocating under the frangipani tree on the lawn.

Much of her social life and the business life of her stepfather centered on the
Canal, as the town of Luganville was known. The town had grown considerably
during the American occupation, when thousands of troops passed through
Santo, including James Michener, the novelist who wrote *Tales of the South
Pacific* while looking across the sea to Ambae, which he dubbed "Bali Hai." The
French District Agency was in the Canal, as were the commercial houses of
Burns, Philp; Barrau; and others. Angela partied with the boys from "the Batch,"
Burns, Philp's bachelor accommodation. Sometimes, everyone came down to
Venui for parties.

The parties on Venui were legendary. One of Angela's contemporaries, a man
who still lives on Santo, remembered lolling in the tepid bay at Venui, sipping
champagne served to them by the policemen. Another settler, a woman, recalled
one of the British district agent's parties: the men were to bring a bottle and the
women were asked to bring a dish. Angela and Mrs. Maxwell made no pretense
of being good cooks. When all the delicacies brought by settler and missionary
women disappeared into the kitchen, never to appear on the table, it was rumored
that the Maxwells were saving the food for themselves. Parties went on all night.
Following a bull roast on the beach, the guests were given rooms to change their
clothes, then danced until dawn. One woman remembered that rain at dawn once
shrank her crepe de chine dress to an indecent length.

When I met her in July 1994, Angela lived in a sixteenth-century row house
in a village near Winchester. Each door on the street was painted a different color
and had a knob squarely in the center. The inside of the house was cheerfully
cluttered, filled with books and mementos from her time in the islands. Will Stober and I interviewed her while her friendly boxer dog snored loudly. In my more
traditional fieldwork, I have had many taped interviews punctuated with roost-
ers crowing, children crying, and even pigs squealing, but this was the first snor-
ing dog.

One of the mementos on Angela's bookshelf was a ladder about ten inches
tall. I recognized it from a photo she showed me and Will from the 1940s. It was
the "social ladder" and was given to her mother as a joke when the gossips of
South Santo alleged that she was a social climber. Angela's mother was probably
anything but a social climber. However, she did like a good party and she was a

Figure 60 (left). Margaret Rodman (left), Angela Eaton, and the boxer dog that snored. Photo by Will Stober, with permission.

Figure 61 (below). Angela Eaton's "social ladder." Photo from Angela Eaton collection, with permission.

self-proclaimed rebel. (It is alleged that the distinguished Australian master mariner and artist, Brett Hilder, once described her as "the most dangerous woman in the Pacific.") I was surprised that Angela regarded her mother's rebelliousness as coming out in her use of "bamboo" (actually wild cane, I think) to line the shutters of the verandah as is evident in the photo of the social ladder. Native materials were used to make a social statement in this Western-style house. "She wanted that bamboo background," Angela told me, "because she thought it looked cool, and she was always trying to be a little bit rash."

Angela's mother took considerable social risks. She refused to rise, as everyone else did, when the British resident commissioner entered the room. "I will rise for my sovereign and no one else" she insisted, even when her husband pointed out that the British resident commissioner was her sovereign's agent. There were three bedrooms in the bungalow on Venui and one, the guest room, was known as "the hot box." Angela was allowed to avoid her own hot bedroom and sleep on the verandah with a pet rooster at the foot of her bed. The resident commissioner's office let it be known that British Resident Commissioner Blandy and his wife would appreciate it if the Maxwells would give up their own bedroom so that the Blandys could sleep comfortably. Angela's mother flatly refused. She said, "No, to hell with it, they can sleep in the guest room. If it's too hot, tough luck."

From the Blandys' point of view, the room was indeed too hot, but this proved to be the Maxwells' good fortune. Blandy approved alterations to enlarge the bedrooms (the hot box was 12' x 12') and improve the ventilation. No wonder he was so emphatic in a memo to the superintendent of works: "The alterations will make all the difference between comfort and discomfort. They have my entire approval."[23]

The "British Community" of Non-British People

Ironically, the British community, which the government had moved to Venui to serve, was one with which the kind of people posted to the agency had virtually nothing in common. Most residents called British were in fact British *ressortissants* born in the islands, perhaps with an ancestor from Australia or the United Kingdom. The men in the families tended to establish long-term liaisons with native women. Marriages were most often with members of other settler families or with outsiders found in Australia or Norfolk Island, or visiting the New Hebrides.

The Stephens family was probably the largest family on South Santo during the period when the British District Agency was at Venui. This family received

international attention in 1980 when Jimmy Moli Stephens, a third-generation member of the Stephens family in the New Hebrides and self-proclaimed "Prophet President," led the Santo Rebellion. His obituary in *The Independent* contained unreflective assumptions about race: although Jimmy's Polynesian background gave him "an edge" over Melanesians "in flamboyant oratory and basic leadership skills, it left him organizationally dependent on an extended family, much of his own procreation."[24] In fact, many followers throughout the islands supported Jimmy, as did his numerous wives including the one called the Virgin Mary, who gave birth to a baby in Los Angeles.

No family, as Jimmy's role in the Santo Rebellion suggests, was more of a gadfly, more in the government's face than the Stephens family. Nor was any settler family more literally under the government's eye than the Stephenses, as the incident of John Stephens scuttling his ship suggests. It worked both ways, no doubt, with the Stephenses looking right back at the colonial world of Venui from the shore. T. C. Stephens' sons ran plantations all along the South Santo coast. John's brother, Len Stephens, and his wife, Eileen, an Australian Presbyterian deaconess, lived on South Santo, as did brothers Oliver, Fred, and Tubou (father of Roy, Jimmy, Lily, and Anna, whose 1945 wedding photo is reproduced here).[25] Another brother, George, lived on nearby Malo. Oliver's daughter Vina married Peter Morris, who gave me permission to visit Venui. Three daughters (Violet, Emily, and Caroline) also married and remained in the islands (see figure 62).[26]

The Stephens family saga, oft told in Vanuatu, begins with the story of Thomas Carfield Stephens, who had been an English naval officer, and his wife, Sela Tubou, a member of the Tongan royal family. Sela was a cousin to Queen Salote. Her relatives let her know that any children she had with this English commoner would lose their royal status. To avoid the stigma of having half-white children in Tonga, she and her husband set out for the New Hebrides, where, ironically, the same children were stigmatized as "half-black."

They made a dangerous crossing to the New Hebrides from Tonga in a twenty-six-foot open whaleboat with their first three children, arriving at Erromanga in 1904. Eventually they settled near Tasmalum on South Santo, where T. C. Stephens shared a property with the settler Clapcott, who, like Stephens, came from the Portsmouth area of England. Clapcott was killed by the local people in 1923 either for blocking the route of deceased spirits (the missionary explanation) or for poisoning a ni-Vanuatu married woman with whom he had been having an affair (the islanders' explanation).

T. C. Stephens continued to run the mainland plantation he had shared with John Clapcott, but seeking safety for his family established their home on the off-

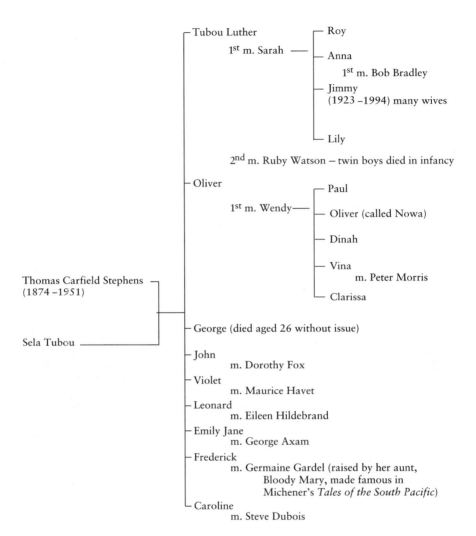

Figure 62. Genealogy of some members of the Stephens family.

shore island of Urelapa.[27] T. C. Stephens built a spacious Australian-style bungalow that was simple, as the British district agent's home was, in terms of utilities but that included a few luxuries, notably a large piano in the living room.

Occasionally Granny Stephens, as Sela became known, would organize a big party that included the government functionaries, and Thomas Carfield would play the piano. Even when she was an old woman, she was strong-minded. Her

otherwise rambunctious sons were very much at her beck and call. George Bristow described her as a regal hostess:

> Only once a year or so she would decide to hold a party, and it was a tremendous party, because she would sort of clap her hands as it were, and the sons would come in and she would give her orders. Then they'd go out and they'd bring in all the fruits of the land, freshwater prawns, and all manner of luxuries for the party. She would organize it. The native girls, the local girls, would be under her thumb. She would invite most of the European population to her party. It was something to remember. She sat in the corner and kept her eyes open to see that everything was going right, giving orders here and orders there, calling Johnny over, or calling Len or Oliver and saying "Mr. So-and-So needs this, and Mrs. So-and-So needs that," and they used to scurry around. She was very much the matriarch.

Granny Stephens continued to preside over the family home at Urelapa after T. C. died in 1951. John Stephens was allowed to leave prison, such as it was, to attend the funeral. Sela's daughter, Caroline, described the Urelapa house as the

Figure 63. Anna Stephens' and Bob Brady's wedding, Urelapa, 1945. L–R: Sela Stephens (holding an unidentified infant), Dinah Stephens (kneeling, Oliver Stephens' daughter), Violet Stephens Havet, Caroline Stephens Dubois, unidentified child (possibly Steve Dubois Jr.), Bob Brady (American soldier), Anna Stephens, Lily Stephens (Anna's sister), Emily Stephens Axam, Dorothy Fox Stephens, Germaine Gardel Stephens (Violet, Caroline, and Emily were sisters whose brothers married Dorothy and Germaine). Photo from Violet Bowhay collection, with permission.

social center of Santo in the 1940s and 1950s, which is hardly surprising given the large number of young people in the family at that time. But most of the socializing was among the settler families themselves rather than with the "government," leaving Angela Eaton to conclude that "the Stephenses didn't have a social life." Although the British government and the "British" settlers were neighbors, their worlds seldom intersected.

Social life on Santo was, in Angela's words, "a mess, but it was a wonderful mess." It was a mess compared to her later years in Nigeria, or even her experience in Vila, where her social life was structured around the colonial hierarchy. In Santo until at least the 1960s, that hierarchy was nonexistent, as the only expatriate colonial personnel were the two district agents. Maxwell gave a party on the Queen's Birthday, the French gave one on Bastille Day, and otherwise everyone had to organize their own fun. Although the entire population of South Santo was small, there was what Angela called "a half-caste barrier" that kept mixed-race, British *ressortissant* families and the British government on the margins of each other's social lives. The possibility of formal socializing with ni-Vanuatu was so far beyond those margins as to have been inconceivable, although sex between white men and Melanesian women was not.

Race and Place

Reproductive sex between Melanesians and whites produced "half-castes." This term was still in common usage in the 1990s. It was "haf-kas" in Bislama. Racial difference, including the ambiguous categories of hybridity such as the half-caste, has been conflated historically with cultural difference.[28] So the Stephens family did things differently, in Angela Eaton's estimation, because they, or at least the grandchildren, were half-caste, not because they fused Tongan and British etiquette or housekeeping styles. The following exchange between Angela and Will Stober reveals ambiguities and uncertainties that some scholars would regard as typical of colonialism.[29] Clearly Angela and Will, although both "ex-colonials," do not think alike on the question of who is and isn't a half-caste. Will is quite clear: half-caste is mixed race, Tongan and white, as well as the product of such offspring and a ni-Vanuatu. Angela is not unkind but she is confused, and her confusion highlights ambiguity that was seldom so explicitly expressed. Granny Stephens was not "half-caste" for Will but she was for Angela who, in some confusion, asserted that Mrs. Stephens was no princess and, not being what she was reputed to be, she acted like a half-caste. In other words, she was a mimic like a half-caste. Some of the stereotypical associations that whites

commonly expressed to me about "half-castes" when my tape recorder was off stand out in Angela Eaton's musings on the Stephens family.

Will Stober was both intrigued and horrified by the idea of "going native," as his alter-ego Fletcher had done in *Isles of Illusion*, also with considerable ambivalence. To him, "going native" connoted having sex with nonwhite women, a topic with which he was also fascinated. He did not own a video machine, but he made an audiotape for me of the British television series *Ruling Passions,* based on Ron Hyam's book about sex and the agents of the British empire.[30] He posed the first question to Angela on the topic, invoking George Bristow's authority (see figure 64): What does it mean to go native? Angela's first response concerned housekeeping, and her entire answer had to do with people in and out of their domestic or racial place. Mr. and Mrs. Stephens lived differently in their European-style house than "we" would. They hardly ever left Urelapa. They kept out of white colonial space except when they needed to call on colonial authority—for example, to obtain a permit.

Mrs. Stephens knew, and kept to, her place in other ways. She sat uneasily with Angela's mother, sharing lemonade, probably declining an offer of the ubiquitous gin and refusing to allow her daughter to enter the intimate white space of the British district agent's latrine. It is not as if the agency had a fancy lavatory much different from what Lily would have found familiar. They all had simple pit latrines. We cannot know from this exchange what Mrs. Stephens was thinking or even if she really was concerned that Lily not use the agency facilities. Her exchange with Lily is camouflaged by the use of a language that was alien to Angela. Perhaps it was Polynesian. More likely it was the widely spoken Bislama in which all settler families, but few Vila-based administrators or visiting schoolgirls, were fluent.

What we glimpse is not Granny Stephens' character but Angela's views of a matter out of place in racial terms. The Stephenses, she claims, treated their grandchildren "like dirt." To explain why she thought this, Angela came up with what seemed to me at first an odd example. But the story of Lily and the toilet is actually very appropriate to Angela's argument. It is a story about a particular kind of matter, dirt, specifically urine or excrement, and where it belongs, namely away from the British district agent's house.

The uncertainty about whether Mrs. Stephens would have used the agency facilities seems connected to an ambivalence about her racial status. Angela insists that she was "regarded as a half-caste." A typical half-caste characteristic is mimicry, acting white but not quite.[31] Angela stumbles over this problem of difference. It goes without saying that Angela regards the Stephenses as social inferiors. The Mrs. Stephens of Angela's story is sensitive to this, restricting Lily's movement, literally, without Mrs. Maxwell's doing so. In fact, Mrs. Maxwell,

WILL STOBER: George Bristow says that old man Stephens was the English naval gentleman to the end. . . . He didn't go native, he might have married a Tongan girl.

ANGELA EATON: He went native in certain ways. The house . . . wasn't run like an English . . . house. And all the offshoots of his half-caste children, they treated them like dirt.

STOBER: Who did?

EATON: He and his wife.

STOBER: Are you saying that they treated their grandchildren like dirt?

EATON: Yeah, because they were half-caste. They didn't—what's the example I can use?

STOBER: So were their children for that matter. I mean, their own children were of mixed blood. All the Stephens brothers and girls were obviously of mixed blood, by definition.

EATON: That's right, they were all half-caste. For example, once old Stephens . . . and his wife [who] rarely left Urelapa . . . came to visit Joe to get a permit, or something. And Mommy invited them up to the house. . . . And Lily . . . one of their granddaughters . . . came with them. . . . And Mommy brought them onto the verandah, and they all sat down rather awkwardly, and had a glass of lemonade. . . . And Lily asked to go to the lavatory. And my mother said, "Oh, yes," and she was about to lead her to our toilet when Mrs. Stephens said, "No, no." And she said something in . . . Polynesian, we didn't know what language, to Lily. And she said to my mother, "No, no." And Lily went out into the plantation. Now, Lily was not allowed by her parents to use a white lavatory, because in their eyes half-castes should not use white toilets. Now, that was old Mrs. Stephens herself.

MARGARET RODMAN: Would Mrs. Stephens have used the lavatory herself?

EATON: I don't know. . . . I don't think so. . . . A tremendous gulf there.

STOBER: This is all very curious. A gulf between—it's a bit much, isn't it? The white Englishman, pure bred. The pure-bred Tongan "princess."

EATON: But . . . John Stephens was a far more sophisticated half-caste. You see, you've got to realize that there were the primitive half-castes, like old Mrs. Stephens, who never ever—

STOBER: But she wasn't a half-caste, this is the thing.

EATON: Well, she was a Tongan, but she was regarded as a half-caste. Joe said she was no princess, that was her story that had come through. She wasn't a princess, she was a Tongan. But . . . they didn't regard themselves as lower than us. They were different to us. John Stephens was the true half-caste. He was sly, devious, and when it suited him, he would become native, and when it suited him, he would try and become white. And nobody trusted John Stephens at all. He had all the vices of the half-caste.

Figure 64. Musings on half-castes.

the self-styled rebel, probably would happily have shown Lily to the loo. It is an apparent contradiction then that a deferential Mrs. Stephens did not think she was lower than the Maxwells, just different, yet she was so deferential.[32] Angela struggles to find a resolution, turning to an imagined difference between "sophisticated" and "primitive" half-castes to defuse Mrs. Stephens as relatively harmless compared to her "true" half-caste son, the notorious John.[33]

Half-castes could not be trusted, according to the racial stereotypes to which many whites in the New Hebrides subscribed at that time. Angela expressed with remarkable candor the assumptions that seemed implicit in many less direct statements I heard about people of mixed race in the New Hebrides. Sophisticated is bad in this inversion of evolution. The half-caste devolves or dissipates. His sophisticated evil is evident for Angela in the fact that he could move between racial identities; but note that while he could "become" native when it suited him, he could only "try" to become white. John is untrustworthy, exhibiting "all the vices of the half-caste." These arise, I would say, not from John's racial background as Angela alleges but from the untrustworthiness of the ambiguous boundaries that enclose the term "half-caste," ambiguities evident in the exchange among Will, me, and Angela.

Uneasy in the Islands

The Santo Rebellion accompanied the official end of colonialism in the New Hebrides. In so doing, it underscored the fact that colonialism was not monolithic. The rebellion revealed the depth of divisions between and among islanders, settlers, and the Condominium. Some of the fault lines were those of the Condominium itself—French versus English. Others, such as sectarian divisions, were products of missionization. Still others reflected old feuds among indigenous factions of islanders.

Jimmy Stephens, as leader of the Nagriamel movement, epitomized these tensions. He advocated *kastom* but also Christianity. He spoke for the "black" man but acted like a white man in many ways. (He never pretended to speak for women.) He dressed in a shirt and trousers; his assistants wore loincloths and carried briefcases. Despite his smiling demeanor, his Santa Claus beard, and his twinkling light eyes, Jimmy Stephens was deadly serious in the demands he made on behalf of ni-Vanuatu and in his threats of violence to back them up. Some of these demands were spatial: in particular, the "dark bush" had to return to the islanders. The "dark bush" meant land that had not been domesticated—that is, cleared, planted, or mined.

From the earliest days of the Condominium it was obvious that extensive land alienation had occurred on paper. At one time there were allegedly expatriate claims to more land than existed in the entire archipelago. The land issues arising from this alienation were the raison d'être for the Joint Court and the grand buildings described in chapter 2. The court and the Condominium had never succeeded in resolving these issues. So here was Jimmy, grandson of an Englishman and a cousin of Queen Salote, pressing the cause of the ni-Vanuatu and running some settlers, of similarly mixed-race backgrounds, off the land.

Other settlers were forced by the French to leave. One evening in July 1995, I sat in a Santo restaurant listening uneasily to tales of restaurant violence during the rebellion. Had there been saloon doors, I would have expected a lone gunman to burst through them at any moment. Santo really did seem to live up to its nicknames, La Frontiera and Le Far West. One British *ressortissant* told me how in 1980 a French settler had shoved a table into his stomach as he sat eating his dinner, pinning him to the wall. The hapless diner's wife (a Francophone) was in the back of the restaurant. Alerted to the situation by ni-Vanuatu kitchen staff, the wife grabbed a large knife and raced into the dining room to defend her husband. The assailant took one look at the woman and her knife and fled. Some, such as this attacker, were deported after the rebellion, when the tables, so to speak, had turned in favor of the Anglophones.[34]

It seems appropriate that when the evacuation of British *ressortissants* came during the rebellion, it took place on South Santo, the bastion of British settlement, and, for awhile, of British government. Evacuees were told to make their way to Tangoa, the Presbyterian mission's island off the south coast. To guarantee safe conduct, Jimmy Stephens issued stickers to put in the vehicles' windows. Evacuees were not sure if this was a help or a hindrance. One evacuee who had lived in Santo for many years had a better idea. He marked his car with a large red cross, so it was always safe for him to drive. The drive to South Santo must have been poignant for these people. They crossed plantations, the grassy floor littered with fallen nuts but still groomed by cattle. They drove past plantation houses, simple affairs, much mended and moved. They might have glimpsed the little islands off the main island, including Venui, where no sign of the British presence would have remained.

On the Move Again

The British district agent had long since moved to Luganville, in yet another attempt to be where the action was on Santo. By the end of World War II it was

clear that the town of Luganville was the place to be. Thanks to the American presence during World War II, the streets of Luganville were laid out in a grid pattern and were wide enough for tanks to pass each other. Quonset huts were, and still are, everywhere, providing housing and commercial space and even accommodating the municipal water supply.

The American PT boat base where the Sarakata River meets the Segond Canal provided a *pied à terre* for George Bristow, who took over as British district agent for the Northern District in late 1954. Bristow felt isolated on Venui, not only socially, but in terms of doing his job. When I spoke with him in England, he said,

> Well, it was hard work, I mean just driving down through the plantations for twelve miles, I think it was, to this place called Beer. It was delightful when you got there, but then I never felt easy all the time I was living on Venui. I always wondered, "What's happening in the Canal?" You know, what sort of mayhem is happening that I should have something to do with? So I'd find myself being dragged back there.

Out of sight was not out of mind. The colonial gaze was still important, and Venui commanded a view of the coast, but not of the town. Gradually, the administrative office and then the British district agent's residence moved from Venui to Luganville. By the time John Field replaced George Bristow as British district agent in 1957, the prison and the police remained on the little island, but the British district agent lived near the Condominium radio station, along the Segond Canal southwest of town. Field supervised the creation of a new district agency, with offices next to the French in Luganville, and a residential complex, called the British Paddock, on the eastern outskirts of the town where a U.S. naval gun installation during World War II had literally commanded the view up and down the Canal. The site, unlike Venui, had more than adequate space for a parade ground. Field argued for modern designs and construction methods that would allow for air conditioning. He was also concerned to keep the land open to encourage the breeze and allow enjoyment of the sweeping view.

The establishment of the Paddock was the culmination of a long process. As early as 1952 there had been proposals to move the agency away from Venui to the Canal. One nonstarter was the suggestion that the British district agent locate on a site immediately above the French District Agency south of town. The French would not have accepted such symbolic dominance. How could the flags fly at equal height if the British were up the hill?

Home at Last

The former French District Agency, southwest of Luganville along the Segond Canal, is probably the only site in Santo that could immediately open as a historic house. The office, which forms the seaward side of a rectangular compound, was built on the site of the first hotel in Santo. (There is still only one "real" hotel.) Inside the office was a sign from World War II warning that each damaged coconut palm costs Uncle Sam $30. A matched pair of portraits flanked the desk: two ni-Vanuatu policeman—one French, wearing a red casquet, and the other British, wearing a green beret with red pompons.

The former prison forms one end of the compound. Long replaced by a larger and more secure facility in town, the little prison was still in perfect condition when I walked into *namba sikis,* the solitary confinement cell, in 1995. The other two, larger cells were each intended to accommodate about four prisoners. In contrast to British sites, although it may be just coincidence, the servants' quarters are on the highest ground with the best view.

The house, a classic in colonial design and probably built from a ready-cut kit, had shady verandahs, louvered windows, and tongue-in-groove ceilings. The furnishings looked as if they were the same age as their owner, the nonogenarian Mme Leroy. She had come out to the New Hebrides as a tourist in the 1930s, met Miguel Leroy, a plantation manager, and married him on Malakula. They bought

Figure 65. French District Agency (exterior). Author's photo.

Figure 66. Mme Leroy (left) and Mme Stuart, 1995. Author's photo.

the house in which she lives in 1968, after the French District Agency was relocated to central Luganville. In 1995, Mme Leroy was frail and hard of hearing, but determined to remain where she was. Hélène, a ni-Vanuatu woman who had worked for Mme Leroy for thirty-five years, baked a sponge cake and made coffee for me and my landlady, Mme Stuart, who had brought me to visit her friend "Mimi." It was on this occasion, as I was photographing the old sewing machine,

the archways, the verandahs, that Mme Leroy kept protesting that this was just an ordinary house, "Ce n'est pas très interressant." "Si," my landlady insisted, shouting for her friend's benefit; "c'est interressant—pour *elle!*" Indeed it was.

I was in my element, for the house said so much about the past and about its occupant. There were very few family photos or mementos. Mme Stuart said she had taken her own photos and papers to Noumea for safekeeping during the rebellion, but Mme Leroy had burned hers. Her husband was still alive at the time—he died in 1983—but they had no children for whom to keep such things. They did not know what would happen and they did not want their personal things "going all over the place."

Lacking personal mementos did not mean lacking a personal touch. The interior of this house looked as well-worn and well-preserved as its occupant. Like an old stuffed animal, the house looked loved. The very bright red roofs seemed to sit oddly on the old buildings, like new packaging. But the roofs, almost blinding in the tropical sunlight, made a strong statement, which may have been just what Mme Leroy wanted. They said, "I'm still here. There is no more Condominium. There is no French government here anymore. But I'm still here and this is my home." As we drove away in Mme Stuart's air-conditioned car, a thrilling contrast to the hot and dusty trucks I had ridden in for weeks, she told me that her friend Mimi has an apartment in France and a house in Brisbane, but she is not content there. Her life is in Santo, in her house far from the land of her childhood, a house on an island that has become her home.

■ CHAPTER 8

HOUSES FAR FROM HOME

This book has adopted an unusual methodology, the ethnographic study of British colonial administration through the spaces that a unique colonial process constructed. It is an anthropological approach that uses the historical design and use of space as a window into understanding colonialisms' cultures.[1] The situation was unique: the Condominium of the New Hebrides in which Britain and France shared jurisdiction over but did not divide an archipelago of some eighty islands from 1906 to 1980. The research method, however, has wider applicability.

This colonial research on the spaces of British administration in the New Hebrides has shown how a theoretical concern with multilocality can be developed and grounded. This approach shows how the remembered presence of different places shapes people's housing experiences; it also explores the range of meanings that a single place can hold for different people.[2] The methodological focus is on houses as both socially constructed, and thus revealing of larger processes, and as material forms that help shape, and are shaped by, the experience of later occupants.

As a multi-locale method, it builds on other contributions to contemporary theory in anthropology.[3] Marcus has outlined multi-locale approaches that follow the object *or* follow the people. Here I have tried to follow the people through

the objects and the objects through the people. That is, I have examined houses as objects in people's memory and in archival sources over time as well as following the issues that emerge discursively as houses are built, changed, and lived in. This puts into practice James Clifford's idea of traveling theory.[4] Colonial space both expressed and helped to shape colonial ideas, as knowledge was produced and circulated between the Colonial Office in London and the New Hebrides. As we have seen, officers' memories of other postings often surfaced in the New Hebrides as did policies developed for other parts of the British empire. Within the New Hebrides, debates about housing between the British and the French as well as among the British themselves often reflect or fuel other issues.

Residential and administrative buildings themselves were the organizational focus of each of the sources of information for this project—of the interviews with retired colonial officers and their families, of the archival research, and of the listing of historic sites in Vanuatu. Each chapter has explored the history of a particular building and the people and issues—cultural, administrative, political—connected to it. Buildings literally are the architecture of the book.

The structure of the book takes advantage of the idea that buildings "have the perfect memory of materiality."[5] Houses and offices bear witness to past decisions, and their present forms hold clues to all the changes that followed their creation. Buildings, however, are not texts. They contain stories, but people tell them; and those stories of colonial experiences, hopes, fears, and plans describe a culture of colonialism, which is what this book has been all about.

Buildings, like people, have life histories, and these life histories often connect buildings and people to each other and to the political events of the times in which they live. The main story that the buildings in this book tell is that of the Anglo-French Condominium of the New Hebrides. This is a story in which the details matter. Each building as well as each tale has, at any point in time, a position in the administration of the New Hebrides, whether French, British, Condominium, or Melanesian. Through the buildings one sees the construction, modification, and use of a particular administrative project, the Condominium, at the intersection of (although often also on the margins of) French and British colonial interests. Also evident are individual arguments and positions. These are ostensibly about buildings, but they are also about many other things. Throughout the book, the insularity of the British social world in the islands is evident. This insularity reveals a great deal about the colonial process, as discussed in the next section, but it also points to the limitations of the study. These are discussed in the subsequent section, as is the need for further research. The final section draws together some of the themes of the book, exploring how in constructing, modifying, and using British houses, people expressed and contested ideas about

colonial rule, about Melanesians, about the French, about Americans, about other parts of empire, and about prospects for independence.

Insular Worlds

An approach to British colonialism in the New Hebrides through buildings high-lights the insularity of the social lives of British administrators and their families. Sometimes this insularity was literal, when they lived on little islands such as Irir-iki or Venui. To an extent, it was evident in the siting of their houses—for exam-ple, in the desire to be close, but not too close, to the French, or in the clustering of British houses in the Paddock or Shepherd's Bush by-the-Sea. By and large, British officials and their families socialized with each other. There were excep-tions, notably some close friendships between British and French counterparts. But socializing with islanders, missionaries, and settlers tended to occur only when a British official was on tour.

Insularity was compatible with the enclosed style of the prefabricated houses, but the climate was not, nor was French taste. The French judge in the early days of the Condominium refused to have a bungalow of British (Australian) design as it was unsuitable for French habitation, being too enclosed. A more open, villa style of house was preferred. British housing, with hot, unlined verandahs subject to the glare of the sun, or, once the verandahs were enclosed, with dark interior rooms, was not necessarily to British taste either. Nor was the modern housing that supplemented it in the 1960s. In fact, some occupants strongly disliked it, as we have seen; but it seemed necessary or at least unavoidable. People put up with housing shortages, buildings in need of renovations, and crowded accommoda-tions, although not always without complaint. Housing, as we have seen, was in fact a major source of complaint throughout the Condominium.

Throughout the book there is a sense that housing had to be appropriate to one's station and one's culture. This sensibility produces and reinforces insularity both between the British and others and among the British according to their po-sition in the colonial hierarchy. The need for suitable housing was abundantly clear to the early British official Romilly (see chapter 2). Later, a resident commis-sioner's wife also expressed the sense that her husband's position in society in-creased their insularity (see chapter 3). The discussion in chapter 7 of whether a settler child could use the toilet at the British district agent's house also reflects such concerns. In each of these cases, and in other discussions of housing through-out the book, tension is evident between the need to act appropriately to one's sta-tion and the desire to reach out, to enlarge one's social world at least a little. The

allocation of housing according to rank and seniority fits well with this sense of what is appropriate.

The connections British officers' families maintained (or created in some cases) to England as Home also comes out clearly in the material throughout the entire history of the Condominium. All other houses are postings; they exist in relation to that Home. These relationships among buildings and places through the people who dwell in them are instructive for understanding dimensions of identity, as well as for conveying a sense of the often imaginary, insular center that held for people living overseas.

Limitations of the View from British Houses

It should be clear by now how the houses of British administrators in the New Hebrides can frame an ethnography of colonialism, and that what they frame is a small social world, linked with others but insular nonetheless. The limitation of this approach may also be apparent, but it deserves further exploration because it points to the need for further multi-sited research. What an approach through British colonial space cannot teach us is much about the world beyond the British, especially the unofficial worlds of French- and English-speaking settlers, missionaries, and Melanesians. The project I have followed here of working through official British houses is limited to the view that the British had from the windows of those houses. The interviews and the archives convey British officials' sense that others were looking at them, but what that gaze revealed about the British colonial presence cannot be seen from within British houses or from within this study. Methodologically, the next step is to go outside, to enter other houses, read other documents, and explore the memories of other people in positions quite different from those of British officials in the colonial period.

In the research and in writing this book, I chose to focus on British officials, on those for whom England, not the New Hebrides, was Home. But I carried with me a lesson I learned in Paris, one that will shape my future work. The lesson was that not everyone of European background in the colonial New Hebrides had lived in "houses far from home." Ronald Corlette-Theuil, whom I interviewed in Paris in 1994, made this very clear. His family traced its immediate roots to the island of Malakula in Vanuatu, and more distantly to Ambae, France, and to the Isle of Man via Australia. Corlette-Theuil and I had corresponded extensively about the project before I met him. He described himself as living in exile in Paris, unable to carry on the family plantation in the islands because of difficulties with local people, uncomfortable in Australia, where racism

had alienated him as a schoolboy, and uncertain about his future in a literary job in France. His letters, in an elegant copperplate script, had been very helpful, providing precise descriptions of plantations and settlers' homes in the islands. Despite this willingness to help with my research, when I finally met Corlette-Theuil face to face, he told me that he had almost refused to write or see me when he read the title of my project. How could I assume that for all people of French or English extraction, their houses in the New Hebrides were "far from home"? Was I ignoring the fact that families like his had lived in the islands for five or more generations? Their houses were not "far from home." They *were* home.[6]

Applying the same approach to settlers' homes in the islands as I have followed here for British officials would contribute another dimension to understanding "how Europeans imagined themselves in the colonies and cultivated their distinctions from those to be ruled."[7] Such distinctions were not simply between ruler and ruled, but among rulers. Settlers in the New Hebrides as elsewhere were historically specific participants in "imagined communities" that sometimes included government, missions, indigenous people, and Vietnamese, and sometimes polarized them.[8]

Construction, Modification, and Use

How have the houses far from home in this book taught us about the British officials and their families who lived in the New Hebrides? In three ways: through construction, modification, and use. These ways of learning through houses in turn reveal a number of themes.

First, there is the history of a building's construction. This reveals political purposes, whether to express high hopes for a new form of government (chapter 2), the power of the gaze from the British Residency (chapter 3), the ambiguities of imprisonment (chapter 4), tensions between Americans and British in World War II (chapter 5), or the extension of government control through district administration (chapters 6 and 7). The construction history also suggests the importance that particular people placed, at various times, on impressing the French, impressing the islanders, meeting British standards, or saving money. Linkages between the New Hebrides, London, Sydney, and New Caledonia are evident in the not-always-smoothly-functioning chain of supply for building materials and in the tender processes. The question of what is suitable for colonial officials and for the distinctive Anglo-French situation of the Condominium is amply debated through construction processes. The construction of the Joint Court buildings (chapter 2) was an opportunity to make, and to contest, a series of assertions in built form

about the "juristic experiment" that was the Condominium. So, too, the question of physical incarceration and social rehabilitation was debated through the building of prisons. The debate in chapter 4 over the suitability of constructing a grass house as a prison reveals underlying questions of categorization, containment, and the definition of both prisoners and homes. The construction process of the White House in chapter 5 is a succinct statement in built form about the efficiency with which the American military superimposed itself on the British administration.

Second, the houses in this book have much to teach through stories, documents, and physical evidence of their modification. The White House, the prison, the Residency, and indeed all of the buildings central to the book are as much about modification as about their initial construction. The Tanna house (chapter 6) is an especially clear illustration of the ambiguities that colonial officers experienced about dwelling and working, ambiguities that the presence of a wife and children highlighted. There, the office initially was the open verandah. Then the area of the verandah used as an office was enclosed, becoming part of the house. Islanders thus were allowed farther into colonial domestic space on official business, but eventually neither the officer nor his wife felt comfortable with this arrangement. The officer's wife in her pajamas hearing islanders come and go in the office next to her bedroom door found it all too much. Colonial boundaries were then modified along Condominium lines. A separate office was constructed, one that shared a party wall not with the bedroom but with the French district agent.

Some modifications to the British Residency also occurred as a response to the presence of wives. This in turn was an index of both changing conditions of employment and the degree to which the New Hebrides seemed under control, or "safe" for women and children. The Colonial Office felt that the British Residency had to be improved when the first married resident commissioner arrived in 1924. The first resident commissioner's bulldog used to walk right through the screening on the Residency doors. The second resident commissioner was not bothered by the holes in the screens, nor did mosquitoes worry him. But by 1924, the Colonial Office authorized such upgrading as could be accomplished at "no great expense."[9] Keeping costs down was always a priority when one was making modifications to British colonial houses and offices in the New Hebrides.

Other modifications resulted from conflict. The modifications of the "hot box" at Venui, described in an interview as well as in the archives, point to a stubborn little power struggle between the district agent's wife and the resident commissioner. Forcing the British resident commissioner to sleep in a small, hot guest room instead of allowing her husband to offer their own bedroom led to the renovations of the guest room that the district agent's wife had wanted all along.[10]

A larger, in fact international, struggle is evident in the changes to the White

House and the British Paddock during World War II described in chapter 5. Through archival documents, the White House is revealed as a space that British officials tried to create but were unable to control. The Americans, for their part, bypassed the ponderous slowness of the dual colonial bureaucracy. When the Americans plowed the paddock and turned it into a corn field, British government personnel were powerless to do anything about it because their objections were simply ignored. They were mutually constructed as civilians, not as part of the military effort. The British resident commissioner thus had virtually no influence on the Americans but had to maintain his authority with his own personnel—in fact, with more of them than before because of the influx of officers from the Solomons.

The White House and the paddock tell a great deal about how Americans intervened in and disrupted British space, ran roughshod over British colonial authority at the local level while cooperating with London at higher diplomatic and military levels. The American reputation for efficiency is evident in the rapid completion of a house that the British were building very slowly. The marginality of the New Hebrides except for its temporary significance as a strategic military site is evident in the way it is occupied, upgraded, then left to return to its marginal position in the postwar world. For the Americans, its importance was purely strategic, and temporary, lasting only until the battle of the Coral Sea was won. For the British and the French, the importance of the islands was far more complex if still marginal. It was historically nuanced by other wars and other diplomatic agreements, such as the Entente Cordiale. The Paddock was emblematic of the British side of a colonial equation that struck a balance with the French while never being able to work efficiently with them or without them. The White House, on the other hand, was testimony to the efficiency with which the American military superimposed itself on the British administration without seeking a balance at all.

The houses in this book also teach through their silences on the subject of modification. People frequently spoke of the rigidity or intransigence of the spaces and the little that one could do to make them feel like home. Housing in the later colonial period was the most often criticized—for example, Shepherd's Bush by-the-Sea in chapter 5. But some objected to the gloominess of older houses with deep verandahs that blocked light to the interior rooms. Escape was an alternative to modification, and the British often took the gin or the tea out under the frangipani tree not only in response to earthquakes, as Angela Eaton described in chapter 7, but to extend domestic space, as islanders do, to the more comfortable outdoors.

Other modifications reflected the adaptation of imported housing styles to

the climate of the New Hebrides. While designed for heat, the Australian prefabricated buildings that were a mainstay of British housing in the islands were not designed to cope with humidity or the glare of sunlight reflected off the sea. Insulating verandah ceilings and adding louvers were the most common modifications to these buildings. The enclosure of parts of verandahs to create extra bedrooms or offices was also very common. Like porches everywhere, verandahs fill in by stages; people can always visualize the next thing they want to do to their house but rarely, especially in the case of peripatetic administrators, plan beyond their immediate needs.[11]

A third way in which the houses central to this book teach about their occupants and about colonial processes is through the use to which the buildings' spaces are put. Use overlaps with modification. For example, the increasing political importance of socializing is evident in a shift from using the British Residency simply as government housing to using it more for entertaining and guest accommodation. Where once three officers shared the Residency (King, Jacomb, and Hallowell), by the 1940s an annex was required for accommodating the visiting dignitaries brought to the islands by World War II and the American presence. The obligation to socialize on a scale considered quite large for the small town of Port Vila had already led to widening the Residency verandah in the 1930s. The British resident commissioner at the time, G. A. Joy, had expressed his concern not to erect a social wall around the Residency.[12] Later, in the 1960s, efforts were made to include Melanesians at parties; during the 1970s, a renewed effort to get along with the French included more socializing. The guest lists, decorating motifs (Melanesian-style rugs), cuisine (food served on banana leaves), and menus (sometimes assertively non-English) all frame political changes that eventuated in independence for Vanuatu in 1980.

The uses of the White House shifted from its intended purpose as housing for British officials to a hospital and later housing for American troops during World War II to the first accommodation for female staff in the British administration. The Joint Court building went from courthouse to apartment building to theater to demolition. The president of the court's house became American Island Command headquarters in the early 1940s, then the Joint Court house, and finally the Supreme Court of Vanuatu.

Interviewing a variety of people who had lived in the same house at different times—following the people through the object—led to interestingly multi-vocal results. Descriptions of the houses revealed diverse memories and divergent feelings. The extreme insularity of district administration in the New Hebrides is apparent in the loneliness that afflicted some, but not all, residents of the Tanna house and in the tiny but energetic social world of Venui Island. Every house and

every posting elicited different views. The Turners loved the White House. Others found it dark and gloomy. Some felt that the old Residency was uncomfortable; others viewed the new Residency as a motel; still others liked them both. These personal preferences with regard to housing are not surprising in themselves, but they open the door, so to speak, to other differences with regard to what British officers and their families thought they were doing in the New Hebrides. For example, descriptions of the layout of the district agency might reveal details about gender roles, racial boundaries, or the importance of education. The colonial mission as one of working with "backward peoples," contradictory feelings about the category "half-caste," and uncertainty about imprisonment were some of the topics that came out through discussions of housing and other buildings. The cultural lenses through which British administrators and their families looked out their doors were evident in discussions of their use of housing, as well as in its construction and modification.

These lenses were colored. Racial boundaries in the use of space helped to create and maintain inequalities basic to colonial rule.[13] Racial boundaries also contributed to the insularity of British social worlds. Initially, British space was white space, in which natives had to be off the streets of Port Vila at night. Inside British houses there could be house girls but no other Melanesians, although prisoners could be close to the house exteriors. Later, as spaces for the political development of Melanesians expanded, they began to be entertained in British houses and to be provided with British houses of their own. The transition to independence was in part a spatial one in which Melanesians came to use nearly all of what had once been British, French, and Condominium official and domestic space. Like their British predecessors, ni-Vanuatu administrators and their families call other islands home: not England, but Ambae or Malakula, Santo or Tanna. And like the British posted overseas who might never have lived in England but called it Home, many ni-Vanuatu civil servants have spent little time in the island homes that are such important touchstones of their identity. Instead, they live in many of the houses described in this book, and these remain houses far from home, albeit for new residents.

Notes

■ Chapter 1: *House of Bamboo*

1. Michael Jackson (1995:155) makes a similar point with regard to what he learned from Australian Aboriginal people: "But in the end, home is not a place that is given, but an experience born of what one makes of what is given, and the work is always before us all of becoming 'bosses for ourselves'."

2. I acknowledge the riskiness of this approach. Some academics, including Caren Kaplan (1996:65–100) would dismiss all of these terms as "modernist tropes" that cannot productively be part of postmodern or postcolonial theories. In exploring the history of a particular colonial form, however, I believe that they remain productive metaphors to explore and critique because of their multiple meanings in participants' discourse and because of the shifting relationships between some of the terms.

3. Kaplan 1996:161.

4. Rosaldo 1989:70.

5. Spatial practice, in Lefebvre's sense "embraces production and reproduction, and the particular locations and spatial sets characteristic of a group of people" (1991:33).

6. In John Noyes' words, with regard to Africa, it seemed natural for them "to look upon the world and see only colonial space, . . . to move through the landscape and cross only colonial space, . . . to write about the world and mean only colonial space" (1992:24).

7. Lowenthal 1985:210. See also Boyarin 1994:22 for discussion of memory as a process of creative collaboration between present consciousness and past experience.

8. Clifford 1989:179.

9. Marcus 1995; M. Rodman 1992.

10. Marcus 1986:171.

11. Des Chene 1997:73.

12. I visited as well in 1993 and 1995, but by then the house had been destroyed and rebuilt, a project that dimmed its light-projecting effect.

13. Clifford 1992:99. For further discussion of the spatial practices of anthropological fieldwork, see Clifford 1997.

14. Clifford 1992:101; emphasis in the original.

15. The real names of participants in the research are used with their written consent.

16. BESA is an acronym for the British Ex-Servicemen's Association.

17. According to the *Oxford Companion to Ships and the Sea* (Kemp 1976:893), trop-

ical storms have different names in different oceans. They are called hurricanes in the western North Atlantic, eastern North Pacific, and the western South Pacific, where Vanuatu is located. In the Bay of Bengal, south Indian Ocean, and northwest of Australia, such storms are called cyclones. They are typhoons in the western North Pacific.

18. I describe this project in M. Rodman 1998a.

19. A York student, Joseph Macchiusi, also wrote his 1996 M.A. thesis using archival material from my files. Jean Mitchell, a doctoral student, received funding under my SSHRCC grant to conduct research on urban space and gender. She did this research in Blacksands, outside the capital of Vanuatu, Port Vila, from 1996 to 1999.

20. This research is described more fully in other publications (M. Rodman 1985b, 1997a).

21. The preceding three paragraphs appeared, with minor changes, in M. Rodman 1997a:4–5.

22. This is what Foucault (1972) and others (e.g., Mitchell 1991) would call the the the colonial "gaze," emphasizing the power involved in commanding such views.

23. Bolton 1999.

24. Noyes 1992:7.

25. It is important to note de Certeau's distinction between place *(lieu)* and space *(espace)* here because I shall be dealing with both. Place is order. It is the way objects—such as houses and offices, streets and parade grounds—are distributed. "The law of the 'proper' rules in the place: the elements taken into consideration are *beside* one another, each situated in its own 'proper' and distinct location. . . . [A place] implies an indication of stability" (de Certeau 1984:110; emphasis in the original). Space, on the other hand, is dynamic. It is a "practiced place" in which time, movement, and other vectors intersect. It has none of the stability of the "proper" place. Space is enacted, or enunciated. The contrast with place is analogous to the contrast between *parole* and *mot* or *connaissance* and *savoir*.

26. De Certeau 1984:36.

27. On Tanna, women, whatever their race, are still expected to avoid the *na gamal* in the early evening when men gather there to drink kava (Latin: *Piper methysticum*), a plant that is a member of the pepper family. The ground root of the plant is used to make a drink that induces relaxation and contentment. The dried root is exported as "kava-kava" for sale to health food stores (see Brunton 1989, Lindstrom 1991).

28. Foley 1993.

■ Chapter 2: *The Condominium*

1. Harcombe 1991:22.

2. The terraces are at heights of approximately five, twenty-five, fifty, and over fifty-five meters (Bennett 1957:121).

3. Gwendolyn Wright (1991) uses the image of Celesteville to discuss colonial space in her book on metropolitan French urban design in the colonies.

4. The phrase "wishful thinking" refers to Nicholas Thomas, who calls for anthropologists to follow a path that is different from the large and growing literature on colonial and postcolonial discourse. Instead of viewing colonialism as a hegemonic ideology, what he advocates, and what I am trying to write here, is "an ethnography of colonial projects: that presupposes the effect of larger objective ideologies, yet notes their adaptation in practice, their moments of effective implementation and confidence as well as those of failure and wishful thinking" (1994:60).

5. See Anthony King (1992:347–353) for discussion of the meanings of "colony,"

"colonist," and "colonialism." He underscores the importance of analyzing colonial relations as a *space* of production whose cultural practices and products can affect the metropole as much as the colonies (King 1991). This point is superbly demonstrated in his study of the bungalow as a house form adapted by the British in India and exported around the world (King 1984).

6. See Noyes 1992 on spatiality in German Southwest Africa and Carter 1987 about the creation of empty space in the white settlement of Australia and the ways new places were named. See also Said 1993:78–81 for discussion of the creation of empire in the coincidence of ideas about what a place might become and the actual control of that place.

7. Romilly's letters from Africa and the Pacific were edited by his brother, Samuel (Romilly 1893:334).

8. The quotation comes from Morrell 1960:204. One suspects that only diplomats with a well-developed sense of humor could devise this travesty of civil authority. This thought is from an unpublished portion of a manuscript by Jean-Marc Philibert and me. The manuscript appeared in condensed form in Philibert and Rodman (1996), and this passage by Philibert was among those eliminated. For exploration of British naval policies of benevolent intervention in the Pacific, see Samson 1998. For historical information on Vanuatu see Henningham 1992; Jolly 1991, 1993; MacClancy 1981; Morrell 1960; Scarr 1968; Shineberg 1967; and Ward 1948. For the postcolonial period see Miles 1998 and Philibert 1981, 1992. For an overview of arts and culture see Bonnemaison et al. 1996.

9. See Coffier 1988 on traditional architecture in Vanuatu for discussion of the range of "native" housing.

10. Romilly 1893:361. See also Cawsey 1998, a descendant of MacLeod and a defender of the trader's good character, whose account tells a rather different story.

11. Romilly 1893:349.

12. Romilly 1893:349; Morrell (1960:349).

13. Scarr (n.d.:12).

14. Information in this paragraph, as well as the quotation, comes from Deryck Scarr's unpublished report for the British Residency (n.d.:11–12).

15. Deputy-Commissioner Rason to Mr. Lyttelton, 21 September 1905 (Public Records Office [hereafter PRO] FO 534/101, no. 77, only enclosure).

16. Deputy-Commissioner Rason to High Commissioner (hereafter HC) im Thurn, 6 June 1905 (PRO FO 534/101, no. 67, only enclosure).

17. Some professed to speak for natives, as when Fred Bowie wrote the British resident commissioner on 28 October 1909 to forward a petition signed by fourteen native chiefs requesting the appointment of a Native advocate (PRO FO 534/112 [9796], no. 27, enclosure no. 5).

18. T. F. Swallow to Captain Rason, 11 September 1905 (PRO FO 534/101, no. 98, enclosure no. 2).

19. Morrell 1960:353.

20. Roseby 1911:7.

21. Ibid.

22. Ibid.

23. Jacomb 1914:88.

24. MacClancy 1981:80.

25. Oliver 1962:250.

26. These four high officials were usually a governor, an attorney general, a chief justice, and a colonial secretary (Jacomb 1914:74).

27. Jacomb 1914:74.

28. Ibid.

29. Woodcock 1976:213.

30. Letter from Reid Cowell to Will Stober, 24 May 1991, declining to prepare a submission for Stober and Keith Woodward's project on the history of British district agents. Courtesy of Will Stober.

31. Cowell's play is called *Pandemonia, or a Franco-British Fantasy*, 2.1, p. 28.

32. This research draws upon archival material in the Records Branch of the British Foreign and Commonwealth Office, which has rarely if ever been used by researchers on the New Hebrides since it was relocated from the Western Pacific High Commission holdings in Fiji in the late 1970s. Other sources used here include files from the British Public Records Office, the Mitchell Library, the Faculty of the Built Environment Resource Centre at the University of New South Wales, and libraries at the Australian National University.

33. Thomas Roseby, British judge, used this phrase in a speech to the president of the Joint Court on 15 November 1910, published in the *New Hebrides Magazine* (January 1911:6).

34. Henningham 1992:12.

35. The French maintained a small hospital in Port Vila staffed by a military doctor.

36. Gwendolyn Wright has shown how French colonialism in the early twentieth century embraced urbanism "in efforts to make colonialism more popular among Europeans and more tolerable to the colonized peoples" (1987: 291). See also Fuller 1992 for a discussion of Italian colonial architecture, Vale 1992 for a comparative study of buildings in colonial capitals and Rabinow 1989 for more discussion of architectural dimensions of French colonialism. See King 1995 for discussion of Rabinow, Wright, and others writing on colonialism and urban space.

37. Wright 1991:6.

38. Noyes 1992:215.

39. Examples of Presbyterian boosterism include the following comment as part of an announcement of recent weddings: "The old excuse, 'I could never bring a wife to a place like this' is becoming obsolete (*New Hebrides Magazine*, April 1907:5). The cautionary remarks about settlement come from the first report of the Executive Committee for the New Hebrides British Association (*New Hebrides Magazine*, August 1908:5).

40. Scarr n.d.:10.

41. Jacomb n.d.: vol. 2, pt. 2, 1907:23. In 1911, the *New Hebrides Magazine* reported "the number of voters on the French roll for Vila is 116 while that on the British roll is 39." Nearby Mele had 1 English and 93 French voters enrolled (April 1911:22).

42. *New Hebrides Magazine* (August 1906:3).

43. Ibid. (January 1907:2).

44. Both quotations in this paragraph come from Jacomb n.d.: vol. 2, pt. 2, 1907:29.

45. Jacomb 1914:64.

46. New Hebrides British Service archive (hereafter NHBS) 79/1908, 28 March 1908, British Resident Commissioner (hereafter BRC) Merton King to the French resident commissioner (hereafter FRC), probably still Charles Bord, FRC since 1904, who was replaced briefly by Jean-Martin Colonna and then by Charles Noufflard later that year.

47. The final quotation is from Jacomb 1914:58.

48. BRC King to C. Lucas, Foreign Office, 14 February 1910 (PRO FO 534/112, no. 32. Private).

49. Oliver 1962:251.

50. The Ifira Island Trust has exercised traditional rights to land in the Port Vila area since independence.

51. Western Pacific High Commission archive (hereafter WPHC) 27/21/11, Joint Estimates for 1912–1913.

52. NHBS 232/1908, 5 June 1911, minuting, British Judge to BRC King.

53. NHBS 33/1907, 21 December 1907, BRC King to High Commissioner.

54. "European" was crossed out in the handwritten draft of the English legislation. The French draft, in a parallel handwritten column, avoids the issue, referring simply to "les indigenes engagés" (employed natives).

55. Jacomb 1914:58.

56. NHBS 227/1908, folder VI, Bills of Lading 1908–1911.

57. French New Caledonian carpenters in the 1908–1910 building boom included a M. Julian or Julienne, who built the Joint Court, and Georges Raveton, who built the post office. British carpenters included Walter Baxter and James Foster, who was dismissed and replaced by G. T. Parry in 1909. The Scots carpenter spelled his own name as both McKenzie and MacKenzie.

58. D'Obrenan 1939:82–83.

59. MacClancy 1981:91.

60. See Bennett 1957 for discussion of the geography and history of Port Vila and the only other municipality in the New Hebrides, Luganville, also known as Santo, the shortened name of the island of Espiritu Santo on which it is located.

61. WPHC 700/1926, 2 March 1926, BRC to FRC.

62. Jacomb 1914:13.

63. WPHC 612/1908, 29 May 1911, BRC Merton King to British High Commissioner. The land for (a) through (d) was purchased from the Société Française des Nouvelles Hébrides for £1,462-15-3; land for the Joint Court (f) was acquired from the French government for £206-15-2. The post office and treasury were built on an uncontested, approximately one-acre portion of Miss Annie Petersen's estate for a cost to the French and English of £43-18-11 each. Title to much of her property was disputed with the French New Hebrides Company. The registrar's house was to have been built on this land but was not, in the event, because of the land dispute. Instead, British carpenters using Australian materials renovated an existing house (possibly one of Miss Petersen's cottages already standing) for use by the registrar (NHBS 227 1908, 3 January 1911, BRC Merton King to FRC Charles Noufflard).

64. NHBS 1/I 227/1908, part III.

65. It is not clear when delivery of mail stopped. Certainly by the 1970s, all mail was sorted and placed in boxes for pickup at the post office.

66. The post office initially issued French New Caledonian stamps surcharged "Nouvelles Hébrides Condominium" and English Fijian ones, surcharged "New Hebrides Condominium" (Jacomb n.d.: vol. 2, pt. 2, 8 June 1908:84).

67. NHBS 1/I 232/1908, letter 24/1/17, Deschamps to BRC.

68. Alexander 1927:189.

69. Jacomb n.d.: vol. 2, pt. 2, 5 November1908:98.

70. Alexander 1927:189. Alexander's figures include the cost of furnishing the judge's house, which amounted to about £300. Furnishing the president's house cost £492.

71. WPHC 447/1920, 5 March 1921, Memorandum.

72. This quotation and the one earlier in the paragraph come from Jacomb 1929:7.

73. MacClancy 1981:82.

74. Material in figure 12 comes from WPHC 1068/09, 12 August 1911, BRC to HC; WPHC 1920/1922, 21 July 1922, J. F. N. Green, Colonial Office, to Under Secretary of State, Foreign Office; WPHC 2581/1922, 6 October 1922, BRC to HC; and NHBS 2/1929.

75. Alexander 1927:189.

76. The story of Dr. Borgesius' housing draws on the following archival documents: WPHC 1920/1922, 21 July 1922, J. F. N. Green, Colonial Office, to Under Secretary of State, Foreign Office; WPHC 2581/1922, 6 October 1922, BRC to HC; and NHBS 2/1929.

77. Venables Vernon wrote to BRC King in late November 1908, while on board the SS *Pacifique* en route Sydney from Noumea. The architect had gone to Noumea, and he describes the complex process of discussing tenders there for the proposed houses of the British judge, public prosecutor, and the president of the Joint Court in the New Hebrides. He met on separate occasions with the British consul to New Caledonia, Mr. Manning, with the French governor of same, M. Richard, and with his director of public works, M. Perras. Vernon's letter conveys the roundabout nature of the process, which lent itself to delays and errors. In addition, because the *Pacifique* did not sail in January, the height of the hurricane season, it was unlikely that builders could leave Noumea for the New Hebrides until February in any case. (The possibility of passage on another vessel, the *Oui-Oui,* is mentioned.) In sum, the wonder is that anything was built (NHBS 227/1908, 28 November 1908, H. Venables Vernon to BRC Merton King).

78. The Sydney architects prided themselves on providing a wide range of help to clients in the islands. They arranged for the shipment of toilets and paint, typewriters and clocks. They even provided detailed advice, complete with diagram, on how to fix a septic system. No job was too small. "Please accept my assurances," Venables Vernon wrote in a postscript to BRC King, "that I am glad to have such work as the Porch [widening at the British Residency]; tho' small, it is of course all work and we have never jibbed at anything: occasionally we have to give advice on a fowl yard fence or on a tear in a piece of wallpaper and though there are men who specialize it cannot be done in the colonies—nor by a young man" (NHBS 227/1908, 10 March 1909, Vernon to BRC King).

79. NHBS 227/1908, 10 March 1909, H. Venables Vernon to BRC King. Raveton took "only" four months longer than expected to build the post office. It took him longer to complete the British judge's house: it was scheduled for completion on 1 October 1909 but was not ready until 5 March 1910. He charged too much: the estimated cost was £3,000 but the actual cost was £4,048 (WPHC 447/1920, 5 March 1921, Memorandum). Further, Mr. Vernon raised doubts about Raveton's abilities: "from a friend in Noumea I hear that he is not a tradesman but intends to hand over the work to a mason, Delpratt," an act that Vernon feared would double the cost of the house.

In October 1908, the Sydney architects, Joseland and Vernon, sent foreman Walter Baxter, "a builder w/ many yrs. experience" out to supervise work in the New Hebrides. He was one of a series of carpenters sent out from Sydney to the New Hebrides (NHBS 227/1908, 14 October 1908, Vernon to BRC King). Some carpenters, such as one named James Foster, did not work out. Venables Vernon expressed his regret about this to Merton King: "I am exceedingly sorry that Jas. Foster turned out as he did. His face did not attract certainly, but he appeared to work all right at MacKenzie's (Sydney)" (NHBS 227/1908, 28 April 1909, Vernon to BRC King). The architectural firm then engaged another British carpenter, G. T. Parry, who had worked with Lever Brothers in the Solomon Islands.

80. NHBS 283/1908, 6 June 1911, Director of Works K. McKenzie to BRC King.

81. From the archival context it seems likely that the original architects for the French judge's house were Joseland and Vernon.

82. WPHC 1555/10-1, 23 September 1911, BRC King to HC.

83. NHBS 50/11/2, 24/6/43, British Judge Egan to BRC Blandy.

84. Jacomb 1914:74.

85. Ibid., 59–60.

86. Ibid., 84–85.

87. NHBS 118/28, 15 May 1928.

88. Stober's 1995 notes for NHBS 50/11/34.

89. The British and French judges were Condominium officials in their capacities as officers of the Joint Court rather than in their other roles as heads of the national courts.

90. NHBS 232/1908, 7/9/23, British Judge O'Reilly to BRC King.

91. Stober, 1995 handwritten notes for NHBS 50/11/13.

92. WPHC 3053/1927, 10/04/1927, Additional Expenditures.

93. WPHC F22/03/27/1950, Rents Payable by Govt. Officers, 1947–1954.

94. Jacomb 1914:195.

■ Chapter 3: *The British Residency*

1. It would be interesting to collect comparative material on the frequency with which the British chose small islands as administrative headquarters elsewhere in the empire (e.g., Auki in the British Solomon Islands Protectorate, Levuka in Fiji, and the islands that comprised Lagos, Nigeria).

2. The Presbyterians may have considered Iririki to be mission land, but the nearby Ifira islanders never relinquished their claim to the island. After independence, Iririki reverted to Ifira islanders, through the Ifira Island Trust, as the customary owners.

3. Sir Roger du Boulay (BRC 1973–1975), personal communication, 27 January 1994. Sometimes these sites were vacant and made available to colonizers because local people considered the places to be dangerous spiritually. See Achebe 1959:138–143 for a description of villagers' attempts to foil missionaries by granting them the "evil forest" as a site for their church.

4. NHBS 282/37, 14 September 1937, BRC to BDA Southern District. There is no indication in this correspondence at what time the flag was lowered. By the time of independence in 1980, the custom had changed, such that the flag was raised at sunrise and lowered at sunset. Andrew Stuart, the last BRC, described a symbolically rich flag-lowering ceremony on the eve of independence.

5. NHBS 227/1908, folder IX, 13 January 1903, Alexander Dean and Sons, Builders and Contractors, to Captain E. Rason, British Resident, New Hebrides.

6. In 1910, Merton King purchased two blocks of land on Efate on which to construct housing and offices overlooking the growing town of Vila (Lands Records Office, Vanuatu Government, ex-title no. 7). One parcel of slightly more than eight acres was purchased 29 March 1910 from Walter Tanner, agent for Burns, Philp Pty. Ltd. The other, just over fourteen acres, was purchased from J. W. Kerr acting for Gustavus Petersen. Annie Petersen also sold King a portion of ex-title no. 26, although she was not paid by the British government until 1936.

7. By 1913, a new prison designed by Joseland and Vernon (see chapter 4) had been moved to the mainland.

8. The Telephone Regulation of 1909 established telephone service in Vila and the neighboring plantation communities of Mele and Tagabe.

9. Jacomb n.d., vol. 2, pt. 2.

10. Jacomb (n.d.) to his mother, 9 December 1907, included in his unpublished diary. The text in brackets is struck out in the original. The reference to the electrician indicates that there was some sort of generator-powered electrical system, which may or may not have included lights. The bells were to summon servants. The subtext regarding the

Europeans' dependence on servants deserves, and will receive, further comment in other writing to come out of this project.

11. Even large homes were often called "cottages" in the parlance of the day, as was also the case in North America. Rason may have initiated the relationship with Joseland and Vernon, for folder IX of NHBS 218/1908 contains a memo to him, undated, with an estimate.

12. NHBS 52/2/5, vol. 1, 30 October 1946, Acting Resident Commissioner (ARC) Blackwell to HC.

13. Mrs. Jacomb to Charles Jacomb (Edward's brother), 27 September 1908. From Jacomb n.d.

14. Knox-Mawer 1986:17.

15. WPHC 268/1926, letter dated 5 November 1925. Also letter from Smith-Rewse to WPHC, 23 June 1924, in WPHC 1910/1924.

16. WPHC 3359/1935, BRC Joy to WPHC, letter dated 2 November 1935.

17. NHBS 52/2/5, vol. 1, 30 October 1946, ARC Blackwell to HC.

18. NHBS 10/38, BRC Blandy to NSW Government Stores Dept., Sydney, 5 March 1943.

19. Mrs. Blandy acquired a donkey, which she or her guests used to reach the top of the hill without climbing the 179 steps. When a fine roast dinner was served at the Residency, locals would joke that the dinner might be the donkey.

20. NHBS 52/2/5, vol. 1, 30 October 1946, ARC Blackwell to HC.

21. WPHC 146/6/6, Maxwell Hoskings to WPHC, undated Structural Report on British Residency, Port Vila, NH, attached to WPHC to Secretary of State for the Colonies, letter dated 4 July 1955.

22. WPHC 146/6/6, BRC to Secretary of State for the Colonies, 9 August 1955, saving telegram no. 30/55.

23. Personal communication, John Rennie, 25 March 1996.

24. WPHC 146/6/6, Secretary of State for the Colonies to WPHC, saving telegram no. 441, 11 October 1956.

25. Personal communication, John Rennie, 25 March 1996.

26. Annex to WPHC 146/6/6 PAC 30/8/01, drawn by G. A. Atkinson, B.A. Arch., and attached to saving telegram no. 447, 17 October 1956. John Rennie objected to my comments on the bathrooms in this passage, pointing out that his wife, Winnifred, actively participated in decisions relating to the design of the Residency.

27. By then the British offices, including the resident commissioner's, had long since been established in the British Paddock, on the land Merton King had acquired in 1910. This quotation comes from WPHC 146/6/6, BRC to Hoskings and Pilgrim, 14 December 1955.

28. WPHC 146/6/6, Maxwell Hoskings to BRC, 3 May 1956; emphasis added. In the original, each sentence begins on a new line.

29. WPHC 146/6/6, WPHC to BRC, 4 June, 1957.

30. WPHC 146/6/6, Mike Townsend's summary of Rennie's January 1959 letter. Mike Townsend, then working at the WPHC and later posted to the New Hebrides, sent the summary to the secretary of state for the colonies, 2 March 1959. Rennie pointed out (personal communication, 25 March 1996) that the Australian architects, whose original design was rejected but who ultimately built the Residency, considerably underestimated the construction costs, so the overruns were less than they appeared.

31. Quotations from Margaret Wilkie come from my interview with her, 26 July 1994, at her home near Tunbridge Wells.

32. This and subsequent quotations come from Allan 1973, kindly made available by Sir Roger du Boulay. Reece Discombe brought the small kauri tree as a gift for Betty Allan from

Vanikoro, where he was diving for relics from the shipwrecked frigates, *Astrolabe* and *Boussole,* of French explorer La Pérouse. Discombe was the first to locate the *Boussole.*

33. When I asked Keith Woodward, he too did not know if there was any regulation underlying the oft-mentioned concern about the equal heights of flagpoles. He suggests that it was not a matter for great seriousness in the following anecdote: he remembers being telephoned perhaps in 1954 or 55, "when I was very junior in the British Residency, by M. Jouvé, then Number Two at the French Residency, to ask whether we had any objection to the new French Residency flagpole at the top of the hill (wrecked in 1957 by hurricane Uma and built circa '52) being as a result higher than the British Residency flag. I thought the whole business was so silly that I laughed and said at once, 'No objection,' and did not even bother to consult with my immediate superior, the Assistant Resident Commissioner, or the Resident Commissioner, so they had no chance of objecting, which I am sure they would not have done." (personal communication, 16 September 1999)

34. Quotations from Roger du Boulay come from my interview with him in July 1994 or his letter to me dated 27 January 1994 unless otherwise noted.

35. Quoted from John Rennie's letter to me, dated 25 March 1996.

36. Roger du Boulay's letter to me, dated 1 December 1999.

37. Ibid.

38. For further information on Nagriamel see Beasant 1984. For a brief history of both the Vanuaku Party and Nagriamel see MacClancy 1981.

39. The foregoing is extracted from the original text of Philibert and Rodman 1996. The portions extracted here did not appear in the final version of that text.

40. See Champion 1994 for details on their Colonial Service experiences.

41.The Comaroffs (1992) discuss similar analogies between the English urban poor and African tribes people in their chapter "Homemade Hegemony."

42. Allan 1973.

43. The herds were goats in the days of the first resident commissioner, then cattle latterly.

44. The missionary's job was to check islanders' translations of the Bible into local languages for theological accuracy.

■ Chapter 4: *Prisoners in Grass Houses*

An earlier version of this chapter first appeared in 1998 as " 'My Only Weapon Being a Pencil': Inscribing the Prison in the New Hebrides," in *Journal of Pacific History* 33(1):29–49. This chapter concentrates on male, Melanesian prisoners. White, mixed-race, and female prisoners were far less common, but are interesting in part because of the different spatial arrangements for housing them. Prisons were sometimes built for female prisoners; they were generally grass houses. White and mixed-race men usually were held in a more permanent house; the British prisoners, at least, tended to have, or learn, a trade and to become indispensable to the colonial regime during and even after their prison term (see the case of John Stephens in chapter 7).

1. Jacomb n.d.: vol. 2, pt. 2, 6 June 1908:81.

2. Ibid., 8 June 1908:82. "Mi no savvy" is Bislama for "I don't know."

3. Joint Regulation no. 12, 1962. Consolidated Version of the Native Criminal Code.

4. William L. Rodman, "Gaps, Bridges and Levels of Law: Middlemen as Mediators in a Vanuatu Society," in *Middlemen and Brokers in Oceania,* ed. William L. Rodman and Dorothy Ayers Counts, 89–90. ASAO Monograph no. 9 (Lanham, Md.: University Press of America, 1983).

5. MacClancy 1981:45.

6. The Greig murders are discussed in chapter 6. See also O'Reilly 1957.

7. Jacomb, n.d.: vol. 2, pt. 2, 15 October 1908, 95a–96.

8. His primary British appointment was as chief inspector of labor. He was charged with inspecting the conditions under which New Hebrideans were recruited and employed as labor on plantations and elsewhere. The commandant of the constabulary was a Condominium position (NHBS Civil List, 1914).

9. Jacomb, n.d.: vol. 2, pt. 2, 15 October 1908, 64.

10. Ibid.

11. Ibid., 65. Joe Alcide was actually an African from the Seychelles (Peter Morris, personal communication 8 October 2000).

12. Ibid., 83.

13. Ibid., 70.

14. See figures 2 and 3.

15. NHBS 227/1908, BRC to HC, 27/7/12.

16. NHBS 215/35, Minuting 7/10/35, Commandant of Constabulary to BRC.

17. George Bristow, MBE, interview, April 1995.

18. Personal communication, 24 March 1996.

19. Information on appointments and leaves comes from the NHBS Civil Lists.

20. This and subsequent quotations from the exchange among Joy, Seagoe, and Frater come from NHBS 215/35.

21. See ibid., figure 3, Seagoe's minute showing daily averages.

22. NHBS 33/1907, Regulations Restricting the Movement of Natives at Night in Port Vila. This was also true elsewhere, including Papua (see, for example A. Inglis, *The White Woman's Protection Ordinance* [Sussex: Sussex University Press 1975]).

23. Delpech and Bellaïche 1987:285–286.

24. NHBS 195/34, Archdeacon R. Godfrey to BRC, 9 June 1934.

25. NHBS 298/35, Unrest at North Aoba, Mission des deux délégués à Aoba, rapport Juin 1935.

26. See NHBS 229/30, in which the dead man was roundly hated by the community, the killer was highly esteemed, and the government intervened only because of a missionary's report. Seagoe concludes "since the matter has come before you officially—govt. prestige requires Togalawari's retention in Vila for a few months."

27. In this regard, the debate is reminiscent of Michel Foucault's argument that the prison serves a juridico-economic purpose, namely, the repayment of a debt to society through the deprivation of individual liberty (*Discipline and Punish: The Birth of the Prison* [New York: Pantheon, 1977]). It also has a techno-disciplinary effect as an apparatus for transforming the individual subject and providing clinical knowledge about the prisoner.

28. Jacomb 1914:60.

29. NHBS 2/1928, letter from BRC to HC, 4/1/1928.

30. Jerry Marston, interview, May 1995. Marston later became BDA when Wilkins retired.

31. Keith Woodward, interview July 1995.

32. Imprisonment seems to have been accepted widely as a colonial training ground for politicians. See, for example, Lawrence Hammar's explanation for why going to prison in Papua could be a good political move in "Daru Island—World's Smallest Capital," a paper presented at the Association for Social Anthropology in Oceania Annual Meeting (San Diego, February 1997), 57–58.

33. The "weekend pass" story is paraphrased from Terry and Jill Howe, interview July

1994. The "well-worn path" comes from Stan Combs' written submission, February 1996.

34. Even we equipped a couple of prisoners with spear guns when we were staying in a house in the British Paddock (Santo) in 1978.

35. George Bristow (interview, April 1995) did observe that his wife played chess at home a couple of times with someone before they realized he was a prisoner, but this man was part-European. It is unlikely that a New Hebridean would have been a potential chess partner in one's home in the 1950s, whether or not he was a prisoner.

36. Jill Howe, interview, July 1994.

37. His mother, Rosemary Leaf, was interviewed on another occasion.

38. Edward Leaf, interview, May 1995.

39. George Bristow, interview, April 1995.

40. Islanders, long-term residents, and expatriates would agree that Port Vila remains a world apart from the rest of Vanuatu.

■ Chapter 5: *The White House and the British Paddock*

1. NHBS 50/2, 30 June 1941, Burns, Philp and Co., Ltd., to BRC Blandy.

2. The French in Vila had already had a taste of World War II. The New Hebrides, at the instigation of FRC Henri Sautot, became the first overseas territory to declare support for de Gaulle and the Free French. With the support of Ronald Garvey, who was acting BRC, previously high commissioner for the Western Pacific, Sautot took control of Vichy New Caledonia in a bloodless coup in 1940 (see the chapter "France Libre" in Garvey 1983).

3. Lamont Lindstrom succeeded in the much more difficult, because less well documented, task of analyzing the effect of World War II on ni-Vanuatu. Male islanders' most intensive and routinized encounters with Americans were as workers on American bases in Vila and Santo. Their "war stories," along with those of islanders caught up by the war in other ways, "enunciate present statements of identity and desire, of self and other, and of the past in the present. Most of these island war 'texts', however, are stored in personal memory . . . [and] they circulate orally" (Lindstrom 1989:397).

4. Quoted in Garrison (1983:5); this book provides a full account of the joint effort and suggests its effect on the subsequent creation of the U.S. Department of Defense.

5. Ibid., 93.

6. Wallin July 1967:29. This serialized article, "The Project Was Roses," provides a detailed account of the Seabees' role in the war effort in the New Hebrides.

7. NHBS 50/2, 5 June 1942, Peter Colley, Administrative Officer, to BRC Blandy.

8. Geslin 1956:251.

9. NHBS 50/2, 5 June 1942, Peter Colley, Administrative Officer, to BRC Blandy.

10. NHBS 50/2, 5 June 1942, BRC Blandy's minuting.

11. NHBS 50/3, 3 September 1943, Report of Conference between BRC, George Hill, Judge Egan, and Major J. P. Mandl, Rose's Island.

12. Ibid.

13. NHBS 50/3, 22 June 1942, Peter Colley to BRC Blandy, and 23 June 1942, BRC Blandy to Colley.

14. The Americans used all the other major Condominium buildings as well. The Joint Court became first a temporary hospital, then the Service Command. The president's house, initially occupied by Australians, became III Island Command headquarters. The French judge's house was used for subaltern officers' housing (Geslin 1956:250–251).

15. NHBS 194/50/8, 12 February 1943, BRC Blandy to FRC Kuter. The house in question was no. 22, seemingly a Condominium house. The location is not specified.
16. NHBS 194/50/8, 30 November 1942, A. R. Myatt for General Johnson to BRC Blandy, and minuting; emphasis in the original.
17. NHBS 50/3, 21 July 1942, minuting Police Chief Seagoe to BRC Blandy.
18. NHBS 50/3, 25 July 1942, BRC Blandy to Major Mandl.
19. The lease was dated 16 September 1942.
20. Garrison 1983:83.
21. Alex Mitchell, interview. Northumberland, 24 July 1994.
22. NHBS 50/13, 9 April 1942, Burns, Philp, Vila, to Acting BRC (possibly G. R. Johnson).
23. For example, native clumsiness was blamed on several occasions for overturning lamps or overheating stoves and causing fires. That the Europeans involved were relegating dangerous tasks involving fire to their servants, thus minimizing the risk of causing a fire themselves, is not discussed.
24. NHBS 50/13, 10 September 1942, BRC Blandy to Burns, Philp, Vila.
25. Dunn 1997:28.
26. Ibid., 26.
27. Lady Patricia Garvey, interview, Suffolk, 25 July 1994.
28. Camilla Turner, interview, Holland Park (London), 1 May 1995.
29. For children's and adults' attitudes to ni-Vanuatu prisoners see chapter 4.
30. Freddie Fowler, whom Will Stober and I visited in a nursing home in Daventry in May 1995, was the first to occupy this post. Will wrote up notes on the visit as Fowler's speech was difficult to understand and we worried about whether the tape would be comprehensible. Will ruminated on the question of why Freddie retired to England after a lifetime spent overseas: "Vila was the end of a long colonial life. It was perhaps—my words, not Freddie's—time to lay down the White Man's burden, the carrying of which had maybe been fun and mayhap funny and to seek rest in (what might almost have become another culture) England."
31. Stamford 1993:8.
32. Irène Turner, interview, Holland Park (London), 1 May 1995.
33. Keith Woodward, taped cassette letter, Bath, 14 October 1993.
34. Alex Mitchell, interview, Northumberland, 24 July 1994.
35. Ibid.
36. David Dale, interview, Somerset, 18 July 1994.
37. Rosemary Leaf, interview, Somerset, 19 July 1994.
38. Edward Leaf, interview, Northampton, 6 May 1995.
39. Camilla Turner, interview, Holland Park (London), 1 May 1995.

■ Chapter 6: *The Tanna House*

This chapter is dedicated to the memory of Joël Bonnemaison (1940–1997). Bonnemaison 1994:220.
1. The Wilsons were on Tanna from November 1971 to March 1972 as relief for BDA Gordon Norris, who was on leave (letter from John A. S. Wilson to Keith Woodward, 7 January 2000).
2. TAFEA is an acronym for the southern islands—Tanna, Aneityum, Futuna, Erromango, and Aniwa—that was first promoted by Middle Bush, Tanna, residents as an inde-

pendent nation, a breakaway group from the rest of Vanuatu during the rebellion just prior to independence in 1980. Now TAFEA makes up the southernmost area council in Vanuatu.

3. This and the following quotation come from de Certeau 1984:108.

4. Ross Lewin was better known as a labor recruiter than a trader or planter. Notably, he was involved in the illegal recruiting activities of the ship *Daphne* in 1869 (O'Reilly 1957:256).

5. Quotes and information about Ross Lewin's death and the flight of whites from the west coast of Tanna come from Bonnemaison (1994:197–198), which is the English translation by Josée Penot-Demetry of Bonnemaison's *La Derniere Ile*.

6. O'Reilly 1957:164.

7. Bonnemaison 1994:59. See also Ron Adams 1984 and Kerry Howe 1984 for the history of Tanna. Graham Miller's (1978–1990) multi-volume history of the Presbyterian mission in the New Hebrides also includes information on this period in Tanna.

8. Lindstrom 1990:168. This book insightfully explores the enduring importance of geography to Tannese culture and the ways that Christianity reconfigured the three customary "disciplines" of geography, medicine, and magic. For comparative information see M. Rodman 1985a about why Anglican conversion changed women's houses on Ambae, but the men's house (*na gamal*) remained the same.

9. Bonnemaison 1994:199.

10. I have described this process for the Longana area of Ambae in M. Rodman 1983.

11. Quoted from the *Néo-Hébridais,* 28 May 1910, in O'Reilly (1957:166). My translation.

12. Ibid.

13. Bonnemaison 1994:202.

14. Information in this paragraph draws on Bonnemaison 1994: 203.

15. Condominium agents did not become known as French and British district agents until 18 March 1922, the date of the ratification by Britain (and presumably France) of the Anglo-French Protocol of 6 August 1914.

> Thus the Anglo-French Convention of 20 October 1906 remained in force until March 1922. As the Convention did not provide for District Agents (but the Protocol did) this designation did not, at least technically, exist until 1922. . . . Thus it was not intended at this juncture [when Condominium agents were appointed after 1912] that there should be duplication. Rather the Condominium Agents in each area [four in all] would be responsible to both Resident Commissioners, and were to be paid from Condominium, not national, funds. (Keith Woodward, personal communication, 12 November 1999).

In the final months of the Condominium, from the beginning of 1980 until independence on 30 July, the British and French resident commissioners agreed to replace their district agents with a single "government agent" in each district who was responsible to the incoming government of Father Walter Lini, not to the resident commissioners. Nevertheless, the French resident commissioner retained his own representative at least on Santo, and possibly elsewhere (ex–BRC Andrew Stuart, personal communication to Keith Woodward, 3 January 2000). The government agents on Tanna (Joe Joseph) and Santo (Job Dalesa) were abducted by rebels on 27 and 28 May 1980, respectively. Joe Joseph's assistant, Mr. Tamata, also was abducted. The penultimate government agent on Santo, Rede Henry, had left his post precipitously when a traditional *tabu* sign (a *na mwele* leaf) appeared on the District Agency door.

16. NHBS 39/1924, 20 December 1922, Shrubsole to BRC King. The government had initially signed its lease with an earlier owner, a Mr. Truss. Termination of the lease was to be effective September 1923 for the agency and December 1923 for the police barracks.

17. In May 1923, Shrubsole offered to buy the government buildings on his land at White Sands for £180. This was considerably less than they were worth, he realized, as Mr. Nicol had just had the house painted, but "I must consider what the house is worth to me, and what in the event of my reselling I would be likely to get for it" (NHBS 39/ 1924). He also indicated that the Condominium could retain possession of the house until they could arrange for a new residence for Mr. Nicol.

18. NHBS 39/1924, 10 October 1925.

19. A few months later the FRC counterproposed that, as the French had already planned to post an agent to the Lenakel area, the British and French might as well share a parcel known as the Ross Lewin Estate. In any event, the lease with Burns, Philp, which may or may not have been the same block of land, was signed.

20. NHBS 943/1924, 16 May 1924, acting HC to secretary of state for the colonies.

21. It later appeared that the agreement had been at a higher level, between the two high commissioners, Rodwell and Repiquet.

22. NHBS 39/1924, 11 August 1924, BRC Smith-Rewse to HC.

23. Nicol and his counterpart on Santo, Thomas Salisbury, appear on the Colonial List for 1922 as British district agents, transferred from the Condominium in that year, receiving salaries of £350 and quarters. There was a French district agent by that time on Malakula.

24. Meanwhile, the BRC wrote that it would be best not to try to go ahead with his own side's plans to install a British agent in French space on Malakula (NHBS 943/1924, 15 July 1924, BRC Smith-Rewse to HC). In fact, plans did proceed to establish Charles Marie Gustave Adam as district agent on Malakula, albeit not in the French area in south Malakula but at Bushman's Bay, near the Australian settler Ewen Corlette, on the east coast.

25. Ray Honey, 1970 Report on the British District Agent's Residence, Isangel, Tanna. Prepared for BRC Colin Allan. Unpublished ms. courtesy of the author.

26. NHBS 39/1924, 14 August 1924, BRC Smith-Rewse to Burns, Philp and Co.

27. NHBS 2364/1924, 27 October 1924, BRC Smith-Rewse to HC.

28. NHBS 39/1924, 14 November 1924, BRC Smith-Rewse to Burns, Philp and Co.

29. O'Reilly 1957:135.

30. NHBS 39/1924, 23 December 1924, McCoy to BRC Smith-Rewse.

31. NHBS 2364/1924, 29 January 1925, BRC Smith-Rewse to HC.

32. There is no mention of Mrs. Nicol or the couple's two children in the files I consulted. From O'Reilly (1957:166), we know that Mrs. Nicol was Flora Kerr, whose brother, Graham, became a prominent businessman in Port Vila. Flora Kerr came out from New Zealand to join her brothers Graham and Hugh in 1899. She died in 1943, the year before Nicol's fatal accident.

33. NHBS 241/1931, 11 October 1944, BDA Nicol to BRC Blandy.

34. NHBS 186/1926 contains the information about Pinot's ill-starred posting to Tanna. NHBS 371/1930 contains correspondence about the loan of the FDA's house to Lucy Evelyn Cheesman, an intrepid scientist who claimed to be the first white woman to visit the Big Nambas people of Malakula. On this two-year trip (1929–1930), she collected eighteen thousand faunal specimens representing one thousand species, of which seven hundred had never been described before. She wrote numerous popular books, including *Backwaters of the Savage South Seas* (1933), revised and expanded as *Camping Adventures on Cannibal Isles* (1945). O'Reilly (1957:38) gives biographical information about her.

35. This paragraph and the preceding one draw on NHBS 399/1932, 13 November 1932, BDA Nicol to BRC Joy, and minuting.

36. Bonnemaison 1994:221.

37. Ibid., 222.

38. Ibid., 226.

39. Ibid., 225.

40. Ibid., 227. Nicol's telegram is cited from O'Reilly (1949:201).

41. Bonnemaison 1994:340, n. 5. The biographical entry for Nicol in O'Reilly provides the information about the gate (1957:166).

42. NHBS 241/1931, 13 June 1945, FRC Kuter to BRC Blandy.

43. NHBS 241/1931, 29 January 1946, BRC Blandy to HC.

44. NHBS 241/1931, 15 January 1946, BDA White to BRC Blandy.

45. NHBS 241/1931, 28 August 1946, BDA Johnson to Superintendent of Public Works. Mrs. Johnson was, at least by 1950, a typist working for the British government in Port Vila.

46. NHBS 241/1931, 8 October 1946, BDA Johnson to ARC Blackwell. Remarkably, the anticipated verandah lining had been ordered not by White but by Nicol as far back as 1937.

47. In November 1947, Peter Colley was transferred back to Port Vila and was ordered to bring his whole police detachment with him. He left Jules Jocteur, the FDA, in charge of the security of the British Agency.

48. McClintock 1995:36.

49. One of the daughters also predeceased her father, but the reason is not given in Sir Basil's obituary in the (London) *Times*, 16 October 1974, or the entry for him in *Who Was Who, 1971–1980* (578).

50. Figures for Neven-Spence's salary were not available to me, but his predecessor, James Nicol, received £600 and living quarters in 1944. His successor, Len Barrow, earned £660 and paid rent for his quarters in 1950. (In 1947, salaries were raised by 10 percent in anticipation of the introduction of a policy of deducting rent from salaries. The deduction was at a rate of 10 percent of basic salary up to £1,300 plus 3 percent thereafter.)

51. The quotations and information regarding Colley's enquiry into Neven-Spence's death and his inspection of the Tanna District Agency come from his report to BRC Blandy, 11 May 1948 (NHBS 4/1/18 1948).

52. George Bristow to Will Stober, 24 November 1995. Courtesy of Will Stober.

53. The quoted material is from Sir Basil Neven-Spence's letter to BRC Blandy, 16 June 1948 (NHBS 4/1/18 1948).

54. Gill 1995:50–54. The quotation comes from p. 53.

55. This quotation and others relating to Bob Paul's views in this paragraph come from an e-mail message to me from Marney Dunn, 23 April 1998.

56. NHBS 241/1931, 11 August 1948, BDA Barrow to BRC Blandy. The prison had to be moved in any case because it turned out to be on land that May Eedy, a trader, was leasing from Burns, Philp. The agency's own thirty-year lease from Burns, Philp was due to end in 1953. Some repairs and the addition of electricity to the agencies were delayed until the matter of the lease was resolved.

May Eedy was one of a rare breed of single women who lived and worked in the New Hebrides. She had been on Tanna since the early 1920s, and her son, Ron, was acting chief collector of customs when Bristow arrived in Port Vila in 1950. The N. F. Eedy who had leased the FDA's house on Tanna briefly in 1930 probably was May's husband. By 1950, May had lived a long time as a widow. According to Bristow, she was a strong woman who was not at all inconvenienced by living on her own.

57. When Bristow moved in, the BDA's house was in little better repair than when Barrow had arrived. Most of what he had ordered had not yet been delivered to Tanna. When the louvers eventually arrived, Bristow installed them with the help of Corporal Jack.

Then, Bristow assisted Wally Geappen, who was working for May Eedy at the time, in installing the promised simple electrical system.

58. NHBS 50/11/29, 20 December 1948, FDA Jocteur to FRC Menard. This letter was the threatened follow-up to a letter in October from Jocteur to the head of Condominium Public Works, saying that he would never ask for anything more from Public Works but that if he did not receive satisfaction this time he would complain to the FRC.

59. Interview with George Bristow, 23 April 1995.

60. George Bristow to Will Stober, 24 November 1995. Courtesy of Will Stober.

61. The information in these two paragraphs comes from Bonnemaison (1994). The first quotation is from p. 232; other quotations are from p. 253.

62. This withdrawal from cash-crop production occurred elsewhere in the New Hebrides and could be a response to low prices as well as to the demands of other activities. See my analysis of producer price responsiveness on Ambae in *Masters of Tradition* (M. Rodman 1987).

63. WPHC F 58/16/5, 27 May 1953, BRC Flaxman to HC; 22 May 1954, HC to BRC Flaxman; and minuting.

64. The account of the fire (here and in the following paragraphs) comes from NHBS 241/1932, 10 March 1952, Bristow's report to BRC Flaxman.

65. See especially Fabian 1983.

66. The subheading for this section echoes Joël Bonnemaison's title in *The Tree and the Canoe* (1994) for the chapter in which he describes the demise of white settlers' dreams of success on Tanna.

67. Quotations are from my interview with Ray Honey, 22 April 1995, or from the report he prepared on the Tanna house, 25 September 1970. He gave me a copy of this report.

68. Susan Wallington's father was resident commissioner in the BSIP just before the Western Pacific High Commission was moved to the Solomons from Fiji and the high commissioner began also to perform the role of resident commissioner for the Solomons.

■ Chapter 7: *On Islands off Islands*

1. Sometimes spelled Benue or Venue, the name is used, confusingly, for the island as well as the property opposite it on the mainland.

2. Len and Eileen Stephens.

3. This account of the Greig murders was provided by Violet Bowhay with information given her by Fred Stephens. Both are related to early South Santo settlers. The missionary, Annand, wrote an article for the *New Hebrides Magazine* called "South Santo Murderers Punished" that included a photo of four young, unarmed male islanders captioned "The murderers under arrest." O'Reilly's biographical compendium *Hébridais* includes listings for both Greig and his murderer, Ifurur(e) (1957:84 and 107). See also M. Rodman 1998:29–49.

4. Violet Bowhay, personal communication, 31 March 1998.

5. Circular letter, printed 23 November 1908, quoted in O'Reilly (1957:108).

6. Hybridity of the sort that these settler families routinely produce and have defined for them is the subject of considerable theoretical discussion in Cultural Studies. See, for example, Young 1995. Homi Bhabha's work (e.g., 1994) also frequently addresses this theme.

7. Mixed-race leaders have included a former prime minister, Maxime Carlot Korman; a mayor of Port Vila; and most famously, Jimmy Stephens, leader of the Santo Rebellion.

8. Burns, Philp and Company's *Handbook of Information for Western Pacific Islands*

(1899) provides an account for travelers of the company's route through the New Hebrides and of the ports of call along the way. Later, a brief account of travel by steamer through the New Hebrides is contained in the Report of a Royal Commission on Mail Services and Trade Development between Australia and the New Hebrides (1915). Burns, Philp and Company received a subsidy from the New South Wales government to carry mail, passengers, and freight to and from the New Hebrides, the first subsidy of its kind. A condition of the subsidy was that Burns, Philp withdraw its own postage and replace it with New South Wales stamps (*Pacific Islands Monthly*, 20 November 1930:6). These stamps would have been used for items mailed in Australia; Condominium postage was required on letters and parcels mailed in Vila.

9. Tangis is sometimes spelled Tangisi or Tangice. It is pronounced like the words "tan geese."

10. M. Rodman 1989:111.

11. See M. Rodman (1985b and 1997) for accounts of ni-Vanuatu moving houses.

12. Jane was born of a mixed-race mother. Nellie's mother was a ni-Vanuatu. Ned Hooker later went to Norfolk Island on holiday specifically to find a white wife, returning successfully with a Miss Adams, whom he married. The Hooker girls married Norwegian sailors. Nellie married Mr. Jensen, who was killed by natives on another small island near Santo (Ais) for having sex with native women. Jane married Mr. Engler, who drowned crossing in a boat from Ambae. Nellie and Jane returned to their maiden names because "the Hooker girls" sounded so much younger than "the widows Mrs. Jensen and Mrs. Engler" (personal communication 1998, Violet Bowhay and Dorothy Morris).

13. The British government did not establish a district agency in an area until after the local population was more or less pacified. The missionaries did the work of pacification, sometimes with the assistance of war-weary natives. I have written about the Longana (Ambae) people's desire to end a tiresome and dangerous cycle of killing and revenge with the help of a missionary (M. Rodman 1983). Other chapters in *The Pacification of Melanesia* report similar cases.

14. NHBS 12/32, 19 January 1938, BRC Joy to BDA N. D. Thomas. The five islands were Venui, Tangis, Tangoa, Urelapa, and Araki.

15. NHBS 129/25, Annual Confidential Report for 1929. The first quotation is from HC Eyre Hudson; the second is from BRC Joy.

16. Burns, Philp had leased the island to Samuel E. Wells in 1928 for ninety-six years. Wells subleased it to the Condominium for British use in 1938 for twenty years, renewable. When he died in 1948, Fred Jones bought the original lease from Burns, Philp, subject to the Condominium's sublease (NHBS 51/7/1, 1952, vol. 1, 17 May 1952, Legal Advisor to BRC).

17. The Saxton house would have cost £1,000 without freight, house fittings, bathtub and sink, and the cost of the labor to assemble it. Instead, Hudson's provided a building that cost £840, delivered, with about £75 for house fittings and sanitary fixtures (NHBS 50/11/27 16/2/48, author unclear to BRC, just before handover to BDA Maxwell).

18. The blessings of a long, thick skirt refers to Mary Russell's 1986 book by that title.

19. The information about Beer comes from Violet Bowhay, personal communication, August 1998.

20. The quotation is from Sewell n.d.:25.

21. Stephens built Hendon, the house in the British Paddock occupied by the commandant of police from 1956 on. Colin Simpson, in *Islands of Men* (Sydney: Angus and Robertson, 1955:151), recounts how two other writers (unnamed) described what happened regarding imprisonment on the French side:

A Frenchman had wounded another Frenchman at a party—or something like that happened to get him sentenced to eighteen months. There being no European jail, only a native one, he had to be quartered in a bungalow and, since no white man could be expected to look after himself, given a native servant. His meals were sent in from the hotel at a cost of £45 a month. On Saturday night the prisoner went to the movies. One writer said that the prisoner's sentence was shortened to get rid of him; the other left the impression that the farce went on for eighteen months.

22. Why the British were not afraid of prisoners armed with bush knives cutting the grass under their windows and playing with their children is the subject of chapter 4.

23. NHBS 50/11/27, 8 October 1948, Urgent Memo from BRC Blandy to Superintendent of Works, Port Vila.

24. Bain 1994.

25. Fred Stephens married Germaine Gardel, a relative of the "Bloody Mary" in *Tales of the South Pacific*. Jimmy Stephens' supporters looked after Bloody Mary in her old age on the Gardel plantation near Jimmy's political headquarters at Vanafo, Santo.

26. Violet married Maurice Havet, who managed Sola plantation in the Banks Islands. Emily Jane married George Axam and lived on South Santo. Caroline married Stephen Dubois and settled in Port Vila.

27. Ewan Corlette of Malakula had staked a claim to Urelapa. David Hooker told me that his grandfather and Capt. Frank Whitford later found Corlette's name and a date marked on a piece of copper nailed to a tree on Urelapa. Another Santo-area settler, Matt Wells of Malo, bought the island from Corlette and gave it to Sela Stephens. Wells was "carrying a blanket" for Caroline Stephens, who later, to his disappointment, married Steve Dubois, a French Canadian who, from about 1940, worked at the Joint Court in Vila, (personal communication, David Hooker; O'Reilly 1957:247).

28. Young 1995:26ff.

29. Among anthropologists, Ann Stoler (1989, 1995:99–101) has made this argument particularly strongly. See also McClintock 1995, esp. 15–17.

30. *Empire and Sexuality: The British Experience* (Manchester; New York: Manchester University Press, 1990). Fletcher was "Asterisk," author of *Isles of Illusion*.

31. See Bhabha 1994:85–92.

32. This is a clear reprise of the Victorian themes about racial hybridity that Young discusses in his book about culture and race (1995:10). The whole exchange lends support to the idea that colonial categories were in flux throughout time and space. In fact, they are still in flux in reminiscences about the colonial past.

33. To be clear, I reiterate that John was not a grandchild and thus had no ni-Vanuatu blood. With ni-Vanuatu women he produced what would classically be termed "half-caste" children, but he himself was not in that alleged category of offspring "treated like dirt."

34. Most deportees who wanted to had been allowed to return to Vanuatu by 1995.

Chapter 8: *Houses Far from Home*

1. Thomas 1994.
2. Rodman 1992, 1997a, 1997b.
3. Marcus 1995.
4. Clifford 1989.

5. The quotation is from a favorite book of mine, Stewart Brand's *How Buildings Learn* (1995:2). Despite the title, his book is evidence that buildings teach as well as learn.

6. For descriptions of settlers' lifestyles in the New Hebrides, see Delpech and Bellaïche (1987) and Cawsey (1998).

7. Stoler 1995:99.

8. Anderson 1983; Stoler 1989, 1991; for similar tensions among settler communities in Africa see Nunley 1987: chap. 1.

9. WPHC 268/1926, letter dated 5 November 1925.

10. Interview with Angela Eaton, 23 July 1994. The archival source is NHBS 50/11/27, 8 October 1948, Urgent Memo from BRC Blandy to Superintendent of Works, Port Vila.

11. Brand 1995:vi.

12. WPHC 3359/1935, BRC Joy to WPHC, letter dated 2 November 1935.

13. Stoler 1991; Home 1997.

References Cited

Achebe, Chinua. 1959. *Things Fall Apart*. New York: Fawcett Crest.

Adams, Ron. 1984. *In the Land of Strangers: A Century of European Contact with Tanna, 1774–1874*. Pacific History Monograph 9. Canberra: Australian National University Press.

Alexander, Gilchrist. 1927. *From the Middle Temple to the South Seas*. London: John Murray.

Allan, Colin. 1973. "Notes on the British Residency at Iririki." Unpublished manuscript in author's possession.

Anderson, Benedict. 1983. *Imagined Communities: Reflections on the Origin and Spread of Nationalism*. London: Verso.

Annand, Rev. Joseph. 1909. "South Santo Murderers Punished." *New Hebrides Magazine*. April, 18–20.

"Asterisk." 1923. *Isles of Illusion. Letters from the South Seas*. B. Lynch, ed. London: Constable.

Bain, Kenneth. 1994. Obituary for Jimmy Stevens [*sic*]. *The Independent* (London), March 4.

Beasant, John. 1984. *The Santo Rebellion: An Imperial Reckoning*. Honolulu: University of Hawai'i Press.

Bennett, J. M. 1957. "Vila and Santo: New Hebridean Towns." *Geographical Studies* 4(2):116–128.

Bhabha, Homi K. 1994. *The Location of Culture*. New York: Routledge.

Bolton, Lissant. 1999. "Women, Place and Practice in Vanuatu: A View From Ambae." In L. Bolton, ed., *Fieldwork, Fieldworkers: Developments in Vanuatu Research*. Special issue of *Oceania* 20(1).

Bonnemaison, Joël. 1994. *The Tree and the Canoe: History and Ethnogeography of Tanna*. Honolulu: University of Hawai'i Press. Josée Pénot-Demetry, translator and adaptor. Originally published in 1986 as La Dernière Ile (Paris:ARLEA/ORSTOM).

Bonnemaison, Joël; Kirk Huffman; Christian Kaufmann; and Darrell Tryon, eds. 1996. *Arts of Vanuatu*. Honolulu: University of Hawai'i Press. Originally published in 1996 as *Vanuatu, Oceanie: arts des îles de cendre et de corail* (Paris: Reunion des musées nationaux ORSTOM).

Boyarin, Jonathan. 1994. *Remapping Memory: The Politics of TimeSpace*. Minneapolis: University of Minnesota Press.

Brand, Stewart. 1995. *How Buildings Learn: What Happens After They're Built.* New York: Penguin.

Brunton, Ron. 1989. *The Abandoned Narcotic: Kava and Cultural Instability in Melanesia.* Cambridge: Cambridge University Press.

Burns, Philp and Company. 1899. *Handbook of Information for Western Pacific Islands.* Published by the company's head office, 10 Bridge St., Sydney.

Carter, Paul. 1987. *The Road to Botany Bay: An Essay in Spatial History.* London: Faber and Faber.

Cawsey, Katherine. 1998. *The Making of a Rebel: Captain Donald Macleod of the New Hebrides.* Suva: Institute of Pacific Studies, University of the South Pacific.

Champion, Olive. 1994. Journey of a Lifetime. Worcester: Square One Publications.

Cheesman, Lucy Evelyn. 1933. *Backwaters of the Savage South Seas.* London: Jarrolds.

———. 1945. *Camping Adventures on Cannibal Isles.* London: Harrap.

Clifford, James. 1989. "Notes on Theory and Travel." *Inscriptions* 5:177–179.

———. 1992. "Travelling Cultures." In *Cultural Studies,* ed. Lawrence Grossberg, Cary Nelson, and Paula Treichler, with Linda Baum and assistance from John MacGregor Wise, 96–116. New York: Routledge.

———. 1997. "Spatial Practices: Fieldwork, Travel, and the Disciplining of Anthropology." In *Anthropological Locations,* ed. A. Gupta and J. Ferguson, 185–222. Berkeley: University of California Press.

Coffier, Christian. 1988. *Traditional Architecture in Vanuatu.* Suva: University of the South Pacific.

Comaroff, John, and Jean Comaroff. 1992. *Ethnography and the Historical Imagination.* Boulder, Colo.: Westview.

Cowell, T. Reid. 1956. "Pandemonia, or a Franco-British Fantasy." Typescript by N. Townsend. Unpublished manuscript.

de Certeau, Michel. 1984. *The Practice of Everyday Life.* Berkeley: University of California Press.

Delpech, Christiane, and Félix Bellaïche. 1987. Hier Les Nouvelles-Hébrides. Arles: Imprimerie Perrin.

Des Chene, Mary. 1997. "Locating the Past." In *Anthropological Locations,* ed. A. Gupta and J. Ferguson, 66–85. Berkeley: University of California Press.

D'Obrenan, Charles, V.D.B. 1939. *Le Voyage de la Korrigane.* Paris: Payot.

Dunn, Marney. 1997. *Pandemonium or Paradise? Kath and Bob Paul in the New Hebrides, 1946–1980.* Bathurst, Australia: Crawford Press.

Fabian, Johannes. 1983. *Time and the Other: How Anthropology Makes Its Object.* New York: Columbia University Press.

Foley, Tricia. 1993. *The Romance of British Colonial Style.* New York: Clarkson, Potter.

Foucault, Michel. 1972. *Archaeology of Knowledge.* London: Tavistock.

Fuller, Mia. 1992. "Building Power: Italian Architecture and Urbanism in Libya and Ethiopia." In *Forms of Dominance: On the Architecture and Urbanism of the Colonial Enterprise,* ed. N. Alsayyad, 211–240. Aldershot: Avebury Press.

Garrison, Lt. Col. Ritchie. 1983. *Task Force 9156 and III Island Command.* Published by the author, 181 Pine Ridge Road, Waban, MA 02168, USA.

Garvey, Sir Ronald. 1983. *Gentleman Pauper.* Bognor Regis, U.K.: New Horizon.

Geslin, Yves. 1956. "Les Américains aux Nouvelles-Hébrides." *Journal de la Société des Océanistes* 12 (12):250.

Gill, Anton. 1995. *Ruling Passions: Sex, Race and Empire.* London: BBC Books.

Gouvernement de la Nouvelle Caledonie. 1903. "Voyage aux Nouvelles Hebrides au bord

du croiseur *Le Protet* en Novembre et Decembre 1902." Report dated 15 January 1903.

Harcombe, David. 1991. *Vanuatu: A Travel Survival Kit.* Berkeley, Calif.: Lonely Planet Publications.

Henningham, Stephen. 1992. *France and the South Pacific: A Contemporary History.* Honolulu: University of Hawai'i Press.

Home, Robert. 1997. *Of Planting and Planning: The Making of British Colonial Cities.* London: E & FN Spon, an imprint of Chapman and Hall.

Honey, Ray. 1970. "Report on the British District Agent's Residence, Isangel, Tanna." Manuscript in author's possession.

Howe, Kerry R. 1984. *Where the Waves Fall: A New South Sea Islands History from First Settlement to Colonial Rule.* Sydney: Allen and Unwin.

Hyam, Ronald. 1990. *Empire and Sexuality: The British Experience.* Manchester: Manchester University Press.

Jackson, Michael. 1995. *At Home in the World.* Durham, N.C.: Duke University Press.

Jacomb, Edward. N.d. Unpublished diary. Property of Christine Stober, Birmingham, UK.

———. 1914. *France and England in the New Hebrides.* Melbourne: George Robertson.

———. 1929. *The Joy Court: An Anglo-French Comedy.* London: Braybrook and Dobson.

Jolly, Margaret. 1991. "'To Save the Girls for Brighter and Better Lives': Presbyterian Missions and Women in the South of Vanuatu, 1848–1870." *Journal of Pacific History* 26(1):27–48.

———. 1993. "Colonizing Women: The Maternal Body and Empire." In *The Politics of Difference,* ed. S. Gunew and A. Yeatman, 103–127. Sydney: Allen and Unwin.

Kaplan, Caren. 1996. *Questions of Travel.* Durham, N.C.: Duke University Press.

Kemp, Peter. 1976. *Oxford Companion to Ships and the Sea.* New York: Oxford University Press.

King, Anthony D. 1984. *The Bungalow: The Production of a Global Culture.* Boston: Routledge and Kegan Paul.

———. 1991. "The Global, the Urban, and the World." In *Culture, Globalization and the World-System,* ed. Anthony D. King, 149–154. Current Debates in Art History 3. Binghamton: Department of Art and Art History, State University of New York at Binghamton.

———. 1992. "Rethinking Colonialism: An Epilogue." In *Forms of Dominance: On the Architecture and Urbanism of the Colonial Enterprise,* ed. N. Alsayyad, 339–355. Aldershot: Avebury Press.

———. 1995. "Writing Colonial Space: A Review Article." *Comparative Studies in Society and History* 37(4):541–554.

Knox-Mawer, June. 1986. *Tales from Paradise.* London: Ariel Books/BBC Publications.

Lefebvre, Henri. 1991 (1974 in French). *The Production of Space.* Trans. Donald Nicholson-Smith. Cambridge, Mass.: Blackwell.

Lindstrom, Lamont. 1989. "Working Encounters: Oral Histories of World War II Labor Corps from Tanna Vanuatu." In *The Pacific Theater: Island Representations of World War II,* ed. G. M. White and L. Lindstrom, 395–417. Pacific Islands Monograph Series, no. 8. Honolulu: University of Hawai'i Press.

———. 1990. *Knowledge and Power in a South Pacific Society.* Washington, D.C.: Smithsonian Institution Press.

———. 1991. "Kava, Cash, and Custom in Vanuatu." *Cultural Survival Quarterly* 15:28–31.

Lowenthal, David. 1985. *The Past Is Foreign Country.* Cambridge: Cambridge University Press.

Macchiusi, Joseph. 1996. "Fearing the Unknown." M.A. thesis, Social Anthropology. York University, Toronto.

MacClancy, Jeremy. 1981. *To Kill a Bird with Two Stones: A Short History of Vanuatu.* Vanuatu Cultural Centre Publication, no. 1. Port Vila: Vanuatu Cultural Centre.

Marcus, George. 1986. "Contemporary Problems in Ethnography in the Modern World System." In *Writing Culture: The Poetics and Politics of Ethnography,* ed. J. Clifford and G. Marcus, 165–193. Berkeley: University of California Press.

———. 1995. "Ethnography In/Of the World System: The Emergence of Multi-sited Ethnography." *Annual Reviews in Anthropology* 24:95–117.

McClintock, Anne. 1995. *Imperial Leather: Race, Gender and Sexuality in the Colonial Contest.* New York: Routledge.

Michener, James A. 1947. *Tales of the South Pacific.* New York: Macmillan.

Miles, William F. S. 1998. *Bridging Mental Boundaries in a Postcolonial Microcosm.* Honolulu: University of Hawai'i Press.

Miller, J. Graham. 1978–1990. *Live, A History of Church Planting in the Republic of Vanuatu.* 7 vols. Sydney: Committees on Christian Education and Overseas Missions, General Assembly of the Presbyterian Church of Australia.

Mitchell, Timothy. 1991. *Colonising Egypt.* Berkeley: University of California Press.

Morrell, W. P. 1960. *Britain in the Pacific Islands.* Oxford: Clarendon.

NHBS (New Hebrides British Service) archive. Foreign and Commonwealth Office Records Branch. Hanslope Park, UK.

Noyes, John. 1992. *Colonial Space: Spatiality in the Discourse of German South West Africa, 1884–1915,* ed. Nicholas Thomas. Studies in Anthropology and History, vol. 4. Churs, Switzerland: Harwood.

Nunley, John W. 1987. *Moving with the Face of the Devil: Art and Politics in Urban West Africa.* Urbana: University of Illinois Press.

Oliver, Douglas L. 1962. *The Pacific Islands.* Rev. ed. Garden City, N.Y.: Doubleday.

O'Reilly, Patrick. 1949. "Prophétisme aux Nouvelles-Hébrides: son histoire et son rôle politique et social." *Journal de la Société des Océanistes* 12:107–138.

———. 1957. *Hébridais: Répertoire bio-bibliographique des Nouvelles-Hébrides.* Publications de la Société des Océanistes, no. 6. Paris: Musée de l'Homme.

Philibert, J.-M. 1981. "Living under Two Flags: Selective Modernization in Erakor Village, Efate." In *Vanuatu: Politics, Economics and Ritual in Island Melanesia,* ed. M. Allen, 315–336. Sydney: Academic Press Australia.

———. 1992. "Social Change in Vanuatu." In *Social Change in the Pacific Islands,* ed. A. B. Robillard, 98–133. New York: Kegan Paul International.

Philibert, J.-M., and M. Rodman. 1996. "Du condominium à la république." In *Vanuatu, Oceanie: arts des îles de cendre et de corail.* Paris: Reunion des musées nationaux ORSTOM. Translated and published in 1996 as *Arts of Vanuatu,* ed. Joël Bonnemaison, K. Huffman, C. Kaufmann, and D. Tryon, 314–317. Honolulu: University of Hawai'i Press.

Rabinow, Paul. 1989. *French Modern: Norms and Forms of the Social Environment.* Cambridge: MIT Press.

Rensel, Jan, and M. Rodman, eds. 1997. *Home in the Islands: Housing and Social Change in the Pacific.* Honolulu: University of Hawai'i Press.

Rodman, Margaret C. 1983. "Following Peace." In *The Pacification of Melanesia,* ed. M. Rodman and M. Cooper, 141–160. ASAO Monograph no. 7. Lanham, Md.: University Press of America.

———. 1985a. "Contemporary Custom: Redefining Domestic Space in Longana, Vanuatu." *Ethnology* 24(4):269–279.

———. 1985b. "Moving Houses: Residential Mobility and the Mobility of Residences in Longana, Vanuatu." *American Anthropologist* 87(1):56–72.

———. 1987. *Masters of Tradition.* Vancouver: University of British Columbia Press.

———. 1989. *Deep Water.* Boulder, Colo.: Westview.

———. 1992. "Empowering Place: Multilocality and Multivocality." *American Anthropologist* 94:640–656.

———. 1995. "Breathing Spaces: Customary Land Tenure in Vanuatu." In *Land, Custom and Practice in the South Pacific,* ed. R. Gerard Ward and Elizabeth Kingdon, 53–101. Melbourne: Cambridge University Press.

———. 1997a. "Prologue." In *Home in the Islands: Housing and Social Change in the Pacific,* ed. J. Rensel and M. Rodman, 1–6 Honolulu: University of Hawai'i Press.

———. 1997b. "Conclusion." In *Home in the Islands: Housing and Social Change in the Pacific,* ed. J. Rensel and M. Rodman, 222–223. Honolulu: University of Hawai'i Press.

———. 1998a. "Creating Historic Sites in Vanuatu." In *Identity, Nature, and Culture: Sociality and Environment in Melanesia,* ed. Sandra Bamford. Special issue, *Social Analysis* 42(3):117–134.

———. 1998b. "My Only Weapon Being a Pencil: Inscribing the Prison in the New Hebrides." *Journal of Pacific History* 33(1):29–49.

Rodman, Margaret C., and William L. Rodman. 1983. "The Hundred Days of Sara Mata: Explaining Unnatural Death in Vanuatu." In *Dying in Cross-Cultural Perspective,* ed. Peter Stephenson. Special issue of *Omega* 14(2):135–144.

Romilly, Hugh H. 1893. *Letters from the Western Pacific and Mashonaland, 1878–1891.* Edited with a memoir by his brother, Samuel H. Romilly. Introduction by Lord Stanmore. London: David Nutt.

Rosaldo, Renato. 1989. *Culture and Truth: The Remaking of Social Analysis.* Boston: Beacon.

Roseby, Thomas. 1911. "British Judge's Speech." *New Hebrides Magazine,* January, 6–8.

Royal Commission on Mail Services and Trade Development between Australia and the New Hebrides. 1915. Report. Victoria: Albert J. Mullett, Government Printer.

Russell, Mary. 1986. *The Blessings of a Long Thick Skirt.* London: Flamingo.

Said, Edward. 1993. *Culture and Imperialism.* New York: Vintage.

Samson, Jane. 1998. *Imperial Benevolence: Making British Authority in the Pacific Islands.* Honolulu: University of Hawai'i Press.

Scarr, Deryck, ed. 1968. *A Cruise in a Queensland Labour Vessel to the South Seas, by W. E. Giles.* Canberra: Australian National University Press.

———. N.d. "European Settlement on Efate: Private Report Made for the British Residency."

Sewell, Angela (aka Eaton). N.d. "Five Signs to Siren (a novel)." Unpublished manuscript.

Shineberg, Dorothy. 1967. *They Came for Sandalwood.* Melbourne: Melbourne University Press.

Simpson, Colin. 1955. *Islands of Men.* Sydney: Angus and Robertson.

Stamford, Anne. 1993. *From British Secondary School to Malapoa College.* Distributed by the British Friends of Vanuatu, 67 Beresford Rd., Cheam, Surrey SM2 6ER, UK.

Stoler, Ann L. 1989. "Rethinking Colonial Categories: European Communities and the Boundaries of Rule." *Comparative Studies in Society and History* 31(1):134–161.

————. 1991. "Carnal Knowledge and Imperial Power: Gender, Race, and Morality in Colonial Asia." In *Gender at the Crossroads of Knowledge: Feminist Anthropology in the Postmodern Era,* ed. Micaela DiLeonardo, 51–101. Berkeley: University of California Press.

————. 1995. Race and the Education of Desire. Durham: Duke University Press.

Thomas, Nicholas. 1994. *Colonialism's Culture: Anthropology, Travel, and Government.* Princeton, N.J.: Princeton University Press.

Vale, Lawrence. 1992. *Architecture, Power, and National Identity.* New Haven, Conn.: Yale University Press.

Wallin, H. N., Rear Admiral. 1967. "The Project Was Roses." *Naval Civil Engineer,* May–July, 16–19; 26–28; 28–31.

Ward, J. M. 1948. *British Policy in the South Pacific.* Sydney: Australasian Publishing.

Woodcock, George. 1976. *South Sea Journey.* London: Faber & Faber.

WPHC (Western Pacific High Commission) archive. Held at the Foreign and Commonwealth Office, Records Branch, Hanslope Park, England.

Wright, Gwendolyn. 1987. "Tradition in the Service of Modernity: Architecture and Urbanism in French Colonial Policy, 1900–1930." *Journal of Modern History* 59 (June): 291–316.

————. 1991. *The Politics of Design in French Colonial Urbanism.* Chicago: University of Chicago Press.

Young, Robert. 1995. *Colonial Desire: Hybridity in Theory, Culture, and Race.* London: Routledge.

Index

Page numbers for photographs appear in **bold face.**

About the Author

Margaret Rodman received her Ph.D. in anthropology from McMaster University in Hamilton, Ontario, Canada. She is now a professor of anthropology at York University in Toronto. Her ongoing interest in Melanasia began with her first visit to the New Hebrides in 1969. Issues of housing, place, and identity are central to her research and publications on Vanuatu as well as on urban Canada. This is her third book about Vanuatu.

Published with the support of the School of Hawaiian, Asian,
and Pacific Studies, University of Hawai'i

Houses Far from Home